LIVERPOOL SECRETS

Behind the Shankly Gates

Trinity Mirror Sport Media

Trinity Mirror Sport Media

Published in Great Britain in 2005 by:
Trinity Mirror Sport Media,
PO Box 48, Old Hall Street,
Liverpool L69 3EB

Executive Editor: KEN ROGERS
Production Editor: PAUL DOVE
Art Editor: RICK COOKE
Writers: ALAN JEWELL, GAVIN KIRK,
CHRIS McLOUGHLIN, DAVID RANDLES, WILLIAM HUGHES

ISBN 0-954687159

Printed and finished by Scotprint, Haddington, Scotland

YOU'LL NEVER WALK ALONE

CONTENTS

16 ... DAVID FAIRCLOUGH
'COME QUICK, ONE OF THE PLAYERS
IS DEAD IN THE SAUNA'

22 ... NIGEL SPACKMAN
'A BIG STEP UP, BETTER THAN
BRAZIL AND LAZY ALDO!'

28 ... TOMMY SMITH
'WE'VE GOT TO RUB IODINE
ON YOUR PRIVATES!'

36 ... JIMMY CASE
'WE LET OUR HAIR DOWN
MORE THAN THEY DO NOW'

42 ... JAN MOLBY
'THE DRIVER SAID: 'YOUR KEEPER'S
DRIVING US ABOUT''

48 ... RON YEATS
'DEADLY TRAINING AND A FIRST
RUN-IN WITH SMITHY'

56 ... JOHN ALDRIDGE
'I DID GET THE CALL I WANTED –
13 YEARS LATER!'

62 ... JOEY JONES
'BOB NEVER KNEW I GOT THE
BUS TO HOME GAMES'

68 ... MICHAEL THOMAS
'TRIPS TO THE CHIPPY AND A TEAM
FULL OF CHARACTERS'

74 ... BRIAN HALL
'ASKING FOR EXPENSES AND
SHANKLY ON THE SPOT'

96 ... PHIL NEAL
'BOB'S FIRST SIGNING BUT HE
NEVER SAW ME PLAY'

102 ... PETER CORMACK
'SHANKS PLAYED FIVE-A-SIDE
UNTIL HE WON'

108 ... JIM BEGLIN
'HOW KENNY HELPED US PLAY
THE PERFECT WIND-UP'

114 ... ALAN A'COURT
'SHANKS' SWEAT BOX AND
'LITTLE WEMBLEY''

120 ... IAN CALLAGHAN
'THE HARDEST MAN I
EVER SAW PLAY'

126 ... ALAN KENNEDY
'FOUR HOURS LATE TO SIGN
BUT BOB SHOWED MERSEY'

132 ... DAVID JOHNSON
'NICKNAMES FOR THE BOYS
KEPT THE SPIRIT GOING'

138 ... PHIL THOMPSON
'FISHY TALE THAT KICKED UP
A STINK BEFORE THE GAME'

152 ... ALAN HANSEN
'MEET THE NEW MANAGER,
LADS, IT'S ME!'

158 ... GERRY BYRNE
'THE ECSTASY AND AGONY
OF A WEMBLEY WIN'

164 ... RONNIE WHELAN
'IF YOU'RE HOMESICK THEN
DON'T COME HOME!'

170 ... KENNY DALGLISH
'STEVIE, THE GREAT SCOTS AND
COOKING UP SUCCESS'

180/181 ... PICTURE INDEX

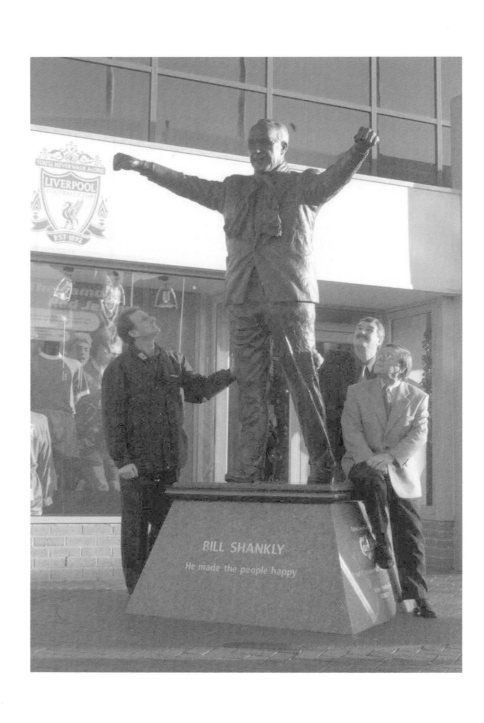

'Above all I would like to be
remembered as a man who was
selfless, who strove and worried
so that others could share the
glory and who built up a family
of people who could hold their
heads up high and say
'We're Liverpool''

- Bill Shankly

The class of '05 . . . former Liverpool players reunite at Anfield for a good cause. Lining up for the 'Tsunami Soccer Aid: Tackling the Aftermath' charity game on Easter Sunday, 2005, are (top row, from left): John Aldridge, Kenny Dalglish, Gary Ablett, Bruce Grobbelaar, Alan Hansen, Jan Molby, Phil Thompson, Neil Ruddock, Ronnie Whelan and John Barnes. Front row: Jason McAteer, David Johnson, Gary Gillespie, Alan Kennedy, Paul Walsh, Phil Neal, a lucky fan

FOREWORD BY PHIL NEAL

CHAIRMAN OF THE LIVERPOOL FC FORMER PLAYERS ASSOCIATION

There has always been a tremendous camaraderie between Liverpool Football Club's army of playing heroes, past and present.

It's well known throughout the game that the Liverpool Former Players Association is an organisation that is second to none. Our charity dinners and functions are full of passion and you feel instinctively that greats like Bill Shankly, Bob Paisley and Joe Fagan are looking down on their boys with a burning pride and sense of true admiration.

Having said that, the LFPA is not about one particular era. It bridges the best part of half a century. Some members have a cabinet full of medals. Others have fewer trophies, but just as many golden memories. What unites us all is a special bond that comes with pulling on that famous red jersey and going into battle in front of the finest fans in the world.

Whenever the Liverpool Former Players Association meets, you can guarantee it is going to be an occasion to savour. No need for After Dinner speakers. No need for any entertainment at all, other than the lads themselves re-living a thousand and one memories.

The stories that come to the fore on these nights are what Liverpool FC folklore is all about. It could be Ian St John or Ronnie Yeats giving us an insight into the remarkable Shanks. It could be Smithy tackling the great days with all of his usual steel or Ian Callaghan commanding respect because of his remarkable statesmanship and appearance record. David Fairclough – or any one of a hundred names – could also be on their feet reliving history and reviving wonderful memories.

I mention those above by name because they have all been key figures for the LFPA. Cally is secretary, David is treasurer and the others have all served as chairmen. I should also mention our hard-working committee members Willie Stevenson, Tony Hateley, Tommy Lawrence, Gerry Byrne, David Johnson, Alan Kennedy and Peter Thompson. Together we work hard to retain the unique spirit that sums up Liverpool Football Club. We all have a genuine respect for the fans who continue to pack out our functions and therefore support all of the LFPA's charity aims.

A donation from this book will be going into that charity fund which has helped many organisations in recent years.

The LFPA secured a guide dog for the blind in the name of the late Nessie Shankly, Bill's wife. Fittingly it was called "Nessie" and continues to do great work. A Sunshine coach was bought for the Variety Club of Great Britain. The Cystic Fibrosis charity was supported at Broadgreen Hospital for a whole year. A unit carries a special plaque in the name of the LFPA and LFC. Support has also been given to the Wirral Sick Children's Fund and another vital organisation, Zoe's Place, which looks after sick children at its West Derby headquarters in Liverpool, thus giving parents a much-needed break.

The Liverpool Former Players Association would like to thank everyone who has supported their activities, not least one of our members Brian Hall, who is our contact within the current Anfield scene; accountant Neil Wilson who also happens to be a fanatical Red and Sue Griffiths, whose secretarial support is invaluable.

Most of all, the former stars of Liverpool would like to thank the loyal Liverpudlians who believed in Bill Shankly's dream; who soared to the outer limits with the great Bob Paisley; who kept their feet firmly on the ground thanks to the guidance of the remarkably down-to-earth Joe Fagan – and who have been roaring in the name of the Mighty Reds ever since through a succession of managers.

Walk through the Shankly Gates. Enjoy this book and revel in its secrets and its humour. Look back with pride and forward with hope in your hearts.

That's what being a Liverpudlian is all about.

In partnership with
The Liverpool Former Players Association

Gary Ablett
Alan A'Court
John Aldridge
Alf Arrowsmith
Alan Banks
John Barnes
Jim Beglin
Bob Bolder
Gerry Byrne
Ian Callaghan
Bobby Campbell
Jimmy Case
Phil Chisnall
Ray Clemence
Peter Cormack
Kenny Dalglish
John Durnin
Roy Evans
David Fairclough
Howard Gayle
Gary Gillespie
Bobby Graham
Bruce Grobbelaar
Brian Hall
Alan Hansen
Tony Hateley
Steve Heighway
Roger Hunt
David Johnson
Joey Jones
Rob Jones
Kevin Keegan
Alan Kennedy
Ray Kennedy
Brian Kettle

Chris Lawler
Tommy Lawrence
Mark Lawrenson
Sammy Lee
Alex Lindsay
Doug Livermore
Mike Marsh
Terry McDermott
Willie Miller
Jan Molby
John Molyneux
Ronnie Moran
Phil Neal
Ian Ross
Ian Rush
Tommy Smith
Nigel Spackman
David Speedie
Ian St John
Willie Stevenson
Paul Stewart
Geoff Strong
Phil Taylor
Michael Thomas
Maxwell Thompson
Peter Thompson
Phil Thompson
Alan Waddle
Gordon Wallace
Paul Walsh
Mark Walters
John Wark
Ronnie Whelan
Ron Yeats
Peter Wall

The spirit lives on ... former players (from left) Ron Yeats, Willie Stevenson, Roger Hunt, Ian Callaghan and Peter Thompson applaud after a rousing version of You'll Never Walk Alone from Gerry Marsden at a Bill Shankly tribute dinner in 2004

'TELL THE MANAGER TO COME QUICK... WE THINK ONE OF THE PLAYERS IS DEAD IN THE SAUNA'

DAVID FAIRCLOUGH

1974/75 –
1982/83
Striker

I t's very difficult to put into words. Growing up as close to the ground as I did, people used to say 'Oh, he'll play for Liverpool one day' but you never believed it was going to happen. It was a bit surreal when it did and it was only probably when you look back and reflect on it that you make more sense of it. I got carried along with it.

I was always at the forefront as a boy. I did well in Sunday league football and schools football and for the city boys. We all wanted to be footballers but for me it happened in a matter-of-fact way. I didn't have to go looking for trials because Liverpool found me. When I went in as an apprentice, Bill Shankly and Tom Saunders said to me 'You have a chance if you keep working'. Whilst that was pleasing to hear at 16, I never took anything for granted and plugged away.

I had moved to Cantril Farm when I made my debut and the next day I went down to watch the Sunday league football and realised how life had changed. I had celebrity status then. It was quite embarrassing, really. While more people want to know you, you can't afford to forget who you are and where you come from. Living in Cantril Farm was a good thing for me. I didn't lose touch.

'HE KNOCKED HIS TEETH OUT AND JOEY GOT SENT OFF. AFTER THE MATCH THEY WERE SEARCHING IN THE MUD FOR THE TEETH'

AN EARLY IMPACT

The Norwich goal in March 1976 was my first league goal. I'd had a couple of appearances in the league and that goal was a relief. I'd scored in the UEFA Cup - my second match - but scoring against Norwich did help me to relax a little bit and give me confidence.

When you are confident, you do get into a bit of a run. The following week I scored two against Burnley. I enjoyed it as it was coming and I tried to play off-the-cuff. Bob was encouraging me to do the things that I was naturally strong at. That was running at defenders, beating them, and I had a good shot with either foot. I was in a good run of form and I tried to make the most of it.

MY BEST MATE RUINED MY DEBUT

I had a little bit of empathy with Phil Thompson, because we'd come from similar backgrounds, and Jimmy Case, who had trained on a Thursday night as an amateur, but Joey Jones was my main friend because he is such a down-to-earth person. I roomed with Joey for part of my early time.

Mad as a hatter, was Joey. Barking. He would talk about what his mum and dad would do. There was no grandiose sense of stardom from him. He never changed and he was a barrel of laughs. He was honest and committed. He was always at the forefront of the joking and the liveliness in the

DAVID FAIRCLOUGH

dressing room. He didn't take the Mickey; it was daft stuff like ventriloquism. He would break the ice all the time. Bob Paisley said after Joey left that 'It was a hard decision to let your mate go. I would have liked to keep him just for in the dressing room.'

He got sent off on my debut at Middlesbrough for headbutting John Hickson. Hickson had slid in to tackle Ray Clemence. While Clem was on the floor, Joey ran in and headbutted Hickson. He knocked his teeth out and Joey got sent off. After the match they were searching in the mud for the teeth. Joey couldn't apologise enough for ruining my day. That was him.

HE KNEW WHAT HE MEANT . . .

When we played Arsenal in the FA Cup semi-final in 1980, I remember being in the team meeting before the first game and Bob Paisley saying that 'You've got to watch out for Osbourne arriving on a late run in the penalty area'. A couple of the lads looked at each other and wondered what he

was talking about.
  'Osbourne?'
  'Yeah, the Arsenal fella. Osbourne.'
  'D'you mean Talbot?'
  'That's it, Talbot'.

For the replay he goes through the team again and said again 'You've got to watch out for Osbourne, arriving late in the penalty area', by which time we realised what he was talking about and nobody corrected him. He did it again before the third and fourth games. Who popped up with the winning goal but Brian Talbot, which proved he knew what he was talking about, even if he didn't always know the name.

Bob wasn't always spot on with the terminology. He could be quite unique. Terry McDermott used to take the boss off a lot, impersonating him. He has spent half of his life doing it.

He was going on one day, pretending to be Paisley saying how much he hates Terry Mac. All the players were laughing their heads off.

Unbeknown to Terry, Bob had walked in and was standing behind him at the door, listening to all this going on.

DEATH IN A GERMAN SAUNA

We were in Munich to play Bayern in a pre-season friendly and drew 1-1. It was great to play in the Olympic Stadium; Karl-Heinz Rumminegge scored and I scored for Liverpool. That's a good memory.

We were in the Holiday Inn in Munich after the game and had a couple of beers. Gradually everyone disappeared. Next morning, the story goes that Bob Paisley and the chairman had phone calls from the staff saying 'Come quickly at once, one of the players is dead in the sauna'. Bob Paisley told the story that he was coming down the stairs thinking 'Who do I want it to be?' Rumour had it that he chose Terry McDermott.

It was quite dramatic. Anyway, it was Jimmy Case who had been having a drink on his own and decided to go and have a lie in the sauna. I think he had his clothes on, with a beer, and fell asleep in the early hours of the morning. He was comatose but eventually they did manage to wake him up.

THE CURSE OF SUPERSUB

You get pigeon-holed and I certainly did - as somebody who could only play 15 or 20 minutes.

It's not something I've ever rested easy about. I think about it all the time. I've never been able to accept it. I'm disappointed with the way it all panned out, if I'm honest.

To a point, I don't think Bob Paisley helped me with that because he over-used me as substitute. He said to me one day 'I'd have you as sub every week if I could'. I said 'I'm getting fed up. I'd rather play in the reserves than be used as sub week in, week out.' That didn't do me many favours.

The fact that you score a goal like that against St Etienne pigeon-holes you even more. The press start using this thing that I was far more effective coming on for the last 15 minutes than 90.

Well, that just doesn't make sense if you think about it. The St Etienne goal and the Everton goal (in '76) did for me.

DAVID FAIRCLOUGH

There were players who had poor games for Liverpool but would be given an extended run to try and get out of it, whereas if I was anything else other than on top of my game, I was always at risk of being the one left out.

I was never given that benefit. It's sad really but I believe that I should have had a much bigger part to play in more games.

THE BIONIC CARROT

I think it was Horace Yates of the Daily Post who

'IT WAS AT THE TIME OF THE 'SIX MILLION DOLLAR MAN' AND I TAKE IT AS A COMPLIMENT. BUT I WOULDN'T WANT TO BE CALLED 'THE BIONIC CARROT' EVERY DAY!'

started that.

The first time I have seen a cutting of it was after I scored two against Burnley in '76 and it appeared in the Daily Post.

It was at the time of the 'Six Million Dollar Man' and I probably have to take it as a compliment. I wouldn't want to be called the 'Bionic Carrot' every day, though.

I was a bit disappointed that John Arne Riise tried to get rid of his red hair recently. I have been asked if I had an affair in Norway 20-odd years ago, the suggestion being that John Arne Riise was my child.

1986/87 –
1988/89
MIDFIELDER

NIGEL SPACKMAN

'A BIG STEP UP, BETTER THAN

Kenny Dalglish is a legend, not just in terms of Liverpool and Celtic, but in football. Having someone like Kenny come in for you as a player was a massive compliment.

Because Liverpool were one of the best teams around at the time, it was a dream come true for any footballer to be wanted by them and Kenny

Dalglish.

It wasn't such a big wrench for me to leave Chelsea as I wanted to play at the highest level I could and Liverpool was the pinnacle of English and, probably, European football.

I was lucky at the time that I had come from Bournemouth to Chelsea and so had played in the old fourth and third divisions, then the old second

BRAZIL – AND LAZY ALDO!'

and first divisions with Chelsea, so my career had always gone upwards.

When I went to Liverpool, though, this was the biggest step I had to make.

You have to learn quickly because you are playing with such great players in training and not just on a matchday.

That teaches you the game.

RON FOR ALL AND ALL FOR RON

I had my best run in the team when Ronnie Whelan got injured during the 1987/88 season when we went on to win the league.

Ronnie and I got on extremely well, as did most of the players at the club then. There was a fantastic team spirit and togetherness, which unfortunately seems to have eroded somewhat ▷

within football over the last few years.

When I first came to the club I was in the team but would get moved around a lot. Ronnie ended up playing at right back or left back and we ended up in midfield together a couple of times as well.

Ronnie was, and still is, a legend in Liverpool. He was a fantastic player for the club and I even think he scored a few more goals than me as well!

BETTER THAN THE BRAZILIANS

The 5-0 win over Nottingham Forest in April '88 has gone down in history as one of those great games.

We ended up playing them three times in the same month. They beat us 2-1 in the league then we beat them the week before the return at Anfield, 2-1 in the FA Cup semi-final. Forest were a good side then.

I remember Bruce (Grobbelaar) making a few good saves early on but then we just went on and played some of the most sublime football where everyone of us knew exactly what was going on. The passing and movement, which is the traditional Liverpool way, was there for all to see.

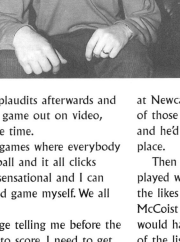

We received some great plaudits afterwards and the BBC brought the whole game out on video, which was unheard of at the time.

It was just one of those games where everybody goes out to play their football and it all clicks perfectly into place. It was sensational and I can even admit to having a good game myself. We all did.

I remember John Aldridge telling me before the game: 'Look, Spacks, I need to score. I need to get this golden boot. I need a few goals tonight.' Good for Aldo, he scored two.

Strangely enough, we played Sheffield Wednesday a week before the FA Cup final and beat them 5-1 away. Alan Hansen didn't play as he was being rested and big Jan (Molby) played at the back. We played some sensational stuff that

day as well but maybe we peaked a week too early before the Cup final.

THE GREATEST OF ALL

If I am to single out one player from the club I would have to praise John Barnes immensely.

Me and Digger were in the same hotel together for a while and got to know each other pretty well being two southern boys and all that.

Being the first black player, with the exception of Howard Gayle, to really make it big at the club, there was a lot of pressure on him. The whole way John handled coming to Liverpool, he came through it all exceptionally well and turned any doubters around very, very quickly.

If we were able to have played in Europe at the time he would have done even bigger and greater things for the club.

People always remember John for his attacking but his all round game was fantastic.

We also have to remember the likes of Alan Hansen who was fantastic for the club, plus the likes of Stevie Nicol who probably didn't get the credit he deserved.

I remember Steve having to play on the right side of midfield up at Newcastle and scoring a hat-trick. He was one of those players that you could have stuck in goal and he'd give 100 percent and not look out of place.

Then there's Ian Rush. What can you say? I've played with some very good strikers in my time, the likes of Kerry Dixon, David Speedie, Ally McCoist and Mark Hateley, plus Mark Hughes. I would have to say, though, that Ian Rush was top of the list.

WELL 'ARD

All the players at the club when I was there were very good. They had to be otherwise they wouldn't have been good enough to be at Liverpool.

Steve McMahon came on leaps and bounds at

NIGEL SPACKMAN

the club. He scored very important goals and was getting a lot of plaudits and got into the England side.

You always need someone in the middle of the park who puts their foot in and Steve was as brave as they come.

There were other hard players at the club who maybe didn't get as much credit for it. Ronnie Whelan was a tough player but was maybe a little more cute than Steve or Graeme (Souness) or the likes of Terry Hurlock and Vinnie Jones who were around at the time. I wouldn't put Steve in the same bracket as these two, though.

He was a fantastic player to have on your team and scored some cracking goals from distance. He was the mainstay of the midfield at the time.

I played with him in the centre most of the time as Ronnie played mainly at full-back when he was fit again.

Competition for places was immense. We had the likes of big Jan (Molby) and John Wark vying for places as well and then Ray Houghton came along which meant Craig (Johnston) couldn't get in the team. It was such a good squad.

Aldo came in just before me then Barnesie and Peter (Beardsley) came in during the summer and Ray (Houghton) a little later. Kenny made some very astute signings to keep Liverpool ahead of the game.

A FEW CROSS-WORDS WITH ALDO

I roomed with John Aldridge who was great.

He did so well to take over from Rushie. His goalscoring record was absolutely phenomenal and full credit to John.

He was a true athlete, a really fit lad. When we were on pre-season or away in a hotel he would come in after light-training and carry on doing sit-ups and press-ups on the floor while I'd be flat out watching the telly. I think he was just trying to impress me.

But as a room-mate he was a lazy sod. He never made the tea and I used to have to do all the running round and look after him. Is it any wonder he played until a ripe old age?

He used to do all the crosswords, John loved doing them.

He would be sitting on the toilet or lying on his bed doing crosswords all the time.

There are some stories I just can't tell you about him, but Aldo was a great bloke and a true Scouser.

A FINAL WORD

The biggest thing in a Cup competition is to get to the final in the first place. To lose in a semi-final is the worst feeling ever. But then to lose in the final for Liverpool was a major disappointment for me.

We were expected to win both of the finals I appeared in - Arsenal in the League Cup in 1987 and against Wimbledon a year later in the FA Cup.

On another day, with a little bit of luck, we maybe would have won but you can't change history unfortunately.

NIGEL SPACKMAN

For me, the Littlewoods Cup final was particularly special as I'd only just arrived at the club at the semi-final stage and came on as a sub. To then be picked to play in the final was a massive boost for me and helped me settle in at the club and be accepted by everyone. It's just a shame we didn't win it.

I keep telling Charlie Nicholas when I'm on the Sky panel with him that he didn't actually score two goals because Ronnie Whelan got one of them via a deflection. Charlie, of course, claims it but he wouldn't get it today. Saying that, I don't suppose Ronnie would want to claim it either!

'ALDO WAS A **TRUE ATHLETE,** A REALLY FIT LAD. BUT AS A ROOM-MATE **HE WAS A LAZY SOD.** HE NEVER MADE THE TEA. HE WOULD BE ON THE TOILET **DOING CROSSWORDS'**

'THE LADS LOOKED STUNNED WHEN BOB SAID: 'WE'VE GOT TO RUB IODINE ON YOUR PRIVATES!"

1960/61
–1977/78
*MIDFIELDER/
DEFENDER*

TOMMY SMITH

Whenever people gather to remember the great Bob Paisley, you will always hear them talking about two things.

It's quite right to say that he could spot an injury from a hundred yards away. Bob could pinpoint a particular problem just by the way you were limping without any need for X-Rays or hospital checks. Of course, he was an outstanding judge of a player and could see things in individuals that others completely missed. For instance, he turned Ray Kennedy from an out and out centre-forward with Arsenal to an international class left sided midfielder. That's quite a switch, but Bob was a master of understanding a player's strengths and weaknesses.

Whenever I think about Bob, one of the first things that comes to mind is another gift he had – for studying the horses. Like me, he loved the gee gees and he would be always coming over to say: "Smithy, I've got a tip for you. But just don't tell that Ian St. John."

Now the Saint was a great player, but he was a jinx when it came to horse racing.

Bob knew plenty of trainers and Ian was always keen to gain some inside information, but whenever he backed one of Bob's tips it lost.

Maybe Bob should have done something about it the day he literally had Ian by the bollocks after our fiery striker was sent off at Coventry.

The Saint was always up for a bit of an altercation on the pitch and he was having this non-stop battle with one of their defenders. After one tangle, the Coventry player responded by sneakily grabbing Ian by the testicles, the Sixties equivalent of the famous Vinny Jones/Paul Gascoigne incident that was captured by a photographer with Gazza wincing in pain.

Not surprisingly Ian lashed out at the lad who went down like a sack of spuds. The Saint was sent off and as soon as the whistle went we all piled into the dressing room to commiserate with our team-mate. The lads were stunned when Bob marched in and said to Ian: "Get you your shorts down!"

Ian looked a bit bemused, but Bob said: "Come on, get them down, we've got to rub some iodine on your bollocks!"

The Saint soon looked as if he had taken a low blow from Joe Frazier, all black and blue in the right places. Bob then summoned the referee and said: "Look at him. No wonder he lashed out."

It went to a tribunal and the referee had to admit there had been clear provocation. Let's just say justice was done.

BUTTED BY GERRY BYRNE: LEARNING MY FIRST CRUCIAL LESSON

Being a local lad and a passionate Liverpudlian, I was naturally keen to impress when I first started training with the first team lads at Melwood in the early Sixties. I remember nutmegging Gerry Byrne, our rock-solid full-back who would become the hero of Wembley in 1965 when he played on in the FA Cup final after dislocating his collar bone.

I thought I would try and impress and was full of it after slipping the ball through Gerry's legs. Minutes later a high ball dropped between us that was there to be challenged in the air. ▷

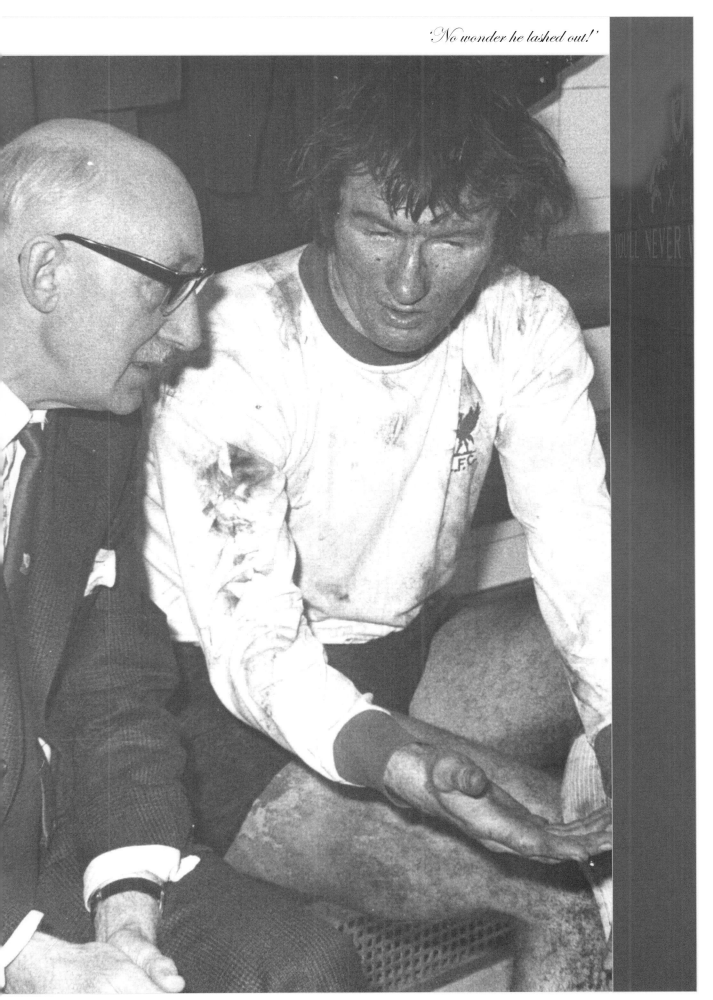

TOMMY SMITH

I leapt with Gerry, concentrating on the ball. Gerry leapt with me, concentrating on my head. He butted me in full flight and I was suddenly flat out on the floor with a crowd around me. The first thing I remember is Shanks standing over me saying: "That will teach you to nutmeg Gerry Byrne son!"

You learn something new every day in football. I had just been given my first serious lesson in how to handle yourself.

SHANKS WAS PROUD OF EVERY CORNER OF ANFIELD – INCLUDING NEW TOILETS

I smile when I read about the proposals for a new world class super stadium in Stanley Park. It brings back a clear picture in my mind of when I was on the Anfield groundstaff as a boy and would spot the boss showing guests around the stadium which was really dilapidated then.

He was really pleased with the changes he was beginning to make because he knew how crucial it was, not only to make Anfield a fortress, but for it to be a ground we could all be proud of.

If only these little tours by Shanks had been captured on film. He would be in the dressing room saying: "This is a toilet. We've got four now. That's twice as many as we used to have. It takes 36 seconds to fill up after you've flushed it. That might not mean much to you, but it's everything to the lads when we're preparing for a game and there's a queue."

Shanks had this thing about toilet facilities. I can remember on one of our European trips. We got to this Eastern European stadium and when we went into the dressing room it looked as if it hadn't been cleaned for weeks. They didn't even have toilet paper. Shanks was ready to call the game off and the UEFA people soon got the message. Suddenly there was an army of cleaners in there putting everything right.

Shanks set standards on and off the pitch. We were Liverpool Football Club and nobody was going to mess with us.

FIRST TACTICS FROM SHANKS

In 1965 I had just turned 20 and was beginning to ▷

▷ break into the first team. Liverpool had this crucial European game against Belgian champions Anderlecht. England had played Belgium just a few weeks before and been held 2-2 and Shanks had been very impressed with the opposition. Three quarters of the Belgian team were Anderlecht players, so the boss knew we faced a real challenge.

I didn't expect to be in the team at Anfield. I can remember that the squad was taken to the Blundellsands Hotel on the outskirts of Liverpool where the boss was going to give his final tactical talk. As I was walking in Ronnie Moran said: "You are playing Smithy."

Shanks indicated that we would be playing our usual 4-4-2, but his caution was clear. He said to me: "Tommy, you will be Ronnie Yeats' right leg tonight. And don't go over the halfway line!"

It was as simple as that although the boss would privately offer me one bit of advice that I carried with me throughout my career. He said: "Tommy, I want you to remember what I'm about to tell you. Don't take any shit from anybody. It doesn't matter who it is."

His words were ringing in my ears against the Belgians. In the match I got stuck in on the Big Man's right hand side. Little things happen that please you when you feel you are on top of your

game. The lad I was marking snapped at one point and said to me: "Nutter!" I was surprised he knew any English, let alone any slang, but it told me I was doing my job. We won the game 3-0.

DROPPED FOR THE FIRST TIME – SO I BLOCK THE DRESSING ROOM DOOR

I've just mentioned my first European game for the Reds. It's funny how firsts stick in your mind. I have vivid memories of being in the first Liverpool team to win the FA Cup; of being the first Liverpool captain to pick up a European trophy, the UEFA Cup in 1973; of being in the first Liverpool team to win the European Cup. But not all the games are happy memories.

I well remember being dropped. The date was February 3, 1973. I suppose it comes to all players, but I was still living by the little phrase Shanks had instilled into me: "Don't take any shit from anyone."

Of course, in my mind that had come to include him and this was certainly the case at Highbury where we were facing up to a tough game against the Gunners. What made it more significant is that I was captain at the time.

We had lost in disappointing fashion 1-0 to our old rivals Leeds and, as skipper, the boss called me in to discuss everything about the game. ▷

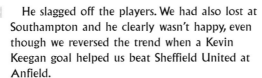

He slagged off the players. We had also lost at Southampton and he clearly wasn't happy, even though we reversed the trend when a Kevin Keegan goal helped us beat Sheffield United at Anfield.

As the Arsenal game loomed, I sensed something was going on in the background. If Shanks used your name when he was discussing tactics, you knew you were playing.

If he talked about the number four or the number six, you knew you were out and I've seen players look shocked and frustrated down the years when this happened.

We travelled to London with no firm indication of what the team was, but I just knew. I was getting more and more wound up inside and Shanks' own words about standing up for yourself were getting louder and louder in my head. I said to myself: "If he is going to be awkward by keeping the decision from me until the last possible moment, I'm going to be awkward."

We used to leave our bags on the bus when we got to away games, but I took mine into the stadium and wedged it across the threshold of the dressing room door. Everyone, including the boss, had to step over it every time they came in. No one moved it.

The team was finally read out and I was fuming.

Peter Cormack asked me what I was doing and I just said: "I'm going home. See you tomorrow."

I finally picked up the bag and was suddenly outside of Highbury where I was spotted by some Liverpool lads. They said: "Where are you going Smithy." I said: "I'm not playing. I'm going home."

This kid just said: "If you're going home, so are we," and so this little group trooped off towards the station, the Tommy Smith Liberation Army! It made me realise what the fans thought of me. It made me even more determined to win back my place.

On the Monday, I was still wound up and determined to get things off my chest with Shanks. Suddenly I heard him calling me from his office.

Before I could utter a word he said: "Smithy, I don't hold it against you. I would have done the same myself." He had completely defused a potentially difficult situation with his man management. We had our spits and spats, but he was a remarkable manager.

TAKING THE LADS TO THE DOGS BEFORE A CUP FINAL

We won the FA Cup for the first time in 1965. We were down at our London headquarters for a couple of days prior to the game and I can remember Bill Shankly taking us to a local dog-track to help us relax. Can you imagine that now, Arsene Wenger or Rafael Benitez actually taking their teams for a night at a greyhound track before a Cup final?

I wanted to put a Tricast bet on, predicting the first, second and third, but incredibly I didn't have enough money. I borrowed the princely sum of £4 off my roommate Chris Lawler. The bet came in and I won £100 which was a lot of money then. I gave Chris a few bob and he was quite happy. I also looked on it as an omen for the cup final against Leeds. I thought: "This is my lucky week."

But it didn't all go as planned. Yes, we won the cup, but we were convinced we were diddled out of our bonus. I was only on £30 a week. The wage structure was hardly complicated. We got the basic plus £1 for every 1,000 fans above 28,000. Therefore if the attendance was 40,000, I would pick up my £30 basic and £12 bonus.

We were on a £1,000 win bonus at Wembley, but we all assumed we would also get a crowd bonus. I was assuming a 100,000 crowd and so a bonus down this front of £72, plus the £1,000 if we won plus my £30 basic – a massive £1,102.

We were so caught up in the occasion that we didn't think about it until we received our payslips. The crowd bonus paid was £2, the same as for our previous home league game. When we pointed out there had been 100,000 at Wembley, they said: "Sorry, the game was on a neutral ground, so that doesn't count!"

'THE KID JUST SAID: 'IF YOU'RE GOING HOME, SO ARE WE' AND WE TROOPED OFF TO THE STATION, THE TOMMY SMITH LIBERATION ARMY!'

TOMMY SMITH

'LETTING OUR HAIR DOWN

1973/74 –
1980/81
MIDFIELDER

JIMMY CASE

My time with Liverpool was a brilliant time, and my outstanding memories will always be of the lads I was with. I played with Keegan, Dalglish and then you had more great players like Hansen and Souness coming through. Playing with someone as good as Ray Kennedy who's my big, big mate was special too.

Everything happened so quickly for me. I went from being an electrician to suddenly playing for the most successful club in English history. Those first few years were something unbelievable.

We just clicked and were an awesome team and

– AND ONE **FINAL REGRET'**

you don't really realise it until you move on and away and you see how things are from a distance - and on the other side. I'm a Liverpudlian and you want to do it for the people.

Obviously, you have personal determination and a professional pride so you push yourself on but it wouldn't be possible without the supporters.

The Kop support is like an extra man. It might be a bit cliched but you ask anyone who plays in front of it and they'll tell you the same thing.

PLAYING THE HERO AND THEN THE VILLAIN

It was always a strange feeling going back as an

opposition player, and funnily enough I always used to play quite well against Liverpool.

Not because I was trying harder or I felt I had something to prove but it was just one of those strange things football throws up from time to time.

The team that employs you and pays your wages has to get your full loyalty and that was something I maintained throughout my career. I always tried my best and tried to win games. I still had my soft spot for Liverpool - just not when we played them.

I scored the winner in that FA Cup run with Brighton up at Anfield, and I remember at the end of that game a reporter said to me that Bob

Paisley had never won the FA Cup, and I told him neither had I! I'm sure if it had been the other way around and Liverpool had won the game I'm sure he wouldn't have lost any sleep over it - and to tell you the truth neither did I. It's because I wanted to go through to the final.

But I never ever got anything but a fantastic reception when I went back to Anfield, and that really meant a lot to me. I always have - even just coming back onto the pitch to draw the raffle the other season.

I left Liverpool on good terms and I hope I was relatively well liked in my time at Anfield by

'I ALWAYS MAINTAINED LOYALTY TO MY CLUB THROUGHOUT MY CAREER. I STILL HAD MY SOFT SPOT FOR LIVERPOOL – JUST NOT WHEN WE PLAYED THEM'

JIMMY CASE

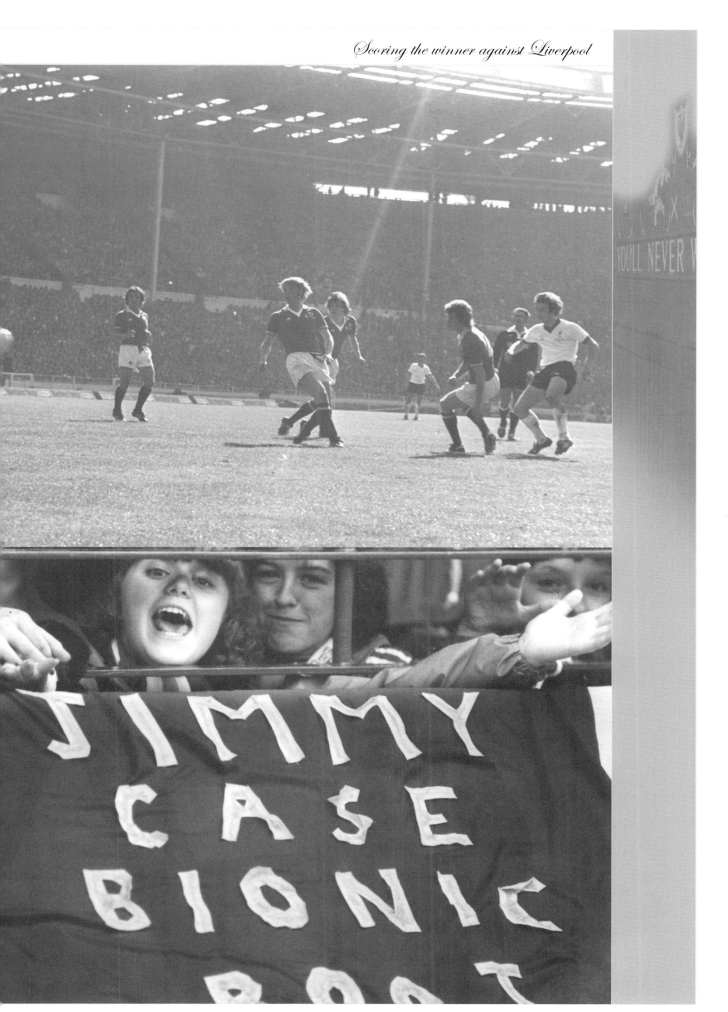

JIMMY CASE

team-mates and the supporters. I certainly had and have a lot of affection for them.

A SOLITARY REGRET

I have so many happy memories of my time at Anfield, there's not much room for regret. Perhaps, the only thing I would change if I could would be the 1977 FA Cup final defeat to Manchester United when we had the chance to do the treble. You have your rivals in football - and our main foes were always United and Everton.

I thought we played well enough to have got the result in the final. But we were unlucky and lost that stupid, freakish goal. But you never know what fate has in store for you. If we'd won that one we might not have won the European Cup final against Borussia Moenchengladbach.

Having won the championship and lost out on the FA Cup we were so determined to win the European Cup. I could see it in everyone's eyes in the dressing room before we went out onto the pitch.

We didn't have to say anything to each other, we didn't have to pump ourselves up, we were just ready.

The support we had that night was the best you'll ever have. Absolutely marvellous they were - it was like a home game for us. We went from one of the most disappointing times to one of the best you'll ever feel. You tend to get things like that in football

though and you have to be able to deal with them or you won't be a player.

RAY THE BIG GAME PLAYER AND MAKING FRIENDS FOR LIFE

'I COULD SEE IT IN **EVERYONE'S EYES** IN THE DRESSING ROOM. WE DIDN'T HAVE TO **SAY ANYTHING** TO EACH OTHER OR PUMP OURSELVES UP. **WE WERE READY'**

As I mentioned earlier one of my abiding memories of my time at Anfield is of Ray Kennedy. Ray arrived at Anfield from Arsenal and he already had this tremendous reputation as a player.

He was a big game player - the type of player who we wanted at Anfield and the type of player that would really add to the squad.

What we didn't know when he arrived at Anfield was what type of bloke he was. He was a diamond and I'm glad to be able to call him my friend.

We had a great laugh back in those days. Don't get me wrong, we were determined to win things and we worked and trained hard but we let our hair down more than footballers can now. There wasn't the same scientific approach.

I'm often asked if I'd like to be a footballer now but it would be impossible for me to consider what I had back then.

I played with some great footballers, I won the biggest prizes going in this game but almost more importantly I made friends for life - among my team-mates and among the fans.

'I TURNED AROUND AND THE DRIVER WAS SAT NEXT TO ME. HE SAID: 'YOUR KEEPER'S DRIVING US ABOUT!"

1984/85 –
1994/95
MIDFIELDER

JAN MOLBY

There were some great characters in the dressing room during my time at Anfield but the biggest was Bruce Grobbelaar. He was a remarkable guy and one of the strongest men I've ever seen. He would get up to all sorts, opening bottles with his eyes, jumping over cars and even moving cars! I remember a couple of times we turned up for away matches and the coach was blocked by cars and Brucie just went and moved them!

Then another time, we arrived at Anfield one day and there was a baseball bat just lying about, so some of us went into the ground and had an impromptu game of baseball at the Anfield Road end but Bruce was so strong that he was not only the first one to hit the ball, he hit it out of the ground!

On another occasion, he drove the team bus. We were on a pre-season tour in Scandinavia and I was sat at the back of the bus. The next moment I turned around and the driver was sat next to me. I asked him what was going on and he said: "Oh, your goalkeeper's just driving us about!"

JOKERS IN THE PACK

The players tended to fall into three groups - those who played the pranks, those who were the victims and the rest. I was fortunate that I tended to come into the last group. We tended to leave all that.

Poor Steve Nicol was the butt of many a joke. I remember one time the lads wound him up. He had been told to go and meet a man from Puma about a boot deal at a service station.

He went off in his best suit and waited for him to turn up . . . and waited . . . and waited. Of course, there was no-one to meet but Steve must have waited there for the best part of the day. We had our scouts out and knew that he'd gone. When he came in to training the next day, one of the lads asked him how it had gone. "Oh, I didn't go," he said. "I thought it was a wind-up." But we knew he'd gone and in the end he couldn't help but tell everyone!

Then there was the classic when Kenny Dalglish and Alan Hansen were driving up to Scotland with him. It was quite a chilly day and it was snowing. One of the lads suddenly said there was a problem with the windscreen wipers and asked him to go and have a look. Of course, Steve got out and they drove off leaving him stranded in his T-shirt!

There was a terrific spirit in the team at that time and it was great to be a part of it.

SUGAR, SUGAR . . .

I used to room with Rushie and he was a nightmare! We would go to the hotel and he would have me doing everything for him. I did plenty of running around. I remember he was very particular about his cups of tea. He had to have one-and-a-half sugars in his tea and it had to be just right. If it had too little or too much sugar in it, he just wouldn't drink it and it would be down the sink!

A DAY AT THE RACES

Quite a lot of the other lads were into golf but I didn't play and I still don't. Rushie and I developed a great love of racing and we used to ▷

enjoy relaxing by going for a day at the races at Chester, Haydock Park or Cheltenham. I remember there were one or two snooker and pool tournaments among the lads while I was at the club. There were some very good players, like Gary Gillespie, and then a group of most of the rest of us who were okay and just had a go but it was all good for the team bonding.

THE LES MIST

I will always remember an incident involving Les Ferdinand. We were playing QPR in a midweek game when Les kicked the ball away and was booked.

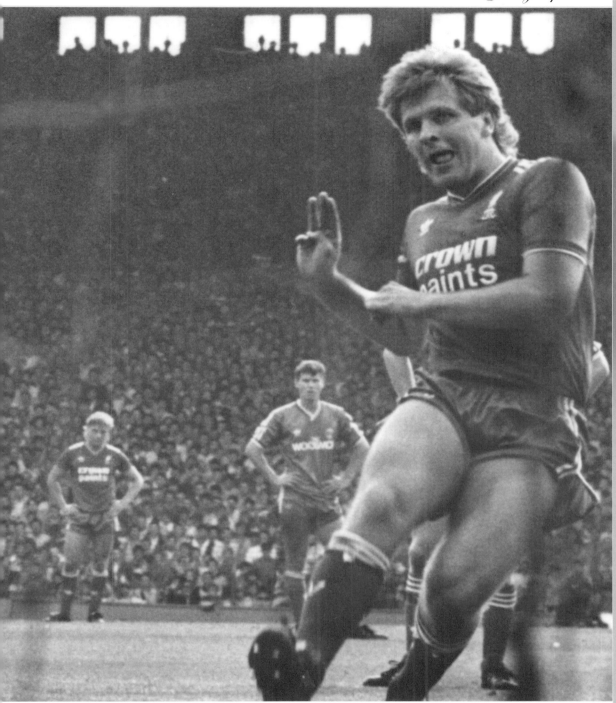

I was about to take the free-kick when I noticed Les was heading for the ref and it looked like the red mist had come down! He just seemed to have lost it and I think he might have done a Paolo di Canio and pushed the ref or maybe worse, so I managed to grab him in a bearhug and calm him down. I think he had a lot of cause to be grateful to me for that!

FASH PUTTING ME ON THE SPOT

Another memory is of John Fashanu. For some reason, I always seemed to take a lot of penalties against Wimbledon and whenever I placed the ball and was walking back to take it, Fashanu always ▷

JAN MOLBY

used to say to me: "I'll have you a fiver, Fat Boy!" Anyway, I think I scored five penalties against Wimbledon so he owes me at least £25 plus the interest!

I'VE NOT GOT IT TAPED!

My best goal for Liverpool is a funny one. It came in a League Cup tie at Anfield against Manchester United in 1985. There was a big dispute between the league and the television companies at the time and no games were being televised.

I remember dispossessing Norman Whiteside in our half and then carrying the ball forward, beating four or five men and then scoring at the Kop end from 25-yards. It was a special moment for me but, of course, there is no footage of it. In a way that might be a good thing because it means I can tell people how great a goal it was!

'WHENEVER **I PLACED THE BALL** AND WAS WALKING BACK TO TAKE IT, **FASHANU** ALWAYS USED TO SAY TO ME: **'I'LL HAVE YOU A FIVER, FAT BOY!'**

But sometimes the more you see goals on television, the less special they feel so at least I will always be happy with my memories of that one!

DIGGER TOPS

I'd say the best player I played with was John Barnes. Obviously Kenny was a fantastic player but he was just coming towards the end of his time as a player when I joined. Barnesie could do some fantastic things with the ball. For three years in 1987, 1988 and 1989 he was sensational. Okay, he may not have consistently hit those heights afterwards but he was still a tremendous player with fantastic ability.

Then Robbie Fowler was just coming on to the scene towards the end of my Liverpool career as well. I was really lucky to play with so many fantastic players.

'DEADLY TRAINING AND A

Liverpool Football Club is famous all over the world. It fills me with pride that I was part of Bill Shankly's famous red revolution that took the football world by storm and laid the foundations for the wonderful club we have today.

When Shanks signed me from Dundee United, he declared that it was part of his plan to build a team up the middle. He had Tommy Lawrence in goal. He brought me in to be a rock in the heart of this defence and he brought in Ian St John to lead the line up front.

He said he would fill in the other parts later. In fact, he already had some exciting young players at that time - men like Roger Hunt, Ian Callaghan and Gerry Byrne. Lads like Tommy Smith and Chris Lawler would come through and the Sixties jigsaw would begin to fall into place.

I was in the army when Shanks moved to get me. Coming to Liverpool brought me out of myself a little bit. Before that I had never been too far from my hometown of Aberdeen. We couldn't afford holidays abroad in those days. Liverpool, as a city, was very different to anything I had experienced before.

And then there was Bill Shankly. Everyone knows he immediately dubbed me his Colossus. I was 6ft 3ins and over fourteen stone and he knew I could become a formidable barrier to English centre-forwards.

Obviously, the club had recognised my potential in games in which I captained the army side. All we did was play football and train. I was the only one in the army side who was not an international. I was only 21 and couldn't believe I was skippering a side with so many star names.

The army could call on men like Alex Young who became an Everton legend and Dave Mackay who became a Spurs immortal. There were a host of others.

We played the Belgian, Dutch and French army

sides. They all had internationals in their ranks and it was great experience for me. I particularly remember the game against the French with a very impressive trophy up for grabs.

We actually played the famous Tottenham side that did the double in '60/61 and beat them. The army life, dominated by football, was great. I never shot a gun in earnest, but I took out a few opponents with my tackling and Shanks clearly believed I could help him with his Liverpool dream.

DEADLY TRAINING - PICK THAT OUT!

I respected him from day one. It's crucial that you want to play for the man in charge. He had basic rules, but he trusted you to stick to them. Very few stepped out of line because you didn't want to get on the wrong side of him.

We were a very fit team. Training is very different these days. Managers spend a lot of time on set pieces. We seldom did that. It was a lot of running, sprinting and exercise. Fortunately for Shanks, we had a host of players with instinctive skills.

You will see a lot of beautiful passing movements in training these days, but ours was a little more competitive. In fact, I would call it deadly. It got a little bit out of hand at times, but I can only remember one serious injury in ten years. Shanks encouraged it because he liked to get the blood boiling. It proved we were fiercely competitive.

We always had a special game the week before the season started. It was a public affair between the first team and the reserves, the Reds versus the Whites. It indicated what the first team was going to be for the big kick-off and it was always a keenly fought affair with people wanting to prove a point.

I can remember a young Tommy Smith, just 17 then, playing against me for the reserves.

'I WOULD CALL IT DEADLY. IT GOT A LITTLE BIT OUT OF HAND AT TIMES. SHANKS ENCOURAGED IT, HE LIKED TO GET THE BLOOD BOILING'

RON YEATS

1961/62 – 1970/71
DEFENDER

RUN-IN **WITH A RISING STAR'**

RON YEATS

Tommy was a striker in those days and had scored a lot of goals at schoolboy level. This cross came over and Smithy leapt with his hands on my shoulders, getting in a header that went right into the top corner. When strikers score, they always shout "YES" as they are coming down. The young Smithy shouted: "Pick that out you Scottish bastard!"

I was going to kill him, but I bided my time. Ten minutes later this ball was played down the line and I knew he would go for it. I came in and hit him with the full weight of a tackle backed up by my fourteen and a half stone.

Smithy was laid out gasping for breath. I stood over him and said: "That makes us quits."

We became great mates after that. We respected each other and he eventually broke into the team and had a great career.

Bill Shankly loved all of this interaction. He was a great believer in communication on the pitch

and it's something that is as relevant today as it was then. I used to say to Tommy Lawrence: "If you are coming out, scream that it's yours and I will get out of the way. Needless goals happen when this communication breaks down in and around the box.

St John the shouter lashes out

Sometimes players ball watch and forget all about the people they are marking. This is when players need to help each other. All it needs is a shout. Ian St. John was our shouter at the other end. He wasn't tall like most conventional strikers at that time, but he was very aggressive. The Saint wasn't a prolific goalscorer, but he got his share and he certainly got other people playing.

He showed his displeasure when crosses didn't come in and would tell Ian Callaghan and Peter Thompson to fire things in more quickly. Thommo, of course, would be beating the same ▷

defender three or four times and the Saint would be going mad.

He formed a great partnership with Roger Hunt. It was tremendous to watch them operate together. When one darted to the near post, the other would instinctively drop to the far post. I get annoyed when I see two players making the same run. It shows they are not communicating and Shanks would not have accepted that.

Behind the scenes things were always happening to boost the team spirit although Alan A'Court once suffered for it. I used to room with the Saint and Shanks used to take the team to a hotel in Lymm as part of the preparation for a game. We must have still been in the Second Division at that time.

It was the Friday night and we went through the usual routine with a cup of tea and sandwiches before we went up to our room about 10pm. It had been a fairly quiet evening and we opened the door and walked in, ready to settle down for the night. Ian walked towards these big cupboards to hang his clothes up.

We didn't know Alan was hiding in the cupboard. Ian's instinctive reaction was to lash out and he caught Alan good style. We had to explain to Shanks why one of his players had been laid out.

Ian later told me that someone had done that to him when he was a child and he had always been frightened of that.

Alan wasn't to know that!

SHANKS' MYSTICAL BODY LANGUAGE

Every day was a pleasure at Melwood. I loved every minute. We had Reuben Bennett, Bob Paisley and Joe Fagan helping Shanks. They were all characters in their own right. The players all got on well. Some, of course, were more personal friends like Ian who I had played against for the British Army when he was at Motherwell. I can remember him biting my ear when we were on the ground. I jumped up and threatened to break his nose. He said: "You can try."

Then he came to Anfield and we became great friends. We played together through a remarkable

football era. The Sixties were special with the Beatles and all of the other Liverpool groups taking the world by storm. Football became different and the fans became very inventive with their singing and chanting. Playing in front of the Kop was an unbelievable experience.

Of course, I became the first Liverpool captain to hold the FA Cup in 1965 when we beat Leeds. I can remember getting back down onto the pitch and immediately taking the trophy to Bill Shankly. I said: "Boss, it's your cup. We couldn't have done it without you."

He said: "Ronnie, as a club and a team we are going on to bigger things."

Of course, he was talking about Europe. That team went on to reach the semi-final of the European Cup in 1964/65 when we lost in controversial circumstances to Inter Milan after beating them at Anfield. In 1965/66 we reached our first European final, but lost to Borussia Dortmund in the Cup Winners Cup.

Shanks would build another team after us and win the UEFA Cup. It was left to Bob to win our first European Cup in 1977.

It all started with Shanks. There is some famous footage of him sitting on the bench, almost mesmerised by what is going on in front of him. He is moving his hands to the left and then to the right. People ask what that was all about.

Quite simply, it was his body language for the team to move as a unit. If the back four pushes up, the midfield pushes up and so on. If the play switches to the other side of the field, the team moves across to defend or attack as a unit. You don't want stragglers anywhere. You want support on the ball and behind the ball.

Shanks would always say that the first line of defence is the forward line. He was right. We were very difficult to beat and had this back up of our wonderful fans.

I used to love it. If we scored at home, the game was over. Opposing teams were always ▷

frightened about going to Anfield.

This is what Shanks wanted. He exploited this psychology. The Kop was like an extra goal. We had a team, on and off the pitch. It clearly struck a chord with everyone who came to the club. It's remarkable how so many players have stayed on Merseyside after their playing days.

When we get together, often at events organised by the Former Players Association, the jokes start flying about. Some of us can remember what happened 30 years ago, but can't remember what happened yesterday!

Stevie G and a case of deja vu

I still work for the club on the scouting side. Liverpool FC has been my life and I want the new Liverpool to enjoy some of the success we had.

I was at the Millennium Stadium when we lost to Chelsea in the Carling Cup. When Steven Gerrard scored the own goal that turned the game, it struck a real chord with me. I can remember scoring an own goal as captain in that 1966 Cup Winners Cup final that proved equally costly.

Dortmund played a through ball and as I chased it with a German striker, I knew I had to get a tackle in. Suddenly I saw Tommy Lawrence flying out of his goal, but I was already committed and the ball flicked up and over Tommy's head. I kept on running, and felt I could get it.

The ball hit the bar and came down, only to hit me on the chest and go in. I saw Steven's reaction when he scored against Chelsea. I knew exactly what was going through his mind. It was even worse for me, happening at Hampden Park of all places. We had beaten Celtic along the way and we felt we could win that final.

The truth is, it happened in an instant and when it came down off the bar I could not get out of the way. You get over it. I knew it was not my fault. I was just desperately trying to prevent a goal.

Shanks was a great philosopher, He would never let you dwell on anything. As one season finished, even if you had won the League, there was no harping back. We always looked ahead to the next challenge. It's something Rafa Benitez also talks about.

People ask me if the 1965 FA Cup final was my greatest day in a Liverpool shirt. The fact is, we were expected to win and we were full of confidence. In the end it went to extra time and

everyone remembers the courage of Gerry Byrne in playing on with a broken collarbone.

Gerry should have been presented with two medals, not one, for the courage he showed. When I finished playing, I turned out for a game in South Africa with a team of ex-internationals. I went down badly and put my whole shoulder out.

The Doc had to stand on my shoulder to put it back in. It was excruciating and I thought about Gerry who had been one of our unsung heroes.

RON YEATS

He is a bit like Jamie Carragher in that respect. Both are hard as nails, although Gerry was remarkably quiet for such a tough lad. Bobby Collins should have been sent-off in the Cup final for the challenge that hurt Gerry, but it was a different game then.

There was a lot of confrontation and we didn't have the cameras picking up every move. Tackling was part of the game and lads would be going up in the air. The difference was they bounced straight back up. Now they are looking to go down and stay down. We never liked to show the opposition that we were hurt. If one of our players stayed down, you knew he was genuinely injured and it was a bad one. I see players going down these days. If you are genuinely injured, you can't run it off at 100 mph. I see people getting carried off, only to be back on their feet in seconds with no apparent reaction. It's just the way the game's changed. I'm just happy to have been part of it all.

'EVERY TIME THE PHONE RANG, I'D BE THINKING 'IS THAT THEM?' I DID GET THE CALL – 13 YEARS LATER!'

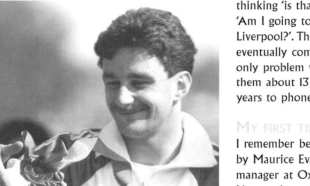

1986/87 –
1989/90
STRIKER

JOHN ALDRIDGE

I've always been a Liverpool fan since I was a kid. My dad was a big fan and so I followed him but it was my uncle who took me to my first game when I was about six or seven.

I was still pretty much a regular when I was playing for South Liverpool.

Before that I played for Cheshire Lines and that gave me more time to go to the match. I would follow Liverpool everywhere, home and away, so I suppose you could say I was a Red-hot fan in my prime.

DON'T CALL US, WE'LL CALL YOU

As a kid I would go to Melwood every Tuesday and Thursday after school and take part in the School of Excellence they had there. It was basically training for all the decent young players in the city, a sort of extended trial for a few months.

Tom Saunders was the head of youth development but this was years before The Academy came along. The likes of Reuben Bennett and Ronnie Moran were there as well and we had some good kids training with us.

I remember before I left Tom pulled me to one side and told me he definitely thought there was a good striker in me and he would be giving me a call to come back. I was made up, what with being a Liverpool supporter and all.

I can remember for a while after, every time the phone rang I'd be thinking 'is that them?', 'Am I going to play for Liverpool?'. The call did eventually come, the only problem was it took them about 13 bleedin' years to phone me!

MY FIRST TIME

I remember being told by Maurice Evans, my manager at Oxford, that Liverpool wanted me. I couldn't believe it. When I pulled on the shirt for the first time, oh my god, that was something special.

My first goal came at the Annie Road against Southampton. It was my home debut and we won 1-0 so getting the winner made it extra special. It came from a Jan Molby free-kick and I ghosted in between two defenders and headed it from just inside the box. Peter Shilton was in goal but couldn't get near it and it went in off the post.

I signed in February '87 but hardly played for

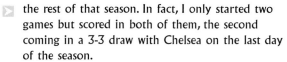

▶ the rest of that season. In fact, I only started two games but scored in both of them, the second coming in a 3-3 draw with Chelsea on the last day of the season.

I didn't play much as Rushie was still there and I think Kenny (Dalglish) had brought me in for when Ian moved to Juventus in the summer.

ABSOLUTELY STUNNING, THE BEST PLAYER I'VE PLAYED WITH

Things began to take shape in the close season (1986-87) when Kenny brought in players like Barnesie, Peter Beardsley and Ray Houghton. They were all very good players and began to provide the service for me to feed off.

It was tremendous playing in that team. There was nobody better. With Barnes on the left and Houghton on the right we all clicked straight away and were so confident. We played some great free-flowing, attacking football.

Barnesie was absolutely stunning, the best player I've had the pleasure to play with and there's been a few good ones over the years.

You would give him the ball and more often than not he would get it into the box. It was just my job to try and get on the end of it.

To win the league so convincingly in the manner in which we did was special. No one could touch us and we went 29 games unbeaten in the league equalling Leeds United's old record.

The league is the one every player strives for in their career so to do it with Liverpool was amazing.

We won it with about three or four games to go and I finished the league's leading scorer with 26 goals which was testament, not to me, but to the attacking force we had in the side.

LEARNING HARD LESSONS ON THE SIDELINES

My second season at Anfield was quite difficult for me as I spent more time on the bench when Rushie came back from Juventus after just a year.

I hadn't missed too many games in my first season and although I was still a Liverpool supporter, it was different watching from the stands as a player.

Of course, you still want the team to win but you want your place back as well.

It's always hard being on the bench when you think you should be on the pitch. That was really tough if I'm honest. ▶

JOHN ALDRIDGE

'MY **SECOND SEASON** WAS DIFFICULT. IT WAS ALWAYS HARD **BEING ON THE BENCH** WHEN YOU THINK YOU SHOULD BE **ON THE PITCH.** THAT WAS REALLY TOUGH IF I'M BEING **HONEST'**

People often said that me and Rushie couldn't play together but that's a fallacy. In that season I still managed around 30 goals and Rushie got his fair share too. I was always quite good in the air so Rushie could feed off me from high balls. We linked up very well and made quite a few goals for each other in most of the games we played together.

IN MEMORY OF THE 96

Of all the goals I scored for Liverpool the ones that stand out are the two in the semi-final replay against Nottingham Forest. They weren't the greatest but it was what they stood for after Hillsborough.

Winning the FA Cup in 1989 wasn't quite as enjoyable as it might have been simply because of what had happened at Hillsborough. It was always at the back of your mind when we played the final.

All we knew was that we had to win it. That was the only goal we had in memory of those who perished.

The final itself wasn't the best of games by any means although it was a thrilling extra-time and we just scraped through.

It was a funny feeling, a feeling that we had achieved something for those who had died. It was special to win the cup but after the initial euphoria of lifting the trophy it soon dawned on us again why we were really there.

Poor old Everton were stuck in the middle of it all but we couldn't have asked for more from them.

The club and their fans were great and really got behind their mates and families because that's what Liverpool and Everton had always been about.

We could sense this out on the pitch that, football aside, everyone was pulling together. Both sets of fans were an absolute credit to the city during that time.

JOHN ALDRIDGE

'BOB NEVER KNEW I GOT

JOEY JONES

I never really believed I would be a professional footballer. I dreamed of playing for Liverpool but I never honestly thought it would happen.

A lot of my mates played football but they were only interested in getting to the local leagues.

I went through the old schoolboy system with Mickey Thomas. I was from Llandudno and he was from Colwyn Bay. We got to the final trial and played North against South. After the match, they told us we weren't wanted. To be perfectly honest, I wasn't arsed because I didn't particularly like school anyway.

I used to knock around with a gang off the estate; we called ourselves the 'Parrots'. We were

THE BUS TO HOME GAMES!'

named after a comedian called 'Parrot face' who used to speak with a funny twang. The majority of us were Liverpool supporters. We used to go on the train to the match.

A lot of people on the estate were from Liverpool. My mum was from the south end. My dad was Welsh but his mum was from the south end as well. There was a lot of Irish there, too.

There used to be lots of fights and I was involved. I'm not proud of it but that's the way it was. I spent a few weekends in local cells.

I've got to be honest, I didn't have much interest in school and I left with no qualifications. I didn't have a job. I didn't know Wrexham were going to take me on. I'd been on trial and not heard anything but they took us on.

The reason I got very pally with Mickey was that we used to get the same bus. I'm quite shy unless I know people and I remember Mickey getting on the bus at Colwyn Bay. As he got on, I always remember him because he had a red and grey school tie and he'd written 'Everton' in biro between the stripes. From that day to this we have been inseparable because we laugh at the same sort of things. The only difference was that he got into trouble when he was older.

I'll only play for Liverpool!

I got into the Wrexham first team at 17. Before then I was on the groundstaff and I couldn't get in the 'B' team. In the local boys' Saturday league, all they used to have was a referee and quite often me and Mickey would end up as linesmen.

We lived in digs together in Borras Park. We earned £8 a week but £5 of that went on digs. It was a real struggle and we often had to bunk on the train. I couldn't drive. My mum and dad didn't have a car. We didn't even have a phone at that particular time.

I remember one day Mickey going out for a bottle of milk and he never came back for two weeks. He buggered off! Honest to God. He hitch-hiked back to Colwyn Bay. That's how we were.

I made my first team debut at 17 and had been in the team for two years. I'd done okay and Sheffield United tried to sign me. I couldn't sign for them. I said 'I don't want to go. I want to stay and I will only play for Liverpool'. I never, ever thought I'd do that, though.

I used to stand out not because of my ability but because I used to roll my socks down. I never wore any shin pads, I had my head shaved and I always wore my shirt over my shorts. That's the way I was. It was only when I went to Liverpool that I started to wear pads.

I came home one weekend, went out on the Saturday night and on the Sunday I'd gone fishing with some of the lads. My dad was standing on the beach. I thought 'What's up? Something bad must have happened.' It turned out that Liverpool had been in touch and wanted to sign me.

I met Bob Paisley at a hotel in Chester and his first words were "Do you want to play for Liverpool?" I just said "yeah, alright". I wasn't bothered about the money. You've got to remember I had been playing for £25 a week and Wrexham had just put up my wages that season to £65. Liverpool came in and said 'We'll give you £100'. If they'd said 'We'll pay you £50 a week', I'd have still said 'Yeah, alright'. That's how much I wanted to play for them.

The next day I went to Liverpool and signed the forms. To say I was overawed was an understatement. All of a sudden, I was sharing a dressing room with players I had posters of on my bedroom wall. I was playing with players who I loved, who I had worshipped. It was a team that everybody would love to play for, whether you supported them or not.

I went over to Holland in pre-season and played well in a game against Utrecht. In the second game against Borussia Dortmund I actually scored two but one was disallowed. They probably thought they'd got another Chris Lawler.

The pre-season went okay and I came back after the Charity Shield. I'd never been on Match of the Day and made my debut against QPR. We lost 2-0 but I actually made a goal-line clearance. That was the first time the fans started chanting my name. I just wish everybody could experience what that feels like.

First team and then the reserves

As the season went on, I did start to struggle. I did the opposite to what a lot of players at Liverpool did. When I signed for them, I went straight into the first team. Normally, they would start off in the reserves for a while. I went into the first team, then I went into the reserves. I did it back to front.

I didn't really want to go and live in Liverpool but I was put in digs in Kensington with a Mrs Lindholm. I'd give her the rent money, then I'd get

> 'I MET BOB PAISLEY AT A **HOTEL IN CHESTER** AND HIS FIRST WORDS WERE 'DO **YOU** WANT TO PLAY FOR LIVERPOOL?' I JUST SAID 'YEAH, ALRIGHT"

JOEY JONES

the bus and go back into town and get the train back to Wrexham on the Bidston line. Then in the morning, I'd get up at 7.30 and go back: Wrexham to Bidston, Bidston to Birkenhead, Birkenhead to James Street and then I'd get the bus and get off at the back of the Kop. I actually did that on match days. Bob Paisley never realised. I got married when I was 21 so this carried on for 12 months. That was just the way it was.

SEEING RED

Some players have favourite goals and favourite saves; I have favourite sending offs. The best was against Middlesbrough in 1975 - the day Davey Fairclough made his debut. The pitch was terrible that day and it was tipping down with rain. It would have been called off today.

John Hickson was one of their main ones up front, a big bustling, Yorkshire centre forward. It was late in the game and I remember the ball coming into the box. Clem has come for it and dropped it. John Hickson went for the ball and Tommy Smith shouted 'Joey, sort it out'. I thought he said 'Sort him out'. So I butted him. I actually knocked him unconscious. I remember all the blood and his teeth had been knocked out.

It was a stupid thing to do but I did it. Imagine the cameras now. I'd have had six months in jail, never mind a ban. I thought he was coming towards me and was going to belt me. It was one of my instincts to hit back so I did. It's not right - I know it's not right - I look back on it now and think how stupid it was.

It was totally out of order and to this day I've never seen John Hickson. I did a talk in Sheffield once and this fella came up to me afterwards and said 'I live in the same street as John Hickson'. I said 'Well, when you see him tell him I'm sorry'. Usually you bump into people in football but I never have.

The best moment for me at Liverpool was simply being there. I supported them for years. Every game I played for Liverpool I cherished. I know it sounds a bit corny but I did. That's why I used to put my fist up to the Kop when I used to run on. It wasn't to cause trouble.

If I had a pound for every time I've been asked about the 'frog's legs' banner, I'd be a multi-millionaire by now. That banner means as much to me as anything from my football career. I saw it when I walked on. It made me feel ten feet tall because out of all those players in the Liverpool team, the Germans will have heard of every one - bar me. They probably thought I'd just climbed over the fence and joined in.

I kept it at home for years. It's in the Liverpool museum now and that's the only place I'd let it go to.

'I'D GET UP **AT 7.30** AND GO BACK. I'D **GET THE BUS** AND GET OFF AT THE **BACK OF THE KOP.** I ACTUALLY DID THAT ON **MATCH DAYS. BOB PAISLEY** NEVER REALISED'

The only place.

I'm still involved in football through coaching at Wrexham. I'd like to play in these charity games but I can't after my heart by-pass operation. Everything I do - and have done - I always try to do the Liverpool Way.

I do genuinely believe that anyone who has played for Liverpool can't help but be influenced by them.

JOEY JONES

'TRIPS TO **THE CHIPPY,** A TEAM FULL OF **CHARACTERS** AND THE NEWS THAT LEFT ME **SHATTERED'**

1991/92 – 1997/98 *MIDFIELDER*

MICHAEL THOMAS

Walking into the Liverpool dressing room for the first time was a weird feeling for me.

I'd taken the championship away from Liverpool two years earlier so I wasn't sure what to expect when I got to Merseyside. I went to Melwood on my first day and it had been all over the press that I was signing for Liverpool, so all the supporters were outside the gates.

Obviously I was a bit worried about the response I was going to get in the city and when I first went in through the gates it was a bit eerie. But as soon as I got into the dressing room it was fine. The lads in there were cracking jokes about the game from 1989, saying things like 'you must be crazy coming here' and 'how much are you on to come here'. They were a great bunch though. They all gave me some stick but I think Ray Houghton, Steve Nicol and Jan Molby, who was always Mr Vocal, gave me the most.

It was all of a welcoming nature though and definitely helped me to settle in. I knew the Liverpool fans would take some convincing. Liverpool fans aren't stupid. They want to see what you can do first before they are convinced about a player. I tried to win them over as quickly as I could and the thing I wanted to do more than anything was to win them a championship medal to repay them for the one I cost them in 1989. I loved them though and loved being part of the club from day one.

The FA Cup run we had that season helped me. I scored the winner in the quarter-final against Aston Villa at Anfield and I scored in the final against Sunderland at Wembley. It didn't appease them totally but it certainly helped!

The club had an air of transition about it when I first got there. Graeme Souness was trying to change things and get rid of players. Everyone was on their toes. Who'd be next to leave? The older players didn't know if they had long left there. So it was a difficult period because we didn't really have a settled side. Saying that, even in that first half-season that I was at Liverpool I think we could have won the championship if we had stayed free of injuries.

The injuries hit home big time from the summer. Everybody was getting injured. When we had all the injuries they looked back at what the training used to be like compared to how it was at the time and it was no different. It wasn't the training. It was just bad luck. It was like a black cloud had come over Liverpool at that time.

ROCK HARD KIT AND OUR SECRET AWAY TRIP CUISINE

Another weird thing for me about coming from Arsenal to Liverpool was that when we were down there we'd train twice a day and every time we trained in fresh kit. But when I came to Liverpool everyone had just one training kit and it was washed once a week.

We'd been sweating into it and they'd just stick it in the dryer and let it dry by itself. The kit would be rock hard and it would stink but it had been that way at Melwood for years. Coming back from away games was completely different at Arsenal compared to Liverpool.

At Arsenal we'd get on the coach and

everything would be prepared for us. We'd have a chef on-board waiting for us and eat a five-course meal as we travelled home. But at Liverpool you'd have the coach stopping off at a chippy on the way home and Ronnie Moran shouting from the front 'who wants fish and chips? Who wants sausage and chips?' Here I was at a professionally run club like Liverpool, one of the greatest teams in the world, and they were organising it like we were a Sunday league side. But it made for a great atmosphere. That side of it was great at Liverpool.

A NEW REGIME AND THE TITLE
THAT SHOULD HAVE BEEN

Things changed when Roy Evans took over from Graeme as manager. It was more relaxed when he was in charge. Graeme was uptight, wanted the best for Liverpool and wanted to win things straight away. At Rangers he'd done that but he couldn't at Liverpool and I think he felt the pressure of that. It got to his heart.

He loved Liverpool though and was desperate to win the championship but he wasn't happy with what he was getting from the players. Roy came in and because it was more relaxed we started to play our football. It was a pleasure to be part of the Liverpool team in 1995/96. We should have won the championship that year. I honestly think to this day now we should have won it. We had a team that could score from any position - well apart from Robbie Jones - but we couldn't defend.

I don't think the young players knew what it ▷

69

MICHAEL THOMAS

took to win a championship. That was my argument with the team. They weren't mentally prepared for it. I came into the team that season when Jamie Redknapp got injured and played in the centre of the park alongside John Barnes. We went on a run of 20-odd games unbeaten but then we lost against Nottingham Forest and I got dropped for the FA Cup semi-final against Aston Villa at Old Trafford a week later. That killed me. I should've walked out. I couldn't believe it. I was crushed. We'd lost one game against Forest and

next minute I was dropped. I wasn't even on the bench either. I don't think anyone could believe it.

To this day, as much as I like Roy and I respect him so much, I think he should've pulled me aside before he announced the team to everyone and told me what he was going to do. I was shocked when he named the team in front of everybody and I wasn't in it. I even thought about walking out of the dressing room and getting a taxi and getting off. The rest of the players couldn't believe it either. Jamie was fit again and straight back in

the team. Was he shocked that he was playing? I don't know about that. I doubt it.

THE NIGHT TORBEN WAS CAUGHT OUT BY SLEEPWALKER JAMO

We had a great bunch of lads at Liverpool during the mid-'90s era. You never knew where you were with David James. One minute Jamo would be ok, the next minute he's lost it and I'm not talking about the ball!

You could never room with him on away trips.

It was too dangerous because Jamo sleepwalks and has little fits in the night. Colin Lee, who he'd worked under at Watford, had told us when Jamo came to the club about his sleepwalking and that he was crazy. I always remember the time when Torben Piechnik came to Liverpool.

We were playing Sheffield United away in the cup and Ronnie Moran forgot about Jamo's sleepwalking and put Torben in with him the night before the game. Anyway in the middle of the night we heard all these shouts coming from their ▷

MICHAEL THOMAS

room. Jamo had got Torben in a headlock and was trying to kill him! We all knew about these fits he had, apart from poor old Torben, but he certainly knew about them by the end of the night.

TRIGGER, MACCA AND ROBBIE'S HORSES AND WAITING ON BARNESIE

Jason McAteer took a lot of stick from the lads. I think Jason likes being silly sometimes. He says things for saying things, if you get what I mean. To actually fight over a nickname like 'Trigger' is when you've got to look at yourself and think 'what am I doing?' Robbie Jones had always been called Trigger, after the character in Only Fools and Horses, since he came to the club but Jason was disappointed when he came in because he told us that he was called Trigger. Rob was like 'you can have it if you want' but we ended up with Trigger and Dave which was the name Trigger in Only Fools and Horses called Rodney by. I was always fond of McAteer though. He was good fun.

One Easter he starts asking questions about why you're not supposed to eat meat. He was like 'but I'm going to McDonald's and I can't go there without having a burger'. He thought about it and then he said 'I'll tell you what, if Jesus was around now he'd have a McDonald's!' I roomed with Barnesie on away trips. He was great. As I was the younger one I had to look after him. I had to get his tea and coffee, answer the door, order the papers and order his club sandwiches late at night. I was like an apprentice who had to do everything for him!

Steve McManaman and Robbie Fowler were always together. They were always putting bets on the horses before games. We'd have the team-talk before a game and they'd be off sorting out tickets for people and putting their bets on the next race. Jamie, McAteer and Phil Babb would all be getting their bets on too. Those five, and one or two others, got labelled as the Spice Boys by the press but I think that was just a sign of the times really. To be fair to them they went out at the right times. They didn't go out partying in the week. They were young boys and they were single. They

had to go out and they did it at the right times but the press seized upon it and were like 'Spice Boys this and Spice Boys that'. In the week they would just go for meals. After training sessions they would go down to the Albert Dock and have their lunch in Est Est Est. So people saw them together having lunch but they were professional in the way they conducted themselves. Robbie and Macca would go and do their own thing. Jamo would just go off with his family and Stan Collymore would go straight home to Cannock.

No-one knew what Stan was thinking. I understand what he says in his book about Liverpool buying a player for so much money that they should work around him but that was never Liverpool's way. He should have known that from the start. Liverpool have always been that way. He can't really moan because he was getting chances in every game and scored enough goals for Liverpool. Maybe he just didn't fit in.

Neil Ruddock was another big character at the club. Razor was Razor. You only have to look at Razor to know what Razor is about. In training sessions Razor thought he was a left winger. He'd play on the left wing or centre forward. To be fair to him when I was a kid playing in London he was at Millwall and he used to play left wing and up front. He used to be really small and really slim but when he started to get bigger they moved him to the back. He still thought he was a glorified centre-forward at Liverpool though.

MISSING A LEADER AND A SHOCK ARRIVAL

The only real leader I ever played with was Tony Adams at Arsenal. He was a leader on the pitch. He carried us.

We didn't have that at Liverpool. It was hard to see who was out there driving us on. John Barnes was a leader in the way he controlled the game, played where he wanted to play and talked to the players but that wasn't the same kind of leadership that Tony gave to Arsenal.

Then we had Paul Ince. He would organise us. I

'ONE **EASTER** HE ASKS QUESTIONS ABOUT WHY YOU'RE NOT SUPPOSED TO **EAT MEAT.** HE THOUGHT ABOUT IT AND SAID: 'IF **JESUS** WAS AROUND HE'D HAVE A McDONALD'S!'

was surprised when Paul signed for Liverpool. I'd heard about it and I though to myself 'he's joining Liverpool from Man United but via Italy. How's that going to go down with the fans?' He fitted in quite well though. At the time I didn't think that we needed him.

He was my best mate there but I didn't think we needed another midfield player. All the press were saying we needed a ball-winner and someone who puts their foot in but that was never our problem. Our problem was at the back and the manager didn't address it. He didn't solve the problem there and I can't understand why he thought getting Incey in would solve it. People thought that he would be the final piece of the jigsaw but he wasn't.

Missed chance under Houllier

I look back at my seven years at Liverpool with positive memories. I had a great time apart from the injuries and not playing at times when I was fit. I think that's what 'peed' me off the most because they'd say it was a squad game and if a

player was playing well he'd keep his place. That wasn't the case. We all had an XI in our heads who we thought would play. But apart from that, Liverpool was a great club with great people.

It reminded me of Arsenal really because it was like a family. There was a special warmth about the club. We were all together but when I went back after leaving it didn't feel the same. It was very cold but I suppose it had to be that way to win the trophies that they did. The funny thing about it is that I would have stayed at Liverpool if I knew what was going to happen in the summer of 1998.

We'd all heard rumours that a new manager could be coming in but it hadn't happened by the start of pre-season. I thought to myself 'I've got to do it now. It's time to go. I can't sit around for another season'. And then Gerard Houllier comes in. I think I would have played a lot more under him. He came into the club and he had no favourites. He signed Dietmar Hamann the following summer so he was looking for a central midfielder. He played who he wanted to play and I think that would have meant I played a lot more.

'ASKING FOR EXPENSES AND

1968/69 –
1975/76
MIDFIELDER

BRIAN HALL

I started life at Liverpool on amateur forms, training and playing with the reserves while continuing my studies at Liverpool University. It got to the stage where I was a regular fixture in the reserve team and doing reasonably well.

My studies stopped in the summer and I was invited into Melwood to train with the first team. This was mid summer so it was pre-season time. I was still living in Preston at the time and travelling by train for training.

There weren't loans from universities then the way there are now so I had to work to supplement my income. That summer I'd been taken on by a bus company in Preston as a conductor and they used to be good to me with my shifts, because I didn't want to miss a session with the senior pros.

Anyway, I turned up for the first day of training knowing I was going straight from the pitch to my work. I'd seen Bill Shankly about the club because he would come and watch the midweek reserve games but I'd never had a conversation with him or been alone with him.

I strode into the dressing room in full uniform with my hat and sat down beside my training gear - and was sat next to where Shankly himself got changed.

He walked in five minutes or so later and stood in front of me. I'd already taken a lot of stick from the lads getting changed for my attire and I was expecting more of the same from the boss. I wasn't disappointed.

He stood in front of me sizing me up for a couple of moments and then said: "You must be the student then?" I was in awe of him anyway but here I was on the spot and I could hardly get the words out. All I could manage was 'yes'.

I NEARLY BLEW MY BIG CHANCE

There was a famous face at Liverpool Uni when I attended, a man called Billy Liddell was the Bursar during my further education.

I'd gone to Uni because I wanted to have something to fall back on if I didn't make it in football and was encouraged to take this option by my father.

I'd been doing reasonably well at the time but I hadn't heard anything about signing a professional contract yet and I was really committed to making

a go of the football. I went to speak to Billy Liddell and told him basically the same thing hoping that he might have some contacts at Tranmere or a smaller club where I would get a chance.

That was all it was, just a passing conversation and it was never brought up again. A few weeks later I got a message that the boss wanted to see me so I went to his office to see what it was he

PUTTING SHANKS ON SPOT'

wanted.

He offered me terms on the spot. The money was perfectly acceptable for the time, twenty pounds per week straight out of Uni wasn't to be sniffed at. But I told him that I'd be staying in Preston for the time being and was hoping for a contribution towards my travelling expenses. Bill wasn't forthcoming. He just got up and walked out. I left his office sure in my heart-of-hearts that I had blown my chance of playing for Liverpool.

He came back in after about four or five minutes and said to me I could have £22 per week and I remember physically shaking trying to put my signature on the contract. I've still got that very first contract at home and the signature looks nothing like what it should do.

I hadn't read the small print of the contract so I didn't know about appearance money or the

BRIAN HALL

attendance bonus and win bonus system. If you were in the first team your wages used to treble sometimes.

To give you an idea of what the money was like, my entire bursary for a year at University was £300 and I got £250 signing on fee from Liverpool. I was absolutely delighted but I still felt I'd lost out to Shankly.

That was a constant theme in my dealings with him. I never ever felt like I'd won an argument or argued my case. He always seemed to twist things around so that you would understand his point, or baffle you with his logic until you were in agreement.

Almost a telepathic understanding!

Everyone always said that John Toshack and Kevin Keegan's understanding on the football pitch was bordering on the telepathic and there's no denying they used to know exactly what the other one did, or was going to do.

Well, when their partnership was its peak a

television programme invited them on to prove, or disprove the theory. It was all done scientifically and they really pushed the boat out. It wasn't live or anything but there was a studio audience there to observe and I'm sure some of the other lads went along for the show.

It was all going really well and the pair of them were really starting to get people excited. They were getting the answers right. They were sat with their backs to each other while cards were held up and the person who couldn't see the card was supposed to receive a message from the other one giving them the answer. What no-one knew was that both Tosh and Kevin could see the cards the other person was getting so of course they were going to get the answer right. They kept it going for as long as they could before they both descended into fits of laughter and came clean.

Dressing room personalities

That was just one of a hundred thousand stories that could have come out of our dressing room.

We were all close, even if that didn't always mean in terms of friendship. I have a lot of friends from the teams I played in now but that's really only come about after the end of our playing careers.

We were brought together by a mutual desire to win and to be successful. We had some big characters in our team but quite honestly none of them came close to Shankly. He was absolutely unique. He would scream and shout at you one minute, turn away for a second and come back to you totally normal as if nothing had ever happened.

He never, ever held a grudge though. He'd have his say and that would be it. Once it was sorted, it was sorted. Not many people would stand their ground with him.

Tommy Smith would occasionally take him on and Larry Lloyd would as well but they tended to be private showdowns rather than anything more public. No-one ever was really brave enough to question his authority in front of the whole dressing room.

Don't get me wrong there were the occasional fall-outs amongst us but surely that's only natural when you have so many competitive young men in such a close environment and even then they were always sorted quickly.

It has always happened and it will always happen. You just can't have the hunger and determination that we had and not expect it to spill over occasionally. That's always been a part of any team sport.

Shanks was always the boss and if he lost his temper there was usually a reason for it, and we understood that.

A FAVOURITE TALE

We were playing against Hull in a League Cup game - a game which was never really top of the agenda. We were winning 2-1 or something like that, when we were given a penalty.

Chris Lawler was the usual penalty taker in the first team but he asked me if I wanted to hit it? I had never taken one for the first team but I used ▶

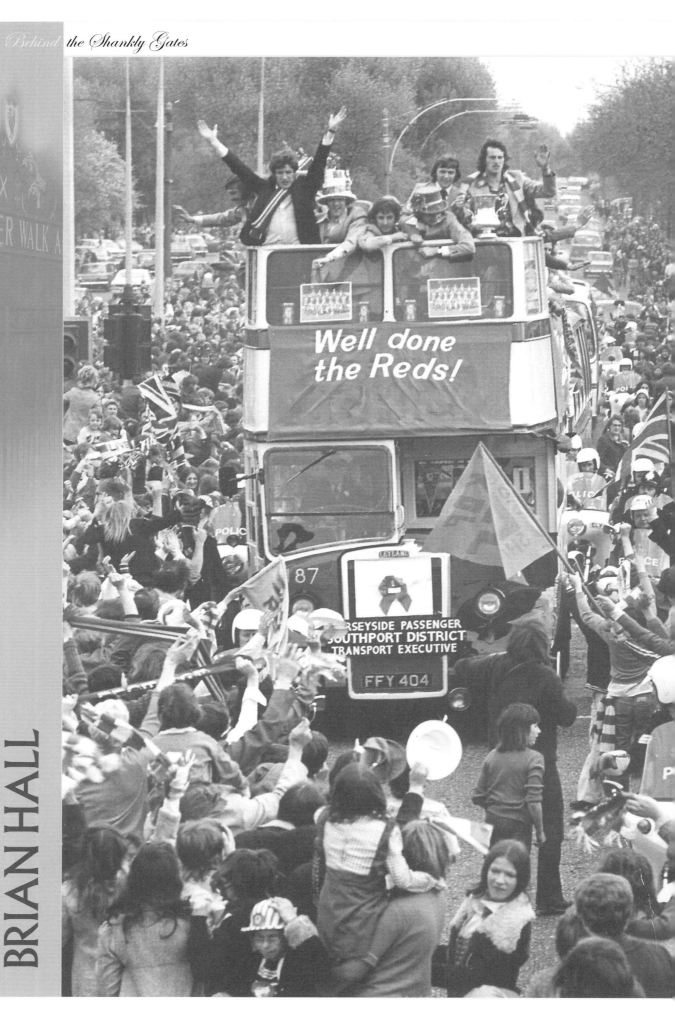

Well done
the Reds!

87

ERSEYSIDE PASSENGER
SOUTHPORT DISTRICT
TRANSPORT EXECUTIVE

FFY 404

BRIAN HALL

to take them in the reserves and I had a really good record with them, so I thought 'why not?'.

You've got to picture this - I know its not easy - but I was taking this penalty at the Anfield Road end of the ground and Shanks was sitting in the Directors' Box. I've stepped up and slotted the ball, side-foot, into the bottom right-hand corner - the goalie's left.

It was a great penalty because it hit the side netting just an inch or so inside the post. It was perfect - or so I thought. It wasn't really important to the team because we'd have won the game anyway but it was important to me.

Anyway, I've gone back into the dressing room very pleased with myself with a big smile on my face.

The boss walks in a couple of minutes after me and walks straight for me.

"That penalty," he said as I looked up expecting

'THAT PENALTY,' HE SAID AS I LOOKED UP EXPECTING A COMPLIMENT, 'FAR TOO NEAR THE POST, SON!' I NEVER TOOK ANOTHER PENALTY AGAIN FOR THE FIRST TEAM'

a compliment.

"Far too near the post son. Far too near the post."

That was all he said to me before walking off and I never took another penalty again for the first team after that.

I've often wondered why he was so unhappy about it and the only reason I've ever been able to fathom was that he must have assumed it was going to go wide of the post. From his angle in the Main Stand it must have looked wide because of the curl with the inside of the right foot and he panicked.

It was a very strange moment, but another example of what set him apart. He didn't just want things done well, he wanted them perfect. I still feel the sense of privilege I've always felt at the chance to work with someone so unique.

THE LIVERPOOL FAMILY

Sweet taste of success ...
toasting the first title under
Shanks after victory over Arsenal
at Anfield in 1964. (Back row,
from left): Alf Arrowsmith,
Ronnie Moran, Gerry Byrne, Ian
Callaghan. Front row: Roger
Hunt, Gordon Milne, Ian St John,
Tommy Lawrence, Peter
Thompson, Willie Stevenson
and Ron Yeats

THE LIVERPOOL FAMILY

Calling all the heroes . . . (top) celebrating the glory of Rome '77 are stars through the decades. From left: Chris Lawler, David Fairclough, John Aldridge, Gerry Byrne, Tony Hateley, Phil Thompson, a proud fan, Sammy Lee, David Speedie and Ian St John. Above (back row) Alan Hansen, Emlyn Hughes, Jimmy Case. Front row: David Fairclough, Ray Kennedy, Phil Neal

Ex-Reds on tour . . . stars pictured top are (back row) Roy Evans, David Fairclough, Phil Neal, Bruce Grobbelaar, John Wark, John Durnin. Front row: Terry McDermott, Michael Thomas, Gary Gillespie, Alan Kennedy, Mark Walters. Above: a rousing rendition of You'll Never Walk Alone at a reunion dinner. With Gerry Marsden (centre) are Ron Yeats, Willie Stevenson, Roger Hunt and Ian Callaghan

THE LIVERPOOL FAMILY

We are the champions . . . a celebration as the league title is clinched at Anfield in 1982. Pictured (to
Mark Lawrenson, Craig Johnston, Phil Thompson. Front row: Sammy Lee, Graeme Souness (obscured

ow, from left) are Bruce Grobbelaar, Ronnie Whelan (back), Ian Rush, Alan Hansen, Kenny Dalglish, ᵠhil Neal. The title was sealed with a thrilling 3-1 victory over Tottenham in the final home game

THE LIVERPOOL FAMILY

The Ex factor . . . (top) heroes one and all with Jessie Paisley to celebrate the 25th anniversary of the 1977 European Cup. Above: Peter Cormack on the ball; all smiles from the two Davids, Johnson and Fairclough; Chris Lawler and 'Sir' Roger Hunt; saluting the great Shanks at Anfield – (from left) Ian Callaghan, Chris Lawler, Ronnie Moran, Kevin Keegan, Roy Evans and the late, great Emlyn Hughes

Power of the Kop lives on . . . pictured (from top) Joey Jones with his famous 'Joey ate the frogs legs' 1977 banner; Jessie Paisley outside the Paisley Gates; Jimmy Case, John Toshack and Tommy Smith reunite to relive the good times; Ronnie Whelan at a charity game; Ian St John, Ian Callaghan, David Fairclough and Brian Hall showing pride in the shirt at Anfield

Head boy ... John Barnes is 'crowned' with the league trophy by Bruce Grobbelaar during a 1988 tour of the city. Also pictured (from left) are Gary Ablett, Alan Hansen, Ray Houghton, Gary Gillespie, Craig Johnston, Ronnie Whelan, Jan Molby (back) and Nigel Spackman

THE LIVERPOOL FAMILY

THE LIVERPOOL FAMILY

Bridging the generations ... the Liverpool players are applauded on to the pitch during a special Anfield tribute to Bill Shankly. Pictured (from left) Ron Yeats, Willie Stevenson, Tommy Lawrence, Tommy Smith, Ian St John, Gerry Byrne, Gordon Milne and Peter Thompson with Brian Hall (right). Below (far left): Sammy Lee and David Johnson; golf pals Alan Kennedy, Ian St John, David Fairclough, David Johnson, Ron Yeats, Tony Hateley and Ian Callaghan; Kevin Keegan and Roy Evans share a joke; David Fairclough, Emlyn Hughes and Phil Neal chat about old times

Ron for all . . . the Liverpool team in relaxed mood ahead of a testimonial match against Newcastle for Ronnie Whelan, at Anfield in August, 1993. Pictured (back row, from left) are Nigel Clough, Stig Inge Bjornebye, Mark Walters, Steve Nicol, Bruce Grobbelaar, Neil Ruddock, Paul Stewart, David Burrows, Mark Wright, Mike Hooper. Front row: Rob Jones, Ian Rush, Ronnie Whelan, Jamie Redknapp and Torben Piechnik

THE LIVERPOOL FAMILY

All together now ... pictured (clockwise) Cally, Smithy and the Saint admiring a new work of Anfield art; Brian Hall, Smithy and Big Ron catch up on Kop memories; camaraderie at a reunion dinner with Kevin Keegan, Alec Lindsay, Jimmy Case, John Toshack and Smithy; on the pitch supporting the Roy Castle Lung Cancer Foundation; in the shadow of Shanks – Brian Hall, Alan Kennedy, Ian St John, Ron Yeats (with Nessie the guide dog), Tony Hateley, David Fairclough, David Johnson and Ian Callaghan; Aldo alone with his Hillsborough memories on the 15th anniversary of the tragedy. Below: the original committee Ian St John, Peter Thompson, Willie Stevenson, Tommy Smith, Willie Miller, Alan Kennedy, David Fairclough and Ronnie Whelan

THE LIVERPOOL FAMILY

Take us as Red ... pictured (right) Terry McDermott, Michael Thomas, John Wark, Gary Gillespie, Paul Walsh, Phil Neal, David Fairclough, a lucky fan, Alan Kennedy, Bruce Grobbelaar, Roy Evans and Mark Walters Above right: Ronnie Moran and Joey Jones share a joke about the glory days

'I WAS BOB PAISLEY'S FIRST SIGNING BUT THE MANAGER SAID HE HADN'T EVEN SEEN ME PLAY!'

1974/75 –
1985/86
DEFENDER

PHIL NEAL

I was the first player the great Bob Paisley signed for Liverpool. I look on that as a real honour although I was stunned when I turned up at Anfield in October, 1974, to meet him for the first time.

He revealed that he had never seen me play! I found that strange to say the least and a negative on day one.

There I was, this young man from Northampton, meeting my new boss for the first time. Liverpool had agreed to pay a £60,000 fee for me. This was a decent fee for an unknown defender. I assumed that the manager had watched me on a scouting mission and had recognised my potential.

What I didn't know at that time was that Bob had complete faith in the Liverpool staff around him. Geoff Twentyman was Chief Scout and he contributed to some magnificent signings down the years. It was Geoff who had spotted me and that was clearly good enough for Bob.

What did give me a boost was when Bob added: "I believe you can play anywhere across the back four."

It demonstrated that they had done their homework on me over a number of games and so

the positive immediately followed the negative. I was just thrilled to be joining the best club in the country and I would finish up playing in more than 600 games, win eight Championships and become the only man to play in all five of Liverpool's European Cup finals. Not bad for a player who was not even watched by the manager before I was signed.

I actually made my debut in a derby match at Goodison against Everton in front of 56,797 fans on November 16, 1974. Bob put me in at left-back in place of Alec Lindsay who had been good enough to play for England. That in itself was an honour.

I only found out I was playing on the Saturday morning. I was going to the game with Tom Saunders with no idea that they were going to plunge me into the side. It was a shock to the system, but my second thought was that I wanted to get out there and prove I could handle it.

I was marking John Connolly who was a skilful winger. We drew 0-0 and that was pleasing. It was a massive leap forward for me.

Bob, of course, was in his first season after taking on what seemed like the impossible task of replacing the legendary Bill Shankly. The team had

lost successive games against Ipswich and Arsenal before the derby, conceding four goals after previously keeping four clean sheets.

Bob was clearly reassessing things. Liverpool had won the FA Cup the previous May. This had been Shanks' parting gift as manager. The team had therefore qualified for the Cup Winners Cup, but they would go out in the third round to Hungarians Ferencvaros. Things were not exactly going sweetly for Bob and in that down-to-earth Geordie voice of his he is supposed to have said: "I didn't want the job anyway!"

It's an interesting quote from a man who, in his nine years at the helm, would go on to win three European Cups, six League Championships, three League Cups in succession and the UEFA Cup. He was also voted Manager of the Year six times.

Clearly, his football judgement was second to none and I remain fiercely proud to have been his first signing – even if he hadn't seen me play!

THE FANS GOT A FREEBIE WHEN WE WON THE LEAGUE

I managed 23 appearances during that first 1974/75 season as Bob Paisley's opening campaign at the helm ended with Liverpool in the runners-up spot. I must have made an impression on the boss because I would be virtually an ever-present over the next

PHIL NEAL

ten seasons. I actually played in every single league game in the eight seasons between 1975/76 and 1982/83. The run was broken when I missed a single game, against Sunderland early in the 1983/84 season. It was business as usual the following year with another full complement of 42 games in 1984/85.

I must admit to smiling these days when I see all of the discussion about the importance of rotation and resting players.

I once sustained a fractured cheekbone, but I still played the following Saturday against West Ham. They were deemed a "footballing" side then and it was thought I could get through against them. It would have been serious if I'd taken another knock, but I played through and the games kept mounting up.

But my only thought during my first full season, 1975/76, was to establish myself and become part of the scene at Anfield. What a year it was. It ended with Bob's first league title as manager and we clinched it on a remarkable night at Wolves. I had begun to understand the humour of the Merseyside fans.

The dressing rooms in Molineux's old Waterloo Road stand opened right out onto the street. It was just a couple of steps up and you were in. There seemed to be Liverpudlians everywhere, many without tickets. Phil Thompson looked out and spotted his two brothers, Ian and Owen.

'THE BOSS LOOKED AS IF HE WAS ABOUT TO EXPLODE. HE SAID: 'IF YOU WANT A CHRISTMAS PARTY, HAVE IT IN THE SUMMER!'

He asked Bob if he could open the door and let them through the dressing room from where they could go down the corridor and into the paddock.

Bob decided to accommodate Thommo and opened the door. After about five minutes it seemed like thousands of people had made their way through, all wishing the lads good luck on the way and heading down the tunnel towards the paddock. Bob said: "Thommo, how many relatives have you got?" It was hilarious.

Little did I know that night that this would be the start of ten to eleven years of phenomenal success.

THE CHRISTMAS PARTY THAT HAD THE BOSS FUMING

We were champions in 1982 and 1983 and were heading towards a hat-trick of league titles in the 1983/84 season when the lads suddenly had to decide on a date for the players' Christmas party, which was always a big thing.

We thought we would have a free week towards the end of November and went ahead to book a function at Tommy Smith's club in the city centre.

However, it all became a bit hectic because of Milk Cup action. We had played Fulham away and even though they were two divisions below us, they held us 1-1. The return leg was on a Tuesday and we had the Christmas party booked for the previous Sunday.

The lads decided we should go ahead with the party on the agreed date, even though the midweek match was looming. The logic was that we would go in on the Monday and work our butts off to ensure we were well prepared.

As it turned out, Gordon Davies equalised for Fulham to secure a second 1-1 draw and when extra time failed to settle it, we faced a third game.

When the gaffer found out about the party he was fuming. We were due to be off the following day, but he said we should all report in at 9am. No one was looking forward to this meeting. The boss finally walked in and said: "Alright, how was the Christmas party?"

We all sat with our heads down until Steve Heighway eventually replied: "Sorry boss."

The gaffer looked as if he was about to explode. He said: "If you want a Christmas party, have it in the summer!"

With that he walked out and slammed the door. That was it. There was no extra training. He had just brought us in to make one bold statement, but we all got the message. We never made that blunder again.

We eventually won the tie at the third time of asking 1-0 and it is now history that we went on to beat Birmingham, Sheffield Wednesday and Walsall before meeting Everton in the first ever all-Merseyside Milk Cup final.

That was quite a season. We beat the Blues, of course, in a Maine Road replay thanks to a Graeme Souness goal.

We also won the league, my seventh title. This was also the year of our fourth and last European Cup final success, the victory over Roma.

Altogether, it was an historic treble. Perhaps we deserved that Christmas party after all.

'SAME AS WEDNESDAY, LADS'

Joe Fagan, like the men who went before him, was a strong character. People possibly didn't realise how strong he was. I remember an occasion when he was in charge. We played really well in the midweek. The weekend game loomed and Joe's team talk was short and to the point.

"You played well on Wednesday lads. Same again."

With that he walked out and shut the door. That was it.

It might sound strange, but it summed up the trust that he had in the players and the backroom staff. That made us feel ten feet tall. He knew we didn't need any complicated discussions. We had all been taught to do the right things and Joe just pointed us in the right direction.

The dressing room almost ran itself. We sorted out any minor disputes and just went out in every game believing we could conquer Europe if not the world.

Joe was big enough and strong enough as a character to believe we could handle it. Of course, if we stepped out of line we would soon know about it.

'SMITHY START A FIGHT!'

Joe Fagan was as honest as they come. He would just look at you and you knew it was time to really work hard. He also had this knack of understanding exactly what was needed.

I can remember when a game was going a bit flat and we needed stirring up a bit. Joe would stand up and shout: "Smithy, start a fight!"

Suddenly we would be up for anything, battling for each other and turning things round completely.

However, there was one game when even a

Smithy fight would not have been the answer. We were playing against East Germans Dynamo Dresden in 1977/78 and beat them 5-1 at home.

It looked as if it would be a formality over there. Then we went one down early on, Ray Clemence had to save a penalty and they hit the crossbar and the post. We were getting battered and were constantly having to look to Steve Heighway as an outlet to relieve the pressure. We ended up winning 6-3 on aggregate, but it was a game I will always remember.

At that time, famous athlete Lasse Viren was allegedly having transfusions of re-oxyginated blood to inspire some remarkable performances.

Dresden had made such a turn-around in form and physical fitness that we wondered if they had been taking advantage of this new and controversial opportunity. The eastern bloc countries were up to all kinds of things at that time. Who knows?

TERRY MAC HAD US ROARING WITH LAUGHTER AT 30,000 FEET

Terry McDermott was good enough as a player to be named Footballer of the Year. He was also one of the funniest people you could ever wish to meet.

We were flying away on one European trip and Terry, as usual, was up and down acting the fool.

Bob Paisley said: "Terry, will you pack it in. You'll get us thrown off."

Terry leapt back to his feet and said: "Not at 30,000 feet boss!"

He was so quick-witted. I can remember a game at Wembley when we played Tottenham in the Charity Shield. Bob had this way of walking, swinging his arm. Terry decided that we would all walk out, swinging our arms in the same way. It was like a Benny Hill sketch.

Terry always had a competitive edge, but it was always mixed with laughter.

One night he was on the bench for England and as the game wore on he persuaded himself he was not going to be used. He got a beef sandwich out of his pocket and started to eat it. Just when he'd finished, Ron Greenwood turned round and said: "Get stripped Terry. You're on."

Not the perfect way to win another cap!

PHIL NEAL

'IT'S TRUE **SHANKS** PLAYED

1972/1973
– 1976/77
MIDFIELDER

PETER CORMACK

Scoring in my first derby game with a header was a great moment for me. We won 1-0 at Anfield in October 1972 and I think I became accepted from then on. I remember Kevin Keegan patting me on the back and saying: "You may not have made it yet, but you've won them over." Larry Lloyd also came up to me as we were walking off at the end and said: "Well done Peter, that's you now."

At the time I didn't realise the magnitude of the derby game. I'd experienced the Edinburgh derby with Hibs against Hearts but nothing like Liverpool and Everton. You don't realise the scale of it beforehand so to get the winner was very special.

FIVE-A-SIDE UNTIL HE WON!'

TWO SHANKLYS

I had the privilege of playing under not one Shankly but two! Bill's brother Bob had been in charge while I was at Hibs. To play for both of them was great. They were both exceptional managers but Bill just had that awe about him. I think when you look at the great managers, you're almost frightened of them . . . the likes of Don Revie and Jock Stein. Shankly had the respect of the players but there was also a slight fear. Nowadays, the top managers like Sir Alex Ferguson and Arsene Wenger have that too. As a player you don't want to let them down.

When I met Bill, he sat me down and said: "Now son, you sign right there." And I just picked up the pen and signed right away. ▷

It was only when I went home and my wife asked me what the details of my contract were that I realised I didn't know! It's not like it is now with all the money they're on and all these stupid agents and all the rest of it. You were just happy to sign for a club like Liverpool and play. To be part of a team that went on to win League Championships, FA Cups, Uefa Cups - there's a lot of players who will never do that in their entire careers.

I had wonderful times. Obviously, I was quite fortunate to be playing in a successful period and I was playing every week. It wasn't like nowadays when you get rested. I never wanted to be rested, I just wanted to keep playing every week.

I can always remember playing all the time and then, in my second year at Liverpool, Shankly called me in and I thought: "Oh, here we go!" I'm sure it was a European game and it was the first time I'd ever been left out. I asked Bill why he'd dropped me and he said: "Ah well, you're looking a bit tired." I said: "Well I've played 72 games and been okay!" I think it must have been his way of kicking me up the backside because I was only left out for the one game and then I came back in again.

'WHEN WE HAD A TEAM **NIGHT OUT** WE USED TO ENJOY A **SING-SONG**. I ALWAYS USED TO ENJOY SINGING, SO I'D ALWAYS GET UP AND **START THE LADS GOING'**

The first time he speaks, it's a lie

At Melwood, the first team always used to train first and then we'd just be finishing and then lads like Sammy Lee and Phil Thompson, who were in the reserves, would go out and there was always a match between the reserves against Shanks's team. Shanks would have Bob Paisley, Ronnie Moran, Smokin' Joe and a few of the others and it's true what they used to say about Shanks keeping playing until his team won!

There was one game which was about five-each or something and Shanks said: "Oh, we'll play for the winning goal." I think Sammy Lee then scored for the other team. Well, the goals didn't have the nets in them and Shanks said: "No, that wasn't a goal. It went through the side." Chris Lawler was stood nearby and Shanks turned to Chris and said: "Chris, was that a goal?" And Chris said: "No it wasn't boss." With that, Shanks turned to the other side and said: "Christ boys, he's been here 25 years and the first time he speaks, he tells a lie!"

Starting off the sing-songs

When we had a team night out, we always used to enjoy a sing-song. I always used to enjoy singing, so I'd always get up and start the lads going! We had some good fun. The spirit was great and the backroom team when I was there were terrific. We had Bob Paisley, Ronnie Moran, Smokin' Joe and Roy Evans. To think that they all went on to be managers must be unique. They were all well-liked and very close to the players and everyone in the squad just got on together. There was never any animosity.

Unfair to pick anybody out

I was fortunate enough to play with some great players. John Toshack, Kevin Keegan and Steve Heighway were all class players as far as I was

PETER CORMACK

PETER CORMACK

concerned and then Tommy Smith and Emlyn Hughes. Alec Lindsay and Chris Lawler were two full-backs who were like midfield players.

They were both very comfortable on the ball, excellent at passing but then again the passing was a trademark of the Liverpool team.

I think it would probably be a bit unfair to pick anybody out as the best I played with because in their different ways, they were all exceptional players.

You had to be exceptional to keep your place in those days - there were no average players at Liverpool.

WE WERE ALL WINNERS

I think the difference when I came to Anfield compared to the other teams I played in was that we were all winners right through the team. We all wanted to win something. I've played in teams where there have been maybe only four winners and it makes a difference.

When I left for Bristol City there were maybe half-a-dozen - guys like Norman Hunter, myself Joe Royle and one or two others but I never played in another team whose players were as hungry to win things. When you fast forward to the present day, I think that's when it's hard for managers to make

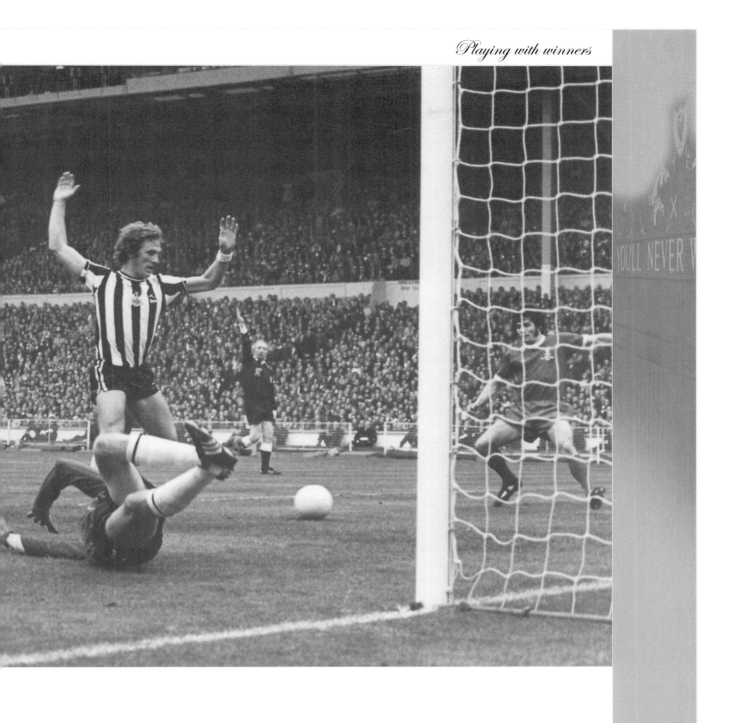

signings because you want to make sure they're all winners.

Maybe a guy who is not quite as good a player but who wants to win things - they're the ones that I'd rather have in my side and I think that's what they managed to do at Liverpool when they brought players on board. It wasn't about money.

Players who came through like Phil Thompson, Sammy Lee and Jimmy Case were all winners.

I know when I wasn't in the team, I wanted the team to lose and that's only because I am a winner. If any player tells you any different, they're lying! Everyone wanted their place back.

'I KNOW WHEN I WASN'T **IN THE TEAM,** I WANTED THE TEAM **TO LOSE** AND THAT'S ONLY BECAUSE **I'M A WINNER.** IF ANY PLAYER TELLS YOU ANY DIFFERENT, **THEY'RE LYING!'**

'ALAN'S TV TREAT, DOUBLE MAGIC AND HOW KENNY HELPED US TO PULL OFF THE PERFECT WIND-UP'

1983/84 – 1988/89
DEFENDER

JIM BEGLIN

O nce Alan Kennedy had moved on, I used to room with Alan Hansen. I don't know whether Alan Kennedy was his mate on the quiet but I do know big Al had me answering the door, answering the phone, working the telly if we didn't have a remote control, I had to do everything! I had to answer the door when the breakfast tray came in the morning to let room service in - Hansen never moved! I just got bullied and ordered around the place, but I got my own back because I was a terrible snorer – well, I still am!

He used to go berserk with me on a Saturday if he hadn't had his full quota of sleep! He loved his soaps. He always used to watch Dallas and Dynasty and he followed Dynasty every week.

On away trips, Al would be the first to leave on a Friday night after dinner at the hotel so he could get back to the room, make a call home to check everything was okay and then be tucked up in bed for the start of Dynasty. He absolutely loved it. He nicknamed me Dex after the Dex Dexter character which was a bit of a wind-up because I was still single at the time and most of the boys were married. I used to go out on occasions and he would try and find out all the little stories and so he christened me Dex. But that doesn't take away from the fact that he was into Dynasty big-time. He'll deny it but he was!

The day Brucie hit me

The biggest character of the lot was Brucie! He was a livewire and just a big, happy character. But I got on his bad side in the FA Cup final in 1986 when he hit me, which wasn't too pleasant.

We got in a bit of a muddle and we were 1-0 down at the time, we weren't exactly picking our game up and Everton were still applying some pressure. The ball came over and ran along the touchline and I thought I'd just shield it from Trevor Steven so Brucie could pick it up.

I was running away from goal but Brucie was telling me not to put my foot on it because he was going to dive on it. But in those days you could get away with picking it up even if I did put my foot on it, as there was no back pass rule then. Meanwhile, Brucie had 'taken off'. He tended to be a bit excitable at times - I think that's fair comment! Anyway, he kind of dived over it and there was a bit of a scramble to get the ball back and he recovered it.

He called me a stupid Paddy or something, so I told him where to go and he hit me! For a moment I was really mad and I thought about hitting him back but then I thought: 'Well hang on a minute, there's 100,000 watching it, a lot more people watching on telly and Brucie is an old jungle fighter!' So I thought I'd better not take him on. Anyway we kissed and made-up - well, we made up!

The craic was good

Brucie was just larger than life and hilarious to be around. He was always coming out with one or two bizarre stories and one or two tall tales as well! He was never far from the centre of attention in the dressing room and they were a good bunch of lads. It was generally a good craic and there was a good social side as well. ▷

JIM BEGLIN

They all enjoyed a night out. Ronnie, Jan, Rushie, Steve McMahon were great characters and Steve Nicol was just daft as a brush.

I remember we always used to take the mickey out of each other. If somebody was interviewed in midweek and appeared on Football Focus or On The Ball, we'd be watching it after our pre-match meal on the Saturday. If there was a slip-up in what they were saying on camera, that always produced major stick. If you made any kind of rick you'd get merciless stick for it.

My all-time favourite comment was from Brucie one night. There was a few drinks on board and for some reason the topic of serial killers came up in the conversation and Brucie listened away. Eventually, he decided he'd have his tuppence worth. He piped up: "What about that one from New York, The Boston Strangler!" That was the kind of thing that you'd get and I remember that one well to this day! Things like that were always good to keep us going. I also had my share of stick for saying daft things but I've gone conveniently blank about what they were!

The wrath of Joe

I was Bob Paisley's last signing as manager and so I didn't really work under Bob. He obviously stayed on to guide Kenny when he became player-manager. Joe Fagan gave me my debut. He was a lovely, quiet man. He was so mild-mannered and so placid as a character, he was just like your favourite uncle. He had a nice way of talking to you . . . until he got cross!

I remember when I got in the side, I was on a high and didn't even think about things because they were just working for me. I like to think things went pretty well for me initially and then it just seemed to catch up with me.

We played Watford at home and I had a shocker of a first half. I was attributed with an own goal when a ball deflected off me but I could have reacted to it quicker. At half-time Ronnie Moran would usually be the one who would hound you and give you stick and Ronnie, being a former left-back, used to love giving left-backs stick!

He would always be on our case and Alan Kennedy used to get it in the neck before me. But

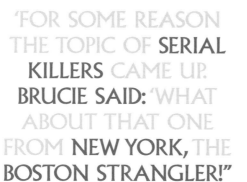

'FOR SOME REASON THE TOPIC OF **SERIAL KILLERS** CAME UP. **BRUCIE SAID:** 'WHAT ABOUT THAT ONE FROM **NEW YORK,** THE **BOSTON STRANGLER!**"

this day, Ronnie ended up saying very little to me. He just said: "He's right you know" because Joe had an almighty go at me and I'd never seen him like that before. He took off at me and basically told me to get a grip of myself and sort myself out and I hadn't seen that side of Joe.

There was another incident as well. We'd played Panathinaikos at home in the European Cup and I'd taken a bit of a blow to the calf. It was heavily bruised but I wanted to play against Villa on the Saturday and he pulled me over on the Friday at Melwood after I had joined in again and told me: "You're not playing tomorrow."

He was obviously thinking on about what was to come and Alan Kennedy had also picked up a knock. I said: "No, I'm fine gaffer, I can play." But he just looked at me and said: "I'm not playing you tomorrow."

I said: "Gaffer, I'm okay. It's a bit sore but it's going down now and I'll be okay." In the end, he put his foot down with me in no uncertain terms. So that was the other side of Joe and when he had to be forceful and say his bit, he could do when it was needed.

Sold a dummy by King Kenny

I think that once Kenny had become manager he had to distance himself. He was player-manager, one of the lads, hugely popular but the more decisions he made, the more he upset one or two players and I think in the end he kind of grew away but he always kept his sense of humour.

I remember we drew away with Luton in the FA Cup in 1987, the year we were defending it.

We drew 0-0 on their plastic and 10 days later they had to come to Anfield for the replay. So we'd done the usual, trained in the morning, gone to the hotel, had our kip and then turned up at Anfield only to find out that Luton hadn't travelled. The weather was particularly bad and the roads were covered in snow and ice and the game was off.

But we had a lad at the time called Alan Irvine. We always used to call him Fraggle Rock, I don't really know why! Anyway the boys decided ▶

to play a wind-up on him with Kenny in on it. Alan didn't know the game was off so Kenny held the usual meeting a little bit earlier and he's basically said that Alan Irvine is playing and talked him up as being the key man. He gave it the works.

Well, bit by bit, you could see the lad getting more nervous. He wasn't expecting to play, he was expecting to either make the bench or be part of the squad so by the end of Kenny's talk, Irvine was looking white! The minute Kenny finished his talk and told us to get ready, he got straight up and headed to the toilet!

Your pre-match visit to the toilet is always an important part of your routine. Anyway by the time he came out, we'd all gone home! So Kenny was always great for craic like that but ultimately, he became more a boss then than a player.

MERSEY MAGIC

I played in a few great games but the FA Cup final would be up there. For me, it ended eight days that were such a high. We'd won the league at Stamford Bridge the week before and particularly in view of what happened to me later in my career with breaking the leg, I look back on that with great affection because my career was so short.

I've still got some tapes of local radio interviews I did at the side of the pitch at the end and I'm talking as if I'm on the most incredible high. For me, you can't get much more of a natural high than that feeling when we had won the double. Of course, seeing my kids born was special as well but that whole period was just unbelievable and we had such a fantastic run.

Everton had beaten us at Anfield in the March and we had a few doubts. I saw Hansen saying he had told Kenny at the time that that team would win nothing. The Press had written us off but we went on an incredible run. I think we won 11 and drew one of our last 12 games.

The Cup was the icing on the cake and because it was Everton, our rivals from the same city, that made it a little bit more special. Driving to the ground with fans cheering, the whole atmosphere was amazing. They say that 98,000 was the official

attendance that day but I think there was more like 120,000 and people were risking their lives to get in. I had about 40 or 50 people over from Ireland - it was just a really special time.

The one little regret I have is that we should have won the domestic treble. We should have won the League Cup as well but got beaten over two legs by QPR in the semi-final. We got beaten 1-0 down there and then we had a nightmare at Anfield. I started off by blasting one against Ronnie Whelan for an own goal and then big Gary Gillespie got an own goal as well and we drew 2-2 and went out 3-2 on aggregate.

On the Saturday after the second leg, we had to play QPR again in the league and we beat them 4-1. There was always a little tradition where we would go out with our Crown Paints sponsored balls. You would basically put Best Wishes and your name on it and then go to your part of the ground and kick it into the stand as a souvenir for someone. As I say, I had been involved in the OG accredited to Ronnie for the first goal of the League Cup game and before the league game, I ran over to the Kemlyn Road side as it was then and booted the ball high into the stand. I was turning around to go back to the warm-up when some Scouse fellow shouted: "Pity you didn't do that on Wednesday, Beglin!"

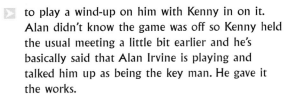

'KENNY SAID **ALAN IRVINE** WAS PLAYING AND TALKED HIM UP AS BEING THE **KEY MAN.** BY THE TIME HE CAME OUT OF THE **TOILET,** WE'D ALL GONE **HOME!'**

SHIRT SWAPS

I've got a few shirts from opposing players. I have Paolo Rossi's Juventus shirt. After Liverpool had won the European Cup in 1984, there was a Super Cup match against Juventus as they had won the European Cup Winners Cup that year. We went across to Turin to play them but the match should never have been played. The pitch at the Stadio Communale was covered in ice and there were little heaters at the side of the pitch trying to melt the ice. I was on the bench and didn't play but it was so cold, we swapped shirts indoors afterwards and I ended up getting Rossi's shirt. When I played for Ireland against Denmark, I swapped shirts with Jan, so I have his number 13 Denmark shirt.

JIM BEGLIN

'GOING UP, SHANKS' SWEAT

L iverpool won the championship in 1947 and got to the FA Cup final in 1950, losing to Arsenal. A lot of those players who were still in the side were going past their prime. In 53/54, when we were relegated to the Second Division, a lot of the Liverpool players were over 30. They had grown old together. Consequently, we struggled a little bit.

When we were in the Second Division, we were playing against Scunthorpe and Grimsby and Lincoln. Any time we came across sides like these, they seemed to raise their game. I remember we were third, fourth - always so near - which was frustrating. We lost to Doncaster, home and away, at Easter in '56. It cost us promotion. That was the way it seemed to go. We were crying out for promotion.

SHANKS ARRIVES

Prior to coming to Liverpool, Shanks had managed three clubs: Workington, Carlisle, Grimsby and Huddersfield. He came to Liverpool with an abundance of background experience. Liverpool was like a sleeping giant.

Phil Taylor, the manager before Shanks, didn't have the experience of being a coach, though he had been captain of Liverpool. He didn't have that inside feeling.

Somehow, we were not quite strong enough. We scored a lot of goals but we let a lot in. I think we paid the penalty for not spending much money. The ground, even, hadn't changed very much. You wondered where all the money was going because we were getting good gates - 35-40,000.

When Shankly first saw the background at Liverpool, he felt that the side was not good

enough. We lost his first game at Cardiff 4-0. He actually said that some of the players had been at the club too long, which wasn't a confidence booster for me because I'd been there about eight years.

He utilised his managerial experience from other clubs and what he did was very simple; he strengthened the side through the middle. He was able to acquire some money and buy Ian St John and Ron Yeats, who cost about £20,000 overall. He got a big 6ft goalkeeper and then he utilised the strengths of what was at the club and we walked the Second Division. That was my most pleasing moment. All through my prime, I'd played in the Second Division and I could have gone to a First Division club but I just kept thinking 'We'll get promotion, we'll get promotion' and it never happened.

ANFIELD'S JAMES CAGNEY

Shankly, in those early days, changed the whole set-up. He re-doctored Melwood and introduced a 'sweat box'. It was a board that was 12 yards square and you'd go in there with a football and you would kick it against one wall and collect it; then you'd turn, kick it against another wall and so on.

He would change and adapt. He might ask you to control and turn or he might ask you to play it first time. He'd have you on the clock. If the ball missed the board, another player would come in and you would have to get the ball off him while he screened it. By the time you came out of there you were absolutely knackered.

We also had what we called 'Little Wembley', which was about 50 yards long and it had a full goal all boarded up. It had numbers on; if you ▷

1952/53 – 1964/65
STRIKER

ALAN A'COURT

BOX AND 'LITTLE WEMBLEY"

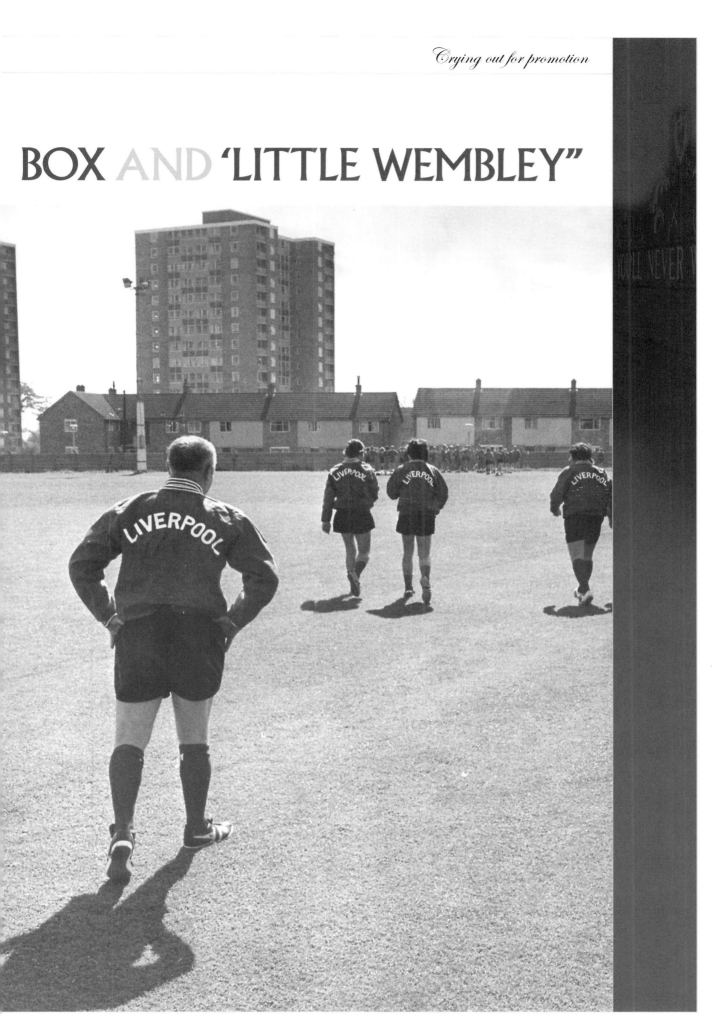

ALAN A'COURT

were aiming for the top left-hand corner, it might be number nine.

If you were aiming for the bottom left-hand corner, it might be number one. It would be on a nice surface that no-one was allowed to go on, unless they were doing some shooting practice.

Off the field, he had a tactics board. In a way, Shanks reminded me of James Cagney because he would stand over it, hunched, going 'Boys, boys', before setting out the plan. He did instil confidence.

BACK WHERE WE BELONG

We were undefeated for the first 11 games the season we got promoted (61/62), winning 10 of them. We were off to a flier. We had a bit of a sticky patch later on and went to Leyton Orient. We were 2-0 down but I scored two late goals for a 2-2 draw, which kept them five or six points away. My happiest moment was when we beat Southampton at home - 4-1 - and we got promotion.

The feeling was a bit of relief and elation. Having strived for seven or eight years, I felt

'I've done it'. I'd played in every game that season.

Once we went into the First Division, it was a different ball game. We finished up in the middle of the table and I played 20-odd games but I didn't think I'd reached my potential. I played better in the Second Division when we won promotion than when I was playing for England in the World Cup in 1958.

In some ways, I think I let myself down a little bit when we came up. I injured my thigh and that didn't help. I think somehow I self-consciously relaxed. I didn't feel I did as well as I could have ▷

'I WAS AS **COMPETITIVE** AS ANYBODY. I ENDED UP **IN THE KOP** SOMETIMES BECAUSE WHEN I **CROSSED** THE BALL, I COULDN'T **STOP RUNNING'**

done but you've got to remember that the club was adjusting; let's face it, there is only one club who can win the league and one who can win the cup. I got the injury and I never got a chance after that because he had got a young team together and signed Peter Thompson.

I missed out on the cup final in 1950 because I was too young and I missed out on the league championship in 1964 because I wasn't involved and the FA Cup in 1965 because I'd left. He only used 15 players in 1964. You aren't going to change a winning team and you didn't have subs.

In some ways I was probably not his type of player in the sense I couldn't mix it. I wasn't frightened of putting a foot in but my way of getting back at a player who was having a go at me was to push it through his legs and go past him. If I tried to kick him or retaliate, my game would suffer so I used my speed and skill. Perhaps I gave out the wrong signals. I was as competitive as anyone. I ended up in the Kop sometimes because when I crossed the ball I couldn't stop running.

He had his own ideas of playing and you've got to take your hat off to him because of the leagues and cups he won.

The one thing I do have to thank him for is when we won the Second Division. I'd jarred my ankle in one game and there is nothing worse. He was never very good with players who were injured; they annoyed him. He didn't want to know. I wasn't scared of not playing but when you are not at your best, the fan screaming 'Wake up!' doesn't know you've had something to upset your balance of play.

It went right up to Friday morning and I'd been doing light training. 'How are y'son?' I said 'I'm struggling a little bit, Bill'. 'Aye, you'll be alright'. I got it strapped up and got through it. I look back and think I'm glad he had the confidence in me to play because I played every game that year.

THE RESULT OF FAILURE

They have team bonding now, with the arms around each other in the middle of the pitch. Players have different characters and, when we were in the Second Division, we had four or five experienced players together and four or five younger players. I think that didn't help the bonding. You needed to be all together.

ALAN A'COURT

You have to go through the rough and the smooth, supporting each other.

The result of failure was felt on the confidence. It's all about self-belief and I think that was the strength of Shanks and Bob. Players on the pitch had to suit each other and it was like that with the managers. Shanks was the rough and brusque figurehead. Bob Paisley was cool, calm and collected. But they were on the same wavelength.

SHANKLY'S OBSESSION

I can remember getting the train coming back from Euston after a match. There were some supporters there, playing a five-a-side. He joins in and the ball went off the platform onto the track. Shanks jumps down to get the ball and got all sorts of oil on his white Mac'.

If anybody wanted to talk football, he would be interested. We were in America and he was talking to this bloke and the bloke didn't know who Tom Finney was. That was it; Shanks just walked away.

He hated footballers playing golf. He said it made you tired and plodding. We did play but we were scared to death and never told him. He'd check on you going to nightclubs drinking. He wanted people to talk and sleep the game. That was his nature. He was totally committed. As a coach or a manager, you have to give two-thirds of your time. There is little time for family.

NO REGRETS

I've seen players come to Liverpool, get two matches and never be seen again. I played 356 games so I must have been doing something right. The Liverpool crowd were always good to me. One man said to me 'You were an honest player'. I thought 'Fair enough, that'll do me'. I made nothing out of the game except the medals, the caps. In material value, I've got a house. But I've had a great time.

'HE WAS THE HARDEST MAN I'VE EVER SEEN – AND I PLAYED A RECORD 843 GAMES FOR LIVERPOOL'

1959/60
- 1977/78
WINGER/
MIDFIELDER

IAN CALLAGHAN

The first character I can recollect when I signed for Liverpool was a tough pro called Jimmy Harrower. He was a very good player, but solid with it. I was just a young player and it would have been in the late fifties.

I was trying to make a name for myself and I distinctly remember this game between the first team and the reserves. Jimmy was marking me and during the game he came over and in a threatening tone said: "Be careful, son!"

It was just the old pro warning the young kid, but I was still surprised. Later I realised that threatening people was part of the game for many people. After all, I roomed with Tommy Smith later in my career.

I got to know Jimmy quite well later on. My best mate at that time was another young Liverpool player, Willie Carlin. He would later play for Blackburn and Derby County.

Willie was in the year before me at school and played for Liverpool Boys and Lancashire Boys. He was a face I knew when I joined the Anfield staff.

Later Willie asked for a club house which was normal in those days as you progressed. They gave him one next door to Jimmy Harrower.

When Jimmy was transferred to a club in Scotland, he knocked on Willie's door and said he was waiting for a delivery of 3cwt of coal, having paid for it before he realised he was on the move. He asked Willie if he wanted to buy it. What Willie didn't know was that Jimmy had gone to the other next door neighbour with the same offer.

Both paid him. A few days later Willie got a knock on the door. It was the coalman, seeking payment for the delivery he had just made. Willie said he had already paid. "You haven't paid me," said the coalman and held out his hand.

It was another lesson in growing up. The game was about men then. The boys had to learn quickly.

A NEW WAY OF LIFE - KEV BRINGS IN HIS AGENT

The game changed dramatically during my time with Liverpool. I made my debut against Bristol Rovers in April, 1960 and I didn't leave until 1978 when I went with Tommy Smith to join John Toshack's Swansea. A revolution happened in between, both at Anfield and throughout the game.

I can remember when Kevin Keegan said he had an agent looking after his affairs. Before that we just plucked up the courage to go in and ask Bill Shankly for a rise. Most of the time we came out thanking him for not giving us one.

Kevin had exploded onto the English football scene. He was probably the game's first real superstar after George Best. Kevin was opening shops, making records and driving a big Jaguar, but considering everything came to him so quickly, he remained as down to earth as the next man. Fame never went to his head.

I can remember when he first joined us from Scunthorpe. We went on tour to Sweden. He was just this young lad and we had no idea how big he would become. Clearly he was a terrific talent, even at that stage.

Kevin was just part of everything that was going on. It was a pleasure to go to Melwood

every day. There was always something happening to keep us smiling and focused. We trained hard and we played hard and while there were wildly different characters in the squad, we got on like a real family.

I WAS A FAMOUS PRO BEING TAUGHT HOW TO WASH MY OWN SHIRT

Gerry Byrne was my first room-mate. He was always immaculately turned out. He still is.

Gerry was one of the toughest players in the game, but he was a gentle giant. We went on tour to America for seven weeks. We had these new style drip-dry shirts and Gerry would insist we

washed them and hung them out to dry in the evening.

Gerry was incredibly organised and he got me into that way of thinking. He moulded me into that way of life. Of course, we had to fend for ourselves. This was not the pampered world of football that we have now in which everything is done for you.

Gerry was a seasoned pro and I was just a youngster. Of course, he became famous for that act of courage in the 1965 FA Cup final when he played on after dislocating his collar bone.

People were shocked, but we knew he was as ▷

hard as nails. He was the hardest man I have ever seen – and I played a record 843 games for Liverpool.

When I think back to that Wembley game, I can remember the agony in his face as Bob tended to his injury and strapped him up. Not many could have gone back out onto the pitch, especially against a team like Leeds who were ruthless at that time. Gerry even played a part in the winning goal.

THE DAY I REPLACED A LIVERPOOL LEGEND

I was pitched into the Liverpool team at just 17. Ironically the man I replaced in that game was my idol, the legendary Billy Liddell. I suppose I didn't understand the significance of it at the time, but I do now.

I'm just grateful that I had possibly the best debut that anyone could wish for. Anything less and I would have been judged against the great man who was good enough

to play twice for Great Britain at the peak of his career.

At the end of that debut match, even the ref clapped me off and I got a standing ovation from the Anfield crowd. That meant so much to me. I wasn't an automatic choice at that point and the following season the club signed Kevin Lewis, but I was on my way.

Billy Liddell was a lovely man, but he didn't talk to me much about the game. He was very quiet and also had a life away from football as an accountant. Later he became the bursar at Liverpool University and was a JP for many years.

But make no mistake. He was a Liverpool icon. I used to watch him in training. Even though he was coming to the end of his career, he was awesome when he fired in shots with both feet. When he got the ball at his feet in a match, you could sense the expectation of the crowd. They always knew something sensational was about to happen.

It was such an honour for me to replace him although nobody could fill Billy's boots.

SHANKS THREATENED TO TELL MY MUM!

I have to say that throughout my career I was never told off once by the legendary Bill Shankly. Well that's not strictly true as I will soon explain.

I can remember him coming to see my parents at our tenement block in Toxteth. I was just a shy lad. He promised my mum and dad he would make me a good pro.

He respected my parents and he looked after us.

The only time he raised his voice to me was during a trip to Bruges. We were staying in this hotel on the big square. Shanks allowed the lads to go out and have a drink, but imposed a midnight curfew.

We came back late and Gordon Wallace was hanging out of the window, pointing downstairs and telling us that the boss was hiding behind the door, waiting for us.

We decided to go in one by one and run for it up the stairs. Shanks saw Ronnie Yeats and Ian St John. He shouted: "You two are always out. I should have known you'd be amongst them."

He then saw Gerry Byrne and roared: "Gerry Byrne, I will tell your wife you've been out."

He then saw me and looked shocked. "Ian Callaghan," he shouted, almost lost for words at first. "I'm going to tell your mother on you!"

You can imagine the stick I got from the other lads the next day.

SHANKS' MASTERSTROKE MADE THEIR FANS FURIOUS

I have played in many great games down the years, but everyone still remembers the 1965 European Cup clash against the mighty Inter Milan at Anfield. We had just won the FA Cup for the first time by beating Leeds at ▶

> Wembley.

It seemed like the whole of Merseyside had turned out to welcome us back to Anfield for the semi-final first leg clash against the Italians. Bill Shankly pulled off a real masterstroke.

He sent Gerry Byrne and Gordon Milne out with the FA Cup and told them to walk around the pitch as the Italians warmed up. Of course, the crowd saw Gerry who had been so courageous at Wembley and still had his arm in a sling. Gordon had missed out through injury and their supporters went absolutely hysterical.

The noise was deafening and it shook the Italians who must have wondered what they had come into. We came out walking ten feet tall and stormed to a 3-1 win. It should have been good enough to take us through.

We then went to the famous San Siro for the return and I have to say that the atmosphere in their stadium was also something else. They won 3-0 and we all know about the dubious refereeing decisions that cost us dear. The whole thing became part of Anfield folklore. These truly were remarkable days in our club's history.

HARD - BUT HE COULD ALSO PLAY

I mentioned that I roomed with Gerry Byrne early on, one famous hard man.

Later I would room with Tommy Smith, another who could put in a tackle. Smithy used to always say I was lazy, but he was just one of those people who couldn't be still. He was hyperactive and there has always got to be a problem to confront with

Smithy. That's the way he likes it.

Breakfast would be sent up to our room. Smithy would be up straight away buttering my toast and pouring the tea. It's not that I was lazy. He just wanted to do everything.

I have always had a great relationship with him. He's a great lad, one of the greatest characters to have played for Liverpool and also one of the best players I have seen.

People always go on about how hard he was – and it's true. But I always add what a good player he was. Remember that skilful run down the right in the 1974 Cup final. He was a good header of the ball (Rome '77) and he liked a 60 yard crossfield pass, although it only came off twice a year!

Seriously, he was a great all-round player and he often doesn't get the credit for that.

We enjoyed some great times together. Even when our careers ended at Anfield, we moved together to Swansea.

We played in an age that people will always remember because it was different. The clothes were different.

The music was different as Beatlemania took over the world. The singing and the chanting was different.

We won everything in sight and we had a succession of sensational players.

The camaraderie between us was outstanding and that is why the Liverpool Former Players Association is so strong as a unit.

It's why we stick together, proud to say that we wore that famous red shirt.

'SMITHY SAID I WAS LAZY BUT HE WAS JUST ONE OF THOSE PEOPLE WHO **COULDN'T BE STILL.** THERE ALWAYS HAD TO BE A **PROBLEM TO CONFRONT'**

IAN CALLAGHAN

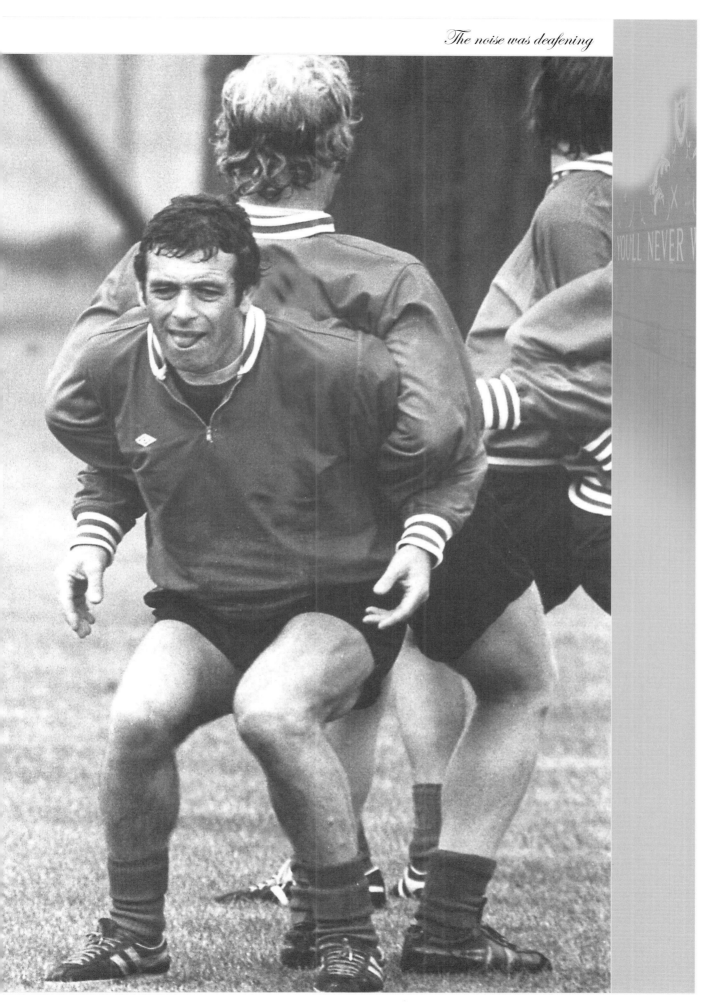

'FOUR HOURS LATE TO SIGN

1978/1979
– 1985/86
DEFENDER

ALAN KENNEDY

I was actually four hours late for the meeting with Bob Paisley and Peter Robinson when I signed for Liverpool in 1978 because I had a problem with my car. The wipers on my brand new Triumph TR7 broke down and it had started to rain. I was driving blindly but I had to make it. I was trying to find a phone - there were no mobiles in those days. I was trying to get in touch but they did stay there.

I was taken to the Atlantic Tower hotel. I went in and I met them and the chairman, John Smith. We concluded the deal within about five minutes. They said 'Right, you've got to have a medical'. I went in the other room, I lay on the bed and the doctor came to me and tested my heart, tested my pulse, looked at my body and said: 'Hey, fit as a fiddle. No problem. You can run all day'. That was it! I thought to myself 'I'm the most expensive full back in the country. I'm going to have the biggest medical.' None of that.

Bob then came out with his classic statement: 'Alan Kennedy. Ahhhh, yes, we'll sign him. £330,000 - a lot of money for a full back but we see the future of Liverpool Football Club in Alan.' Somebody asked the question 'Do you think he'll play for England now?' He says 'Course he'll play for England. If he doesn't play for England, I'll jump in the Mersey.' Then he thought about it because one of the reporters said 'But Bob, you'll drown'. He says 'Yeah, I'll jump in the Mersey when the tide's out'. Unfortunately, I didn't play for England under Bob, it was actually Joe Fagan who got me in the squad in '84.

GETTING OUT OF BAD HABITS

It wasn't what you'd call a great debut. We won 2-1 against QPR and I was absolutely delighted but

Bob and the lads were disappointed because they didn't want to concede and also wanted to score quite a few more. Everybody was disappointed but I was ecstatic: 'A win!' In my last season at Newcastle, I'd not won since Christmas of '77. I was wondering when the next win would be.

I have to say, it took me a long time to get into the 'Liverpool Way'. Bob always said 'Play it simple' while 'There's Alan Kennedy, looking for the 60 yard ball to Terry McDermott.' My triangles were 60 yards long. Graeme Souness and Ray Kennedy would come short for the ball, I'd launch it because I was used to people like John Tudor and Malcolm MacDonald, who would catch pigeons.

It was a daunting task. Liverpool had this philosophy of playing good football and I wasn't used to that. That's no disrespect to Newcastle but they were route one. It was a whole new ball game for me. I think I proved in the first season that what I lacked in accurate passes, I made up for in effort and determination.

I gradually got into the gist of it and learnt a little bit. It only took me seven years to get into the system and then they sold me.

A NEW TEAM GELS IMMEDIATELY

I basically replaced Joey Jones. Joey was a cult figure. He had a tattoo which symbolised Liverpool Football Club. He stood for everything that was good about Liverpool; fighting, determination, playing football the way it should be played. Bob Paisley decided he wanted reinforcements in that particular area and had got me to come in.

Dalglish had come a year earlier, Souness had come six months earlier. Bob felt these were great acquisitions for the club. You lose players and sometimes you get in a better player. ▷

BUT **BOB** SHOWED ME **MERSEY!'**

> It was great because the competition built at the football club and it was healthy competition for everybody.

Even the stalwarts were under pressure. That particular year Ian Callaghan and Tommy Smith left the club, Kevin Keegan and Toshack went the year before. That was a major change-around. You've won the European Cup. How do you kick on from there? All you do is look around and find better players or ones as good as you. That's what they did.

FLIPPIN' 'ECK, IT'S NOT SO BAD

We never gave the defensive record a thought in 1978/79. We conceded three late on in the season at Aston Villa but we knew by then there was some sort of record on.

We lost early on to Forest in the European Cup and Sheffield United in the League Cup.

Because we missed out on Europe, we felt we had to do something special that particular year. Every midfield player came in with about six or seven goals. Bob had got the formula right. We played on some poor, poor pitches in those days but still managed to play some decent football.

We beat Manchester City by five, Norwich by six. It was just incredible, the feeling. That team had only been together a year or so but it worked. We hardly used any players.

There were still complaints from the fans that we weren't playing well enough, even then. Phil Neal came in for criticism from various quarters of the ground, I did, Ray Kennedy did, but when you think about it, you think 'Flippin' 'eck, it

wasn't such a bad team.' Most fans expected Liverpool to win by two or three because they were so superior to the other team.

CARDS ON THE TABLE (BRIEFLY)

We went to Poland once, I think we were playing Lech Poznan. In those days, because it was a communist country, we couldn't use our normal Aer Lingus, so we had to fly British Airways. We were playing cards and I am the world's worst flyer but cards seemed to settle me down.

We were about a mile away from the runway, about to touch down. I've got the best hand you can get: 'Wonderful. Bloody great. Can't lose this one', I thought.

ALAN KENNEDY

As the captain was saying we were a minute from touchdown, all of a sudden he put the engine full on, zoomed down and went back up. The cards were all over the place. 'F****** hell man, what are you doing?' Honest to God, he came over the tannoy and said 'I'm sorry about that ladies and gentleman, we just missed the runway by thirty feet'. I had the best hand ever and ended up on all fours searching for my cards. The game was abandoned. I remember one of the tabloids said '50 feet from death' but I could have killed the captain.

Paris in the spring

I don't think the European Cup final against Real Madrid in 1981 was a dreadful match; it wasn't an

'HE CAME OVER THE TANNOY AND SAID 'I'M SORRY ABOUT THAT, WE JUST MISSED THE RUNWAY BY THIRTY FEET'. I HAD THE BEST HAND EVER AND ENDED UP ON ALL FOURS SEARCHING FOR MY CARDS'

exciting match. People don't remember the pitch, which was in a terrible state. There had been rugby on it the week before and it wasn't well looked after. Finals should have the best pitches and stadiums. I remember Graeme Souness got injured very early on. It was a case of not conceding, that's what we decided on. No goalkeeper was tested.

The manager always encouraged you to get forward. When Sammy Lee picked up the ball, he shouldn't have been in that position in the first place. He left the ball to Ray Kennedy. You don't think about what you're doing, you just do it. You make a run, you may not even get the ball. Bob liked players, such as Terry McDermott, who made runs for the sake of the team, to create space.

Ray threw the ball at me, which hit me directly on the chest. The defender should have cleared it, the keeper should have stood upright, but I had the shot and the ball went in. I just ran and ran and ran; it seemed like it took ages to get to the Liverpool fans. I was fortunate it was at that particular end. It was reminiscent of Kenny Dalglish against Bruges in '78.

Some lads went out that night. I stayed in, being the good, clean little lad that I was. My girlfriend at the time said we were not going out.

PARACHUTE LANDING

Roma had some great players: Cerezo, Graziani, Conte and we felt we were in the minority in terms of fans. We didn't get the better of them, they didn't get the better of us. I suppose Joe Fagan was pleasantly surprised after 90 minutes. What he said was: 'Don't let yourselves down'.

After extra-time, I thought the clock said something like 12 o'clock at night. It just seemed to go on and on and on; it was ridiculously late by the time it got to penalties. Joe was looking for volunteers. I don't think anybody stood out. A couple had been substituted, including Kenny Dalglish. I'd missed them in a pre-season tournament. I'd practised them in training and I was pathetic, absolutely pathetic, but Joe didn't just look at the week before when we were practising;

he looked at the game on the night, who felt confident, who felt decent. The big surprise was me.

Steve Nicol missed his, Phil Neal scored, then Graeme Souness and Ian Rush. I wasn't even thinking about scoring in two European Cup finals. I honestly don't recall what was going through my mind. I wanted it to end there and then. It was frightening, absolutely frightening. Millions of people were watching, 80,000 there on the night. If I could have 'beamed' myself up anywhere, I would have done it. I wouldn't have taken that penalty for all the money in the world but Joe had given me strength, he'd given me the belief that I would be alright. Joe was great at looking at the character of people. He was proved right, the way it went.

I don't know how you describe the feeling; it was wonderful, great. People think it was coolly and calmly placed. It wasn't anything of the sort. It was

'I DON'T KNOW HOW YOU DESCRIBE THE FEELING; IT WAS WONDERFUL, GREAT. PEOPLE THINK IT WAS COOLLY PLACED. IT WASN'T ANYTHING OF THE SORT'

a quick movement, run up, open the body up and place it to the goalkeeper's right-hand side. Nothing made my mind up until that final second.

The lads came running over and I famously did what looked like a parachute jump landing. It wasn't a great way to celebrate winning a European Cup final but it didn't particularly matter. We had a great night afterwards. We were invited to a villa on the outskirts of Rome and all had a meal together - loads of wine. I remember someone said at five in the morning that we had to get back to the hotel and when we did it was absolutely buzzing. Loads of supporters. A wonderful night shared by a lot of people, a lot of our friends and family were there. It was a great laugh, we had a sing-song. I was looking at a picture the other day and the colour of the clothes we were wearing. My God. It was definitely the Eighties, absolutely terrible.

PERMS AND 'TACHES

In those days, it was the fashion. Ten years ago it was bleached blond hair, like Robbie Fowler. It was just a fad. Moustaches were the 'in' thing. Everybody wanted to look like Magnum, with Hawaiian shirts, too. I'm still keeping them. I've got them upstairs in the loft, just in case.

ALAN KENNEDY

'NICKNAMES FOR THE BOYS – 'DOC', 'TOSH', 'TONKA' AND 'OLLIE' ... THE TEAM SPIRIT KEPT US GOING'

When you're born and bred in Merseyside you either support Liverpool or Everton.

I supported Liverpool. Bill Shankly was the manager and I'd go with my brothers and stand on the Kop.

I learnt all the songs, the dos and don'ts, how to support your team and, like every other person inside the ground, wondered what it would be like to play at Anfield. Playing football myself at school, I was always trying to emulate my hero and that was Roger Hunt.

I'd be playing in the streets or the yard and when I scored a goal I'd be imagining I was at Anfield and would run away and celebrate like I was Roger. I was no different than any other kid but obviously I became a professional footballer with Everton and then Ipswich.

I thought I'd missed my chance to play for Liverpool. Shanks had tried to buy me twice from Everton and then a couple of times from Ipswich but it never came off. But finally, in 1976, I did get the opportunity to play in the red shirt of Liverpool at Anfield.

To actually walk down the steps, with a red shirt on, and fulfil that childhood dream was something I can't put into words.

It's virtually impossible to express unless you've actually experienced it yourself. Only then could you know what I mean.

To run towards the Kop end, to score in front of the Kop, to hear them shout your name . . . it just fulfilled all my childhood dreams.

I arrived at Liverpool as an established footballer and an England international but to actually play for the team I supported was something else.

I'm still a Liverpool supporter now. Even though I played for them I'm still passionate about the club.

Of course, it helped to be playing for a team that wasn't exactly struggling.

I was there from 1976 to 1982 and we won three European Cups, four league championships, three League Cups, four Charity Shields and reached an FA Cup final in that time.

That goes a long way to being able to look back now and say they were good days.

JUNGLE TALES AND A RELUCTANT SUPERSTAR

You don't ever win that many trophies unless you're good on the pitch and good off it.

You don't cross the winning line unless you're together and that was something that was always evident at Liverpool. We were comrades on the pitch and comrades off it. Again, that's something special and unique about Merseyside.

It says a lot that so many ex-Liverpool players decided to settle down and stay in this area.

We've got the Former Players Association who meet regularly, we have golf days, dinners, a Christmas get-together and it's nice because we have all remained friends.

When I first came to the club I roomed with Kevin Keegan but after one season he left for Hamburg.

I then roomed with Stevie Heighway but once he had moved to America I roomed with Bruce Grobbelaar. ▷

He was a lunatic, an absolute crackpot. Bruce used to tell me these stories about how he was in the army and would be in the jungle fighting crocodiles and snakes. He was a one-off, was Bruce.

Kevin was magnificent to share with. He was magnificent both on and off the pitch.

He gave a million percent on the pitch and off it he was a bundle of fun. He was a practical joker, good to be with and we had some great banter with him.

Kevin liked a joke and he could take a joke as well. He was definitely one of the boys. I know he was considered as the superstar at Liverpool but he wouldn't thank anyone for calling him that.

He appeared on Superstars but he never saw himself as a superstar. Kevin classed himself as a part of the team, not an individual star.

Liverpool didn't have superstars. If anyone had portrayed themselves as a superstar they'd have been slapped down.

Everyone realised they had a part to play. You always get players who are loved more by the supporters or the media but that didn't affect those individuals in the eyes of the rest of the lads or on the pitch.

A NEW NICKNAME'S IN THE BAG

I was nicknamed 'the Doc' when I was at Liverpool and that was all down to Terry McDermott.

When you're a footballer you're forever getting dressed, undressed, in the shower, out of the shower, in the bath, out of the bath, washing your hair and all the rest of it. There were no real facilities back then so you had to bring a bag with your shaving kit, shampoo and most importantly, a hairdryer.

Because you were washing your hair all the time you couldn't be going out and training or whatever with wet hair so you'd have to dry it.

Some of the lads had perms. They'd have to use these things that I can only describe as like a rake to flip their hair up with. I used to have a hairdryer, a brush, smellies, shampoo and so on and I used to carry it in a black bag.

I also always suffered with sore throats and tonsillitis so I always had Strepsils, Tunes or something like that in there. Now, if you've always got your bag with you, then nobody else brings anything in.

They'd all be like 'we'll just use Johnno's shampoo, or Johnno's hairdryer'.

Terry McDermott was always in there adjusting his perm and using my hairdryer.

Anyway, one day he finds all the Strepsils and Tunes in there and pipes up: 'He's like an effing doctor'. The name stuck and it snowballed from there.

Whenever we travelled away I always carried a bag with me. It was a habit because I always had a book or a game or something like that with me.

Ronnie Moran and Joe Fagan would give me all kinds of pills like paracetamol and whatever else to carry in the bag so if anyone had a headache or anything they'd come to me.

So I became known as 'the Doc' and it stuck. They still call me it now.

That was another great thing about Liverpool - everyone had a nickname.

We used to call Terry 'Cheswick'.

Tez became Chez and Cheswick was from 'One Flew Over The Cuckoo's Nest'.

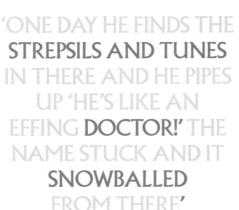

'ONE DAY HE FINDS THE **STREPSILS AND TUNES** IN THERE AND HE PIPES UP 'HE'S LIKE AN EFFING **DOCTOR!**' THE NAME STUCK AND IT **SNOWBALLED** FROM THERE'

As Terry was another lunatic it seemed like an appropriate name.

Kenny Dalglish was known as 'the Ledge' or 'Super' or something else which I won't repeat because he was legend Kenny.

Phil Thompson was called 'Tonka' after the Tonka toys which were known for being unbreakable. Of course that was a Mickey take because all you had to do was blow on Thommo and he'd fall over. Rushie was Tosh because he was Welsh and I'm not going to tell you what Ray Clemence was known as, other than Clem of course.

Phil Neal was known as Nealy but we also dubbed him 'Ollie' after the character in Laurel and Hardy.

He didn't like that but it didn't matter!

DAVID JOHNSON

DAVID JOHNSON

RONNIE THE BARKER AND MR NICE GUY

We used to take the Mickey out of each other unmercifully but it helped to make training more enjoyable. To their credit, the coaching staff at Liverpool realised that.

Their job was to get us prepared - mentally and physically - to win football matches every Saturday. If you didn't have a release, and ours was humour, then you'd be too wound up too far ahead of the game. So I think the relationship between the staff and the players was an intrinsic part of getting us prepared for the games. As long as you concentrated when the serious business started they didn't mind you having a laugh.

Ronnie was the barker (not Ronnie Barker!) down at Melwood. He was the only voice you could hear over four fields - that's Shef-field, Hudders-field . . .

The Kop would be in full song and you could be over the other side of the pitch and still hear Ronnie shouting at you. He and Joe Fagan were like a 'good cop, bad cop' routine at Liverpool. You can't have all Mr Nice Guys at a football club. You won't get anything done.

Joe was Mr Nice Guy - he'd put his arm round you and have a chat with you although he could be hard as well. Ronnie was the one who would give you a bollocking. At the time you'd think he's got a downer on you but now you realise that was just his job.

Too many clubs are run on discipline without humour. That's wrong. Some have the humour but not the discipline. That's wrong too. You have got to have that right balance and that's what Liverpool was all about. We had the right people in the right jobs giving the right balance and that's why we were so good.

DON'T LET ME GO YET . . .

People ask me who the best player I've ever played with is and I have to say Kenny Dalglish. I've also played against him and he's one of the best players I've ever played against as well. I put him up there with the likes of Maradona and George Best in that respect.

I think very highly of Kenny as not only a team-mate but also as a footballer. We scored 85 goals in the league in the 1978/79 season and I was up front with Kenny. That was my best season at Liverpool, especially as between us we had the lion's share of the goals.

The 1981 European Cup final win over Real Madrid in Paris was also particularly special to me but for different reasons. I played in the FA Cup final in 1977 but sat on the bench in Rome. I didn't get on to the pitch but I got a medal. I'd played in all the previous rounds but not in the final. I got the medal and I treasure it but I wanted to play.

A year later I'd played in the semi-final but got injured so missed the final again but got another medal. That meant I had two European Cup winners' medals but hadn't appeared in either final.

So to play in 1981 and walk up the steps as a winner was special to me. My lasting memory is of Joe Fagan coming over to me at the final whistle and saying 'well played son' but I couldn't let go of him. The emotion had taken over and I said to Joe 'don't let go of me yet'. If he had have let go of me I'd have cracked up.

That will always be an emotional moment because that's what winning the European Cup with Liverpool meant to me.

'FISHY TALE THAT KICKED UP

1970/71 –
1984/85
DEFENDER
1986/92
COACH
1999/2004
ASSISTANT
MANAGER

PHIL THOMPSON

I roomed with the worst person in the world, Terry McDermott! Terry was thirsty in more ways than one! Everybody knew that Terry liked a drink but we all did, in fairness. On Friday nights when we used to go to hotels, we always used to have a mini-buffet and it was hilarious.

We'd get in the room about nine o'clock and there'd be chicken sandwiches, cheese sandwiches, beef sandwiches, whatever-else sandwiches and crisps. I'd have a pint of orange and lemonade but Terry would have two pints of blackcurrant and

lemonade - one to drink with his sandwiches and one for through the night.

It would be absolutely awful because although we'd eat a load of sandwiches, there would always be a load left! One night we were away when Terry produced some shellfish and said: "Oh, my dad's given me these cuans." They looked like small snails with shells and you would have a pin which you used to get into them. Terry was sat there with this small plastic bag of them. I just wondered what Terry's insides must have been like with all these sandwiches and cuans!

I remember being sat there and thinking I was

A STINK BEFORE THE GAME!'

going to throw up with this smell of fish. It was just awful but in the end I thought nothing of it and fell asleep. The next morning Ronnie Moran came in to get us up for our pre-match. He walked in the room and said: 'Oh my God! What's that stink!' Terry hadn't covered the cuans up or tied a knot in the bag or anything and it absolutely stank in the room - it was like Grimsby docks!

KIRKBY CLAN AND DOZY DALGLISH!

Terry and I were two lads from Kirkby and as soon as he came to Liverpool, we teamed up and we were room-mates from then on.

Terry was great fun. Squads are made up of different characters. You have the quiet ones, you have the wind-up merchants, you have the funny guys and sometimes you have the ones that you don't get on with but I'd like to think that in our squad, I didn't have too many of those and it was usually an absolute pleasure.

You hear things nowadays about things happening on the training pitch and people having a problem with each other. Yes, we had them but they were very, very few and far between and I think that was the essence of our Seventies team and the camaraderie was top class. ▷

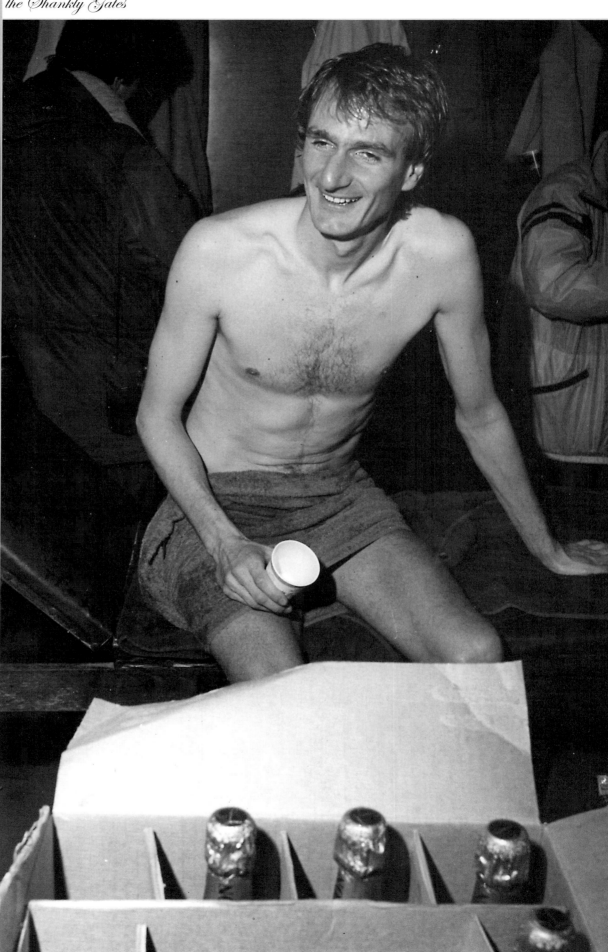

PHIL THOMPSON

Terry was just one of those guys who kept everything going. We used to have some great laughs. On most trips, Terry and I would end up in Kenny Dalglish and Graeme Souness's room and we'd all be joking around and telling stories. As soon as Kenny got there, which was usually about nine o'clock, he would take a sleeping tablet. We'd still be there about 11.30pm and Kenny would be there and you would see his eyes dropping as he started to nod off. That was the way it was. We were a very, very close squad.

TERRY'S GLASS ACT

I remember one night when we were away in some far-flung European city and the lemonade they gave us in the hotel had a corked top on it and we didn't have a corkscrew or anything to get it out, so we did our best to try and push the cork back into the bottle.

Terry was doing that and I don't know what happened but the bottle actually exploded and a piece of glass went into the side of his leg. It wasn't major but it was enough for blood to be oozing all over the place. Luckily, it wasn't anything serious but he had this piece of glass stuck in the side of his leg just below the knee. He took it out and we just laughed.

GEORGIA ON MY MIND

We were in Tbilisi when it was real Iron Curtain and we were down in the depths of Georgia as it is now. The people there weren't allowed to demonstrate or do anything. It was a big game and we were under pressure. It was bang on two o'clock in the morning when we could suddenly hear a crowd coming from a distance and they gathered outside the hotel. They were chanting and singing 'Tbilisi' and whatever. It was absolutely astonishing.

Terry and I could hear the commotion but it was round the other side of the hotel so, lo and behold, we got up and went down to the end of the corridor. We were looking out of a fire escape, looking down on the crowd. I turned around and there was Terry throwing apples and all kinds of

stuff at all these people! He was bombarding them with anything he could lay his hands on! They were there for about 15 minutes, not a policeman in sight, and then they just dispersed!

BRUCIE BONUS

Bruce Grobbelaar was a quite incredible character. It was amazing changing from somebody of Ray Clemence's background, who was steady as a rock, knew his job and was great at it, to this extrovert, Bruce Grobbelaar.

It was from one extreme to the other and it took us a little bit of time to get an understanding together but Bruce went on to be probably one of the most agile keepers there has been. People talk about Peter Schmeichel ranting and raving and everything but Bruce was doing it far before him. He was very, very good.

Bruce was an absolute diamond. He was one of those larger than life characters and we always used to have a laugh. He'd always have a story to tell having been in the army and in the jungle. If you told a story, Bruce would always go one better. If you'd been on holiday to Kenya and you'd seen a tiger, Bruce had fought a tiger! Or had you ever seen anybody shot? He'd say: 'Shot! I actually shot somebody!'

Then there was all that standing on his hands. We used to wind him up, saying: 'Go on, do it for us, do it for us!' He didn't realise that we were winding him up trying to get him to act the clown and everything. We were winding him up behind his back and Bruce would be hamming it up!

CRAZY GOLF

We went out to Tokyo for the World Club Championship against Flamengo in 1981 and it was a memorable trip! I remember Howard Gayle and Kevin Sheedy were with us at the time. They had a three-tiered golf driving range near to where we stayed and the locals took it ever so seriously because they couldn't afford to play on the normal courses over there. We went along one day but before we did, one of the lads had been to a

> **'I TURNED AROUND AND THERE WAS TERRY THROWING APPLES AND ALL KINDS OF STUFF AT THESE PEOPLE. HE WAS BOMBARDING THEM!'**

joke shop beforehand and bought some golf balls!

Everybody took a whole bag of clubs and were dressed up and taking it extremely seriously and there were our lads in pairs of trackie bottoms and T-shirts and we were lashing balls and everything. Then one of the lads hit one of these balls that had been bought and, lo and behold, smoke started coming out of the back of the ball! And you've got all these Japanese people all looking around to see what has gone on!

Even funnier was Howie Gayle He had his club and everything and hit a reasonable first shot. We were playing on the second of the three tiers and with his next shot, the club ended up 30-yards out on the range. It had come out of his hand and was lying there surrounded by thousands of balls! We were all killing ourselves laughing. But five minutes later when we were still hitting these balls, we saw a body inching his way forward, commando-style, out onto the driving range and there was Howie going after his club with balls whizzing around his head!

Tokyo woe

The Flamengo game itself was a shame because Bob was very concerned about us not getting involved in any altercations with the opposition and not doing anything wrong. He wanted us to make sure we upheld the credentials and good name not only of Liverpool, but England. We did that and in fairness to Bob, he held his hands up afterwards and took responsibility for us not being fired up for the game. We went there and treated it too much as a friendly, doing the right thing for the FA's sake and not for our sake.

The game took place in December, right in the middle of our season and, for once, our focus wasn't right. Bob didn't want us flying into tackles because he was concerned about the South American mentality and he didn't want an incident. But we probably went over that line and went too far the other way, but it was all a good experience.

Down to the wire

Coming back from Tokyo, Terry McDermott had a few people going with the trick where you have a very thin wire which you attach to a bank note. You then press a mechanism and it shoots back towards you!

We'd stopped over in Alaska and Terry had this thing and he'd hooked a 10 dollar bill on the end

of it, draped it over the end of the seat and was dangling it in front of people. Just as they were going to pick it up, he'd whisk it away and people would be absolutely shocked!

All these Japanese people and Americans just couldn't understand where it had gone! We were sat in a forecourt lounge killing ourselves laughing and I remember there was this one Japanese fella who was so fascinated by it, he came over and said: 'You show me, you show me, you show me how you do it!' and he loved it!

He sat down with us and was watching everybody being taken in by it. He was sat with all us footballers and watching Terry's prank. One guy came along, slyly looked at the money on the floor, stood next to it and started moving his foot towards it. He was moving his foot ever closer to the note and getting ready to pounce. But just at the moment he was going to put his foot on it, Terry reeled it in and this Japanese guy, who must have been 40 or 50, just fell about laughing. The guy who was trying to get the note looked so embarrassed because he knew that he'd been had!

Carrying too much weight

You could go right through the squad, looking at the different types of personality. Kenny was dry-humoured. He'd always sit in the background, coming up with the comments on the side and everything. He certainly didn't initiate things but would often sit there and just giggle and laugh at all the antics. Alan Kennedy and Stevie Nicol were the butt of a lot of the jokes, particularly Steve.

Nico loved his crisps and his chips. His nickname was Chopsy because he couldn't say chips, he used to say 'chops'! I don't know how it would go down with all the dieticians nowadays, but he just absolutely loved them and would munch his way through something like a dozen bags of crisps every time we travelled from Anfield to, say, Wolverhampton. Nico was a big eater and one of my favourite stories about him was told by his wife.

During one close season, they had gone on a cruise around the fjords of Norway. They'd stopped off in a town and picked up one or two bits of shopping for their cabin - coke, lemonade, chocolates and biscuits for the room, things like that.

Nico's standing there in the shop and his wife's getting something and he's standing there when he sees these scales in the shop and thinks he'll weigh

PHIL THOMPSON

PHIL THOMPSON

▷ himself with it being close season.

Next minute he's shouting: 'Oh, my goodness! Oh, no!'

Then he asks the shop assistant: "Hey Hen! Are these scales right?" She tells him they are and he said: "No! These are at least half-a-stone to a stone out!"

His wife then comes across, looks at him and says: "Steve, you soft sod, you've still got the shopping bags in your hands!" He had both hands full of shopping and was stood there saying: "Hey hen, are these scales right?"

EARLY DAYS

I was only a young kid when I came into the team and I was totally in awe of everything that they used to do. I remember going on holiday at the end of one season with some of the other players when I was only 17.

I was just in my second year as an apprentice and had been on one or two journeys away with the first team and I was invited away on the holiday. I always remember a few years later, Tommy Smith said to me: "You were a right tight sod on that holiday, Thommo." I said: "What makes

you think that Smithy?" He said: "Oh, you hardly put your hand in your pocket!" I said: "Maybe it had something to do with the fact that I was on nine quid a week and you lot were all on £120 a week or something like that!" Smithy admitted he had never thought of that. I think I'd only taken £30 away with me and I was just trying to manage my money.

I was invited on some of those trips in the early days but I was just totally in awe of those lads. I was just like the gopher. They'd be saying: 'Thommo go and get the drinks in', 'Thommo, go

and get some food', 'Thommo, do this' and I was just so pleased to do it because I'd gone from the age of 14 and 15 and being a fan and here I was with Tommy Smith, Larry Lloyd, Alec Lindsay, Chris Lawler - my idols - and there I was sitting in the same bar having a drink with them.

They were a great bunch of lads in different ways and it was great learning from your peers - your Smithys, Callys, Lawlers and everything. I was the younger generation and then there was Sammy Lee and David Fairclough after me if you like. But the good habits that I learned, I would

PHIL THOMPSON

pass on. It was like there were unwritten rules - the competitive edge, the willingness to win and everything like that were just passed on.

Then when your Hansens came along, your Whelans, your Rushes - even your Sounesses - who had all come from other teams, they picked it up too.

They had never been in the situation of week after week after week of win and win and win and win. There was just one mentality and it drove you on. People had come from other clubs where it would have been okay to finish halfway or even just survive, but coming to Liverpool was different altogether and it was a learning process. It was a good learning process but the pressure was intense. I grew up with it so I didn't know any different. The likes of Whelan, Fairclough and Beglin, they'd lived with it too.

We still enjoyed ourselves. We played hard and, if you want, we partied hard. But Shanks and Bob and Joe and Ronnie, they always looked and told us as long as we were performing on the pitch, that was the main thing.

Once things started interfering with that side of things, they would come down hard. And they did. They basically let everyone know what was what. And as you got older and injuries tended to catch up, you'd take care of yourself or you'd know about it - it was a cumulative thing.

Flight at the end of the tunnel

Being made captain was a strange thing. Bob was the manager at the time and I suppose I was in my prime. It was 1978-79 and Emlyn, God bless him, was coming towards the end of his Liverpool career.

There were a lot of players who expected that it was almost my right to be captain of Liverpool and I thought that I was the next progression from Emlyn for various reasons. I played in the same position as him, my game was all about reading the game, encouragement, passion, organising. I was an England international. It just seemed as though everything was right but, lo and behold, the manager gave the captaincy to Kenny. To say I was disappointed was an understatement. But I just got on with my game. It turned out Kenny had told Bob he didn't want the captaincy, as he didn't think it was helping him or whatever - I don't know the actual ins and outs. Then Emlyn came back in for a game or two but had the captaincy taken off him.

On the morning of one game at Anfield, Bob said to me: 'You're going to be captain today' and I was absolutely thrilled. I always remember Phil Neal's words. He put his arm around me and said: 'That's what you deserve and that is your right.' Even now, if I meet Davie Fairclough, he still calls me 'Skip' and it's something that's just always stuck. I like to think I captained in the right manner. It was the proudest moment of my life.

I will never forget that first home game as captain. There I was down in the tunnel and I was absolutely on pins. I was shaking.

In those days, you didn't wait for the opposition before going out. As soon as you were ready, you were off and you were out. So on this particular day, we were first out there and I went down the steps and on to the pitch. I ran down and heard this roar and was thinking it was all for me. I looked up to where I knew my brother stood on the Kop - where I used to stand - to give him a wave. I'd got all the way down to the edge of the penalty box and all these people were waving. I thought: 'Oh, fantastic'. I was waving to my brother and then I turned around . . . and I was the only one on the pitch! The swines had all left me! They probably realised how much it meant to me. Kenny had kept everybody back and they were all at the top of the steps in the tunnel. It was good fun and with 45,000 already in the stadium, it showed the togetherness of that crowd that they could have a laugh at my expense!

Having stood on the Kop, to go on to be the regular captain, lift the European Cup, the league trophy, the League Cup . . . well, they were some of the greatest moments of my life. I captained England six times and I was very honoured to do that. But to be captain of your home town team, especially having been such a fervent Liverpool fan, was something special.

Then it even went full circle as I became reserve team coach, left the club and came back again as assistant manager. It was what dreams are made of. Even Roy of the Rovers couldn't have thought up a story like that.

In the hotseat

There was no way of being eased into the situation when Gerard Houllier was taken ill and I was asked to take over as manager while he was recuperating. It only dawned on me the next day when I was sitting on the plane to Kiev.

Gerard and I always sat together and shared a

large bag of wine gums on flights and he wasn't there. Not only was he not there but we still didn't know at that time how he was going to be. As far as we knew he was still in the operating theatre and it was a big worry. The worry for Gerard was far more than the worry for me and I hadn't really taken it all in.

But the next thing I had to worry about was how I was going to do my team talk. I'd seen and listened to Gerard's talks and hoped I'd learnt from him but that was what worried me most because Gerard always gave a fantastic team talk. I used to hang on to every word because he was so good. He'd have two flip charts which he would use for different things and I thought to myself: 'How am I going to do this?' It played on my mind for months to try and get that aspect right. It worried me and played on my mind - how I was going to do it in the right manner and in a way that was fitting for Gerard?

I started to realise that I was now in charge and that it all rested on me, the decisions that had to be made were down to me. I asked Sammy Lee to do more of what I did, being on the touchline organising things and seeing things. People used to think: 'Oh, Thommo's just ranting and raving on the touchline', but a lot of tactics went into what I was trying to do. Yes, there was a lot of passion that went into it but that was because I wanted to keep the team going when things weren't going well. So I knew I needed somebody else to take on that role because I needed to be thinking from the start. I'd always learnt from Ronnie Moran to try to see things before they happen.

That is the essence of a good coach. It's one thing reacting to things once they have happened but another to try and spot them first. Everybody can be on the touchline when things are going well and you're winning two or three-nil but it's how you react and how the team perceive the management when things are not going right. They want you there helping them. I had a brilliant understanding with Sammy and during all the

time I was in charge, Sammy was a great right hand man to me.

First and foremost, I wanted to justify Gerard. He loved European competition and I wanted us to still be in Europe when he returned, but also still be in contention in the league. So there was a lot on my plate but I used Gerard's illness to galvanise players and the club and at the end of every team talk, on my flip chart, I would put a reminder there about the boss.

I'd remind them who had bought them and made them better players.

We also had some fantastic times. We had some big wins while I was in charge and it was a very, very proud moment but I loved it when Gerard came back! I did enjoy it and it worked because we finished second in the league and went to the quarter-finals of the Champions League but my thoughts were always with Gerard.

I knew he would come back right from day one. People questioned it and talked about whether it would happen but I knew that his passion for his football and his passion for the club meant he would always be back. Nowadays, some people don't think about Gerard's time at Liverpool in a good light but they should remember that time. He came back for the good of the club when it could have been detrimental to his health. People seem to forget what was achieved. We turned things around at the time and helped build up the club's standard to a level that we felt was higher than when we took over and that was all down to Gerard.

Managerial influences

I drew on everybody during that spell in charge. I did think about Shankly, his comments and the motivational side of it and what I took upon me in those times was that I talked more with the players on an individual basis, just as Gerard used to do. I would call them in for chats when it was going badly but also when it was going well so they didn't think they were going to get a right telling off every time they were called in.

When I was assistant manager, I would have

'HE'D HAVE **TWO FLIP CHARTS** FOR DIFFERENT THINGS. I **THOUGHT TO MYSELF:** 'HOW AM I GOING TO DO THIS?' IT PLAYED **ON MY MIND** FOR MONTHS'

PHIL THOMPSON

words with the defenders on what had gone right and wrong in the games and with the other players as well but as assistant manager I didn't feel it was my right to be talking to players individually on a regular basis. I felt that would be going over Gerard's head.

Obviously I knew it was my job at times anyway and I was always available if they wanted to speak to me. But when I was in charge, that relationship with the players was an important aspect of the job.

I remember Danny Murphy as a case in point. We'd had a difficult time leading up to a midweek game at Manchester United and the Saturday before I'd substituted Danny at Anfield.

I did it for his own sake because he'd been getting some terrible stick off the crowd and I thought it was unjustified. One thing you can say about Danny was that he never, ever hid. Although he might not have been playing well, he was always looking for the ball, always wanting the ball. I took him off that afternoon and he sat

down and I remember Sammy started to try and talk to him but Danny could hardly talk, he was so emotional.

So I left it - I just said: 'Well done Danny.' But from that moment, Danny was in my team for the match at Manchester United. I felt that as manager it was important that I played him. The reason was two-fold. On the one hand it was for him because I knew mentally he would see it as a positive and on the other, it was also for the team because I knew Danny could do it. Danny went on to score the winning goal at Old Trafford and he had an outstanding game. I knew Danny would be fired up and he was and it was moments like that, that you think: 'You're learning.' And I was learning from Shanks, Paisley, Fagan.

When you're a manager, a lot of it is the player-manager relationships. As assistant manager, Gerard and I played very much good cop, bad cop. If there was any Mr Angry, I would certainly be that.

Gerard would always talk at half-time and

full-time and if I ever had a go, he would always let it go for approximately one or two minutes, let the lads get that over with and then come in as the calming influence. So it was a good two-way relationship. I remember Shanks and Paisley being like that. Bob was always the bad guy having a moan, but Shanks would then come in and say: 'Come on lads' and be that calming influence. Gerard and I were quite a similar partnership.

MEETING GERARD

The amazing thing about Gerard Houllier and I was that we had barely met before we were asked to work together and, if you want, the club took a big chance.

It was Tom Saunders' idea. He heard Peter Robinson, Rick Parry, the chairman and the other directors saying they wanted a person to do certain things and Tom said: 'The person that you're talking about is Phil Thompson.'

I'd only met Gerard briefly in Valencia. I was over there with Radio City for the Champions League game and I was in the bar chatting to Tom and Ronnie Moran when Gerard passed by. Tom introduced me and Gerard said: 'Oh yes, I know you! I used to watch you from the Kop.' So we chatted for five minutes and then, lo and behold, a couple of weeks later I was told about the possibility of linking up with Gerard and that he wanted to give it a go.

It was a big decision for the club but I could see the reasons why they had made it. They knew how I worked and that I was an honest guy and a loyal guy. Tom Saunders was a very, very shrewd man. In fairness, contrary to what some people may have been saying after we left, we put the smile back on the fans' faces and we won trophies. For young fans who had never seen us win big trophies like the Uefa Cup and the FA Cup before, it was a great, great time and I will never, ever forget that year.

In a way it was a shame that we won the five trophies in the one season. If the success had been spread out over a few seasons everybody would

say: 'What a fantastic time.' We developed the expectations and they were so high when we finished second in the league that we put ourselves under big, big pressure. But that's the name of the game. It's Liverpool Football Club, so you expect that and you wouldn't want it any other way.

We won the League Cup again but, nice as it was, we wanted bigger things but we couldn't deliver the Holy Grail of the Premier League title. With a bit of help and a bit of luck, Rafa can do that because we all want it to come back, Gerard and myself, we're still big fans.

MICKEY MOUSE CUP!

The League Cup came to be very special to us. I lifted it for the first time at Villa Park which was great because it was something which had always eluded us. We'd had some hiccups along the way and then we couldn't stop winning it! But it was actually me who nicknamed it the Mickey Mouse Cup!

My brother-in-law, Jimmy Dutton, gave me a plastic bottle and he'd made the bottom of it into the shape of the base of a cup and put Mickey Mouse's head on the top of it and glued it all together. I took it down to the League Cup final in 1978 when we'd gone to play Nottingham Forest. We'd gone down to Wembley and drew with Forest and then lost the replay at Old Trafford when I upended somebody.

'I WAS **YOUNG,** I WAS **DAFT,** IF YOU WANT, AND I THOUGHT: **'I'M GOING TO GET IT DONE!'** SO MYSELF AND **THE WIFE** GOT IT DONE AT THE **SAME TIME'**

I had taken this little cup with Mickey Mouse on it with me and I remember coming into the dressing room afterwards and it was there in my place and I kicked it all around the dressing room. It got a good hiding! I called it the Mickey Mouse Cup and it stuck from that moment on.

It was great to win it in 1981 and then to win it again and again and again! When I went back to the club as assistant to Gerard, we won it as our first trophy when we beat Birmingham. We went on to win it again against Manchester United in 2003 which was a great, great day. The banners and the celebrations of the Liverpool fans that day were brilliant.

We just outdid the Manchester United club as a whole on that day because we showed them how it should be done to go to a cup final. We showed them how you win and how you party.

And then all you heard afterwards from the people in Manchester, from their paper, from their staff, from the players . . . was that it didn't matter. That's why they played the best team they could have played on the day . . .

THOSE HAIRCUTS

If there was ever a guinea pig, it was me! I can remember the very first game I turned out with the perm was at Wrexham. I can't remember whether it was for England or for Liverpool in the League Cup. Either way, you can imagine the stick that I got! The perm was just starting to come into fashion at that time and we were away somewhere, I think it was a European game and I can remember Tommy Smith - of all people! - suggesting we all get it done together so it wouldn't have the same impact. Of course it didn't happen.

But I was young, I was daft if you want and I thought: 'I'm going to get it done!' So myself and the wife got it done at the same time. We looked like the Hair Bear Bunch! More and more people started getting it done. I remember Bob Latchford getting it done, Bryan Robson, Mick Lyons, Terry McDermott, Phil Neal, Alan Kennedy, Kevin Keegan. It was the times, it was the fashion but did I get some stick for it!

When I was assistant manager at Liverpool, the lads would get their hair done. Some had streaks put in and some had it braided. Sami Hyypia had some streaks put in his hair one day and I said to him: 'How can you mess about with your hair?' and he said: 'Don't you talk to me, what about your perm!?' Then, of course, there would be the autograph hunters at away games and someone would always dig out an old picture of me and the players would be laughing their socks off at this big mop of curls! And, needless to say, Smithy never got his done!

'MEET THE NEW MANAGER LADS – IT'S ME! AND HERE'S A NEW SET OF RULES TO FOLLOW!'

1977/1978 – 1989/90 DEFENDER

ALAN HANSEN

I joined Liverpool in 1977 and when I got there I was scared stiff of going into the dressing room for the first time.

Liverpool were going for a treble and I'd been playing for Partick Thistle. It wasn't like going to another world. It was another world.

But the most important aspect for me going into that dressing room was that they made me feel unbelievably welcome.

There weren't any superstars in the dressing room. Right from the word go it was like I'd been in there for 10 years.

That's one thing I miss about Liverpool. I really don't miss playing but I miss going into the dressing room every day.

The camaraderie we had, the good times, the laughs - as soon as I went into that dressing room I never had a problem. I was really nervous when I went in there but they made me feel so welcome. They were just great guys.

I think everybody who came into the Liverpool dressing room in the 70s and 80s did so with a bit of fear and trepidation because of what the club achieved but no-one had a problem.

Breakfast in bed off Kennedy – and sharing with Dexter

My room-mate for away trips was Alan Kennedy. He was brilliant to share with.

He gave me breakfast in bed every Saturday morning, he answered all the phone calls and answered the door every time there was a knock. I remember one night when we stayed at the Hallam Towers in Sheffield and it was like 10 degrees below freezing and the heating was off.

So I stole Kennedy's duvet but he never complained! He was absolutely fantastic, the best room-mate you could ever have.

I shared with Kennedy for seven years and then after that it was Jim Beglin, John Wark and Ray Houghton.

We used to have nicknames for all the players and there was a fella in Dynasty called Dexter.

He was a suave character and fancied his chances so he was always in front of the mirror.

When I was sharing with Jim I noticed that he always seemed to be in front of the mirror himself every morning so I nicknamed him Dexter and it stuck.

To this day he's still called Dexter by the lads and they'll be like: 'Is Dex coming tonight, is Dex playing today? Dex this and Dex that'.

An unbelievably funny guy

I think you'd probably need about four books to talk about all the wind-ups and practical jokes that were played over the years.

Steve Nicol was often the target of them but he wasn't what I would call a whipping boy.

Nicol came into the Liverpool dressing room and at the time myself, Kenny and Graeme had this Scotland thing going.

We were trying to portray the Jocks as the master race. Nicol came in and he changed all that. But the thing about Nicol was that he was so funny.

He was an unbelievably funny guy. ▷

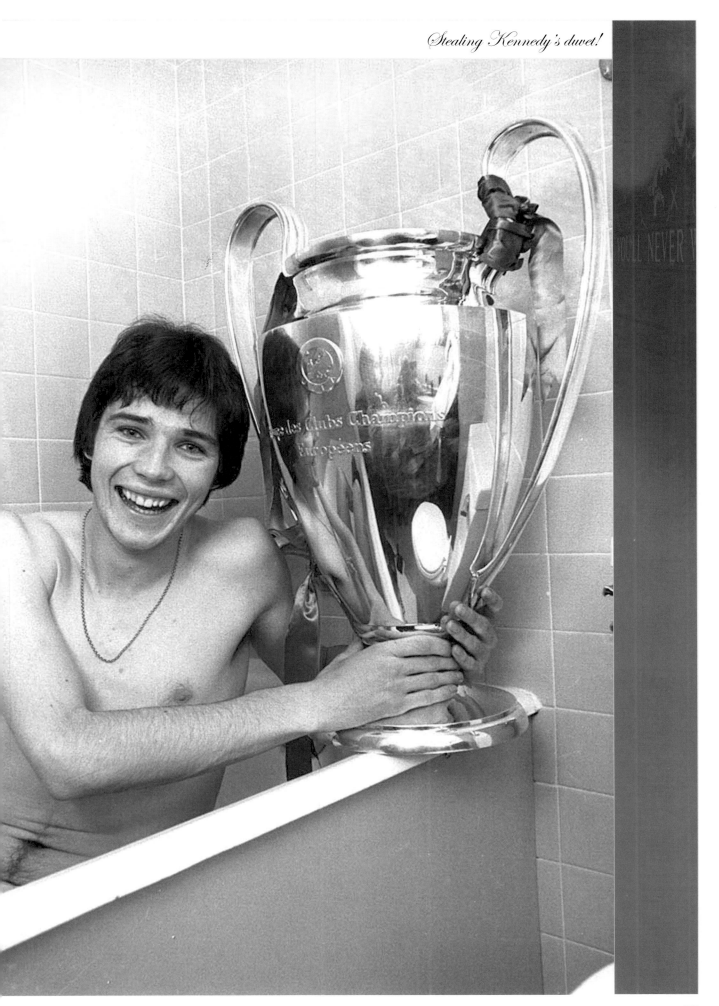

ALAN HANSEN

▶ The combination of Nicol and Bruce in that dressing room was legendary.

Dressing rooms need characters and we had them in the shape of those two.

To be fair to Nicol he sharpened up eventually but when he first came in he was so gullible and they were sending him here, there and everywhere and telling him all kinds of things. He didn't know if he was coming or going.

He was a great player though. If he'd come in and still been gullible but been a dud then we'd have been in trouble but he was a top player.

He's actually one of the boys who I still keep in touch with. He's in Boston and we phone each other every month.

It's funny because if you'd have gone in that

dressing room in, say, 1983 and told the lads that Nicol would become a manager and I would end up on the television then they'd have all laughed at you and said 'not a chance in a million years'.

We laugh on the phone because it's funny how things pan out. I'd say that Nicol and Terry Mac were the funniest in the dressing room.

Terry was another who was brilliant for team spirit.

If you've got characters who make you laugh it makes such a difference.

I used to go in every morning and sit beside Nicol in the dressing room.

I'd be sat there reading the paper and he'd come in and within about 10 seconds he'd have me in stitches. ▷

He was brilliant, although some of the stuff he wore wasn't.

I can remember the time when we went to Japan to play in the World Club Championship and he had this tracksuit on.

He got absolutely annihilated for wearing it.

The thing was it took 16 hours to get to Tokyo and I'm not kidding, people were coming up the plane from the aisles at the front just to look at this tracksuit.

You could see he was gutted, absolutely distraught.

Everyone was saying 'where on earth did you get that from' and he was like 'someone gave it to me'. It was about eight sizes too big and it looked just minging.

After taking all this stick we got to Tokyo and he said 'that's it lads, it's going in the bin' and he chucked it.

We got beaten in the match and came back to England and a couple of days later he came in and said 'you'll never believe this - they've taken it out of the bin and sent it back to me!' That set us all off again.

Did he wear it again? Did he hell. I think he burned it! It was truly the worst, worst, worst thing I'd ever seen.

At least he never had a perm like Thommo, Terry Mac, Nealy and some of the others. They must look at those pictures now and cringe. Unbelievable.

Could you imagine me with a perm? Never in a million years.

I look back at some of the pictures of the lads with those perms and it's frightening.

I'M THE NEW MANAGER!

The best wind up I ever pulled was after Kenny had left as Liverpool manager in 1991.

Ronnie Moran was put in charge as caretaker manager and we'd lost 3-1 at Luton and then 1-0 at Everton in the FA Cup replay.

I was gone myself on the Friday because of my injury so I said to Ronnie 'why don't I go in and say I'm the new manager and give them a load of new rules and regulations'. Roy Evans was in on it too.

So I went in. There was 16 of them in there and I told them I was the new manager and the first new rule was that the pubs they all drank in - in Birkdale and on the Wirral - were out of bounds.

I then told them not to be planning anything for their afternoons because I'd be having them back three times a week working on their ball skills.

And the third one, which was the best of the lot, was that I'd be taping the match on the Saturday and we'd all be coming in on the Sunday, have some lunch and go through the finer points of what had happened.

I'm not kidding you, you should have seen the looks on their faces. It was frightening.

Then I said 'by the way, Steve Nicol's the new captain'. So nobody said anything until Grobbelaar said: 'Right, we're right behind you,' before I went out the door.

Straight away Ronnie Whelan came after me to have a word about the captaincy. I said 'Ron, don't worry. It's a joke,' and he started to laugh.

After that I went down to the players' lounge - and this shows you how quickly news spreads at a football club - and we had these two Irish apprentices.

These two lads burst past me to get into the players' lounge and were straight on the phone to Dublin.

All I heard was: 'Get as much money as you possibly can on Alan Hansen to be the new Liverpool manager'.

I thought to myself 'Christ, I'd better put an end to this before it gets out of hand'.

So I went back to the dressing room and the language coming out of it was unbelievable. It was all about me.

I just went back in and said: 'Boys that was my parting line. I'm actually leaving', but I tell you, not one of the 16 in there had a clue, whatever they say.

It was definitely one of my better acting performances.

'THERE WAS **16** OF THEM IN THERE AND I TOLD THEM I WAS **THE NEW MANAGER** AND THE FIRST NEW RULE WAS THAT **THE PUBS** THEY ALL DRANK IN WERE **OUT OF BOUNDS'**

ALAN HANSEN

'THE ECSTASY AND AGONY

I was an Evertonian when I was a kid growing up in Liverpool.

My uncle used to take me to Goodison Park to watch them, so that was where my loyalties used to lie. That all changed when I became a footballer.

I had trials for Liverpool schoolboys as a teenager but the manager there didn't like me.

I was a full-back but I was made to play outside left in a game. I scored three goals - which was as many as I managed in my entire professional career - and he still wouldn't pick me, not even at left-back.

So when I was 15 I got picked for the Catholic Schoolboys and we were playing a game in Dublin.

A guy called Tosh Moore, who was a school teacher and a scout for Liverpool, spotted me and he signed me up for Liverpool.

I had no qualms about being an Evertonian who was signing for Liverpool.

My first two years at Anfield were as an amateur and then, when I was 17, I signed professional terms.

BOUT OF 'FLU OPENED THE DOOR FOR ME

I made my Liverpool debut in 1957 away at Charlton Athletic and it was because of a 'flu epidemic that I got my chance.

I remember going to the pictures with goalkeeper Tommy Younger the night before the game.

He said to me: 'You stick with me, son, you won't get the flu' and I soon found out why that was. He sat through the entire film smoking a pipe in the cinema!

We lost the game 5-1 and I was unlucky enough to score an own goal. I can't really remember much of the game but I think I did alright.

I was only 19 at the time though so I don't know if I was quite ready to be playing for Liverpool's first team.

When I first went to Liverpool I played under Don Welsh and then Phil Taylor. They weren't a patch on Shanks.

It was when Shankly came that I got my chance at Liverpool. Shanks came in and put me straight into the team and I didn't look back from then.

Shanks was a motivator. His last words, in that famous Scottish voice of his, when we were going out of the dressing room would be 'break their legs boys'.

He didn't mean it, of course, it was just a way of geeing us up.

Reuben Bennett was already there when Shanks came, working as a trainer. Reuben would run round the Melwood training pitch with us and he could run all day.

The team spirit was good under Shankly and I think that had a lot to do with him picking the same team time and time again.

He'd famously say to the press: 'Same team as last year boys' because he would put the same 11 players out on the pitch week in, week out.

We had no rotation then and while some players wouldn't play with injuries, a lot of us did. I think that contributed to our success because we wanted to work hard for each other.

'SHANKS WAS A MOTIVATOR. HIS LAST WORDS WOULD BE 'BREAK THEIR LEGS BOYS!' HE DIDN'T MEAN IT, OF COURSE, IT WAS JUST TO GEE US UP'

LIVING LIKE A MONK AND THAT FAMOUS INJURY

My room-mate used to be Cally. I still meet up with Cally every month or so and have a few drinks.

He was good to share with on the away trips. Cally was a lot younger than I was and he always says that I taught him how to wash and iron.

I still get asked now about playing with a broken collarbone at Wembley and the irony is that I lived like a monk before the 1965 FA ▶

OF A FAMOUS **WEMBLEY WIN'**

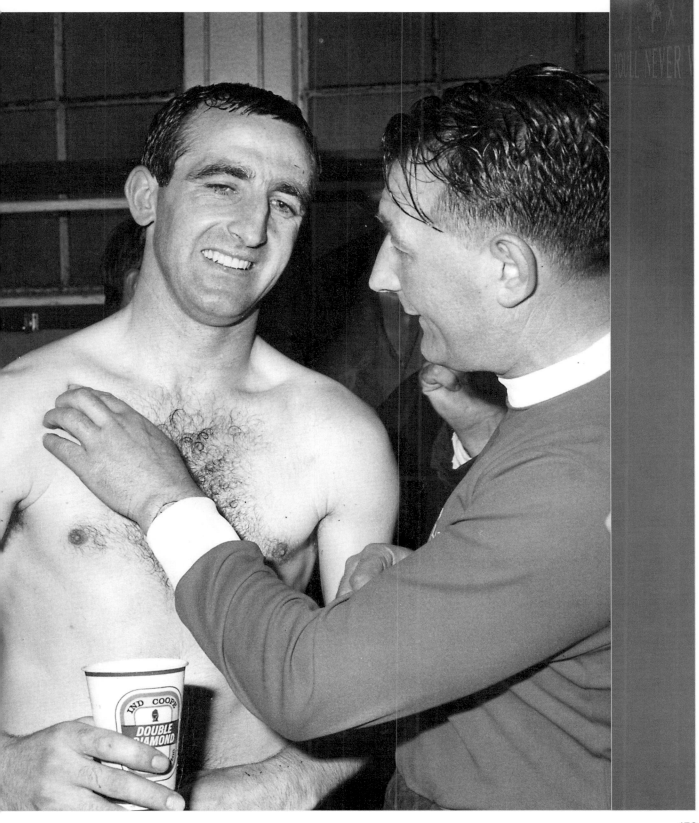

Cup final.

I won't go into my past but I lived like an athlete and abstained from certain things!

So I went into the final feeling as fit as I ever had and I think that's what made me get through the game after I broke my collarbone following a clash with Bobby Collins.

I didn't consider coming off and I don't think anybody could have convinced me to come off.

There's quite a few quotes going about in some of the books that they'd have been locked up now if they'd let me carry on playing with such a bad injury.

It was different in the '60s and at half time they just strapped a cotton wool pad on my shoulder and sent me back out again.

We went on to beat Leeds and win the cup and after the game I couldn't hug anybody nor have anybody come near me because I was in that much pain.

If anyone had so much as touched me I'd have jumped up in the air. I couldn't hug my mates or anything.

I had to go up the Wembley steps walking to one side because the Liverpool fans there all wanted to pat you on the back because you've

won so I had to be careful how I went up.

After that I went to the hospital with Joe Fagan and Reuben to get the injury looked at.

By the time we got back it must have been about 7 o'clock and the party was in full swing so at least I did eventually get to join in the celebrations.

'GO OUT AND WALK ROUND WITH THE CUP'

Unfortunately the injury had ruled me out of the European Cup semi-final game with Inter Milan at Anfield which was played on the Wednesday night. ▷

'IT WAS DIFFERENT IN THE '60S AND AT HALF TIME THEY JUST STRAPPED A COTTON WOOL PAD ON MY SHOULDER AND SENT ME BACK OUT AGAIN'

I didn't know anything about Shanks' plan to have Gordon Milne and myself go round the pitch before the game to show all the fans the cup.

Just before the lads were ready to come out and play he told us to go out there with the cup and walk round the pitch.

So Gordon and I did exactly as we were told and while it didn't really make up for not playing, it was an honour for the both of us.

People still say it was a masterstroke by Shanks because when the crowd saw us with the cup they went delirious. It set them off for the rest of the night. The thing is that I can't remember much about the game itself and the goals we scored because of the pain I was in from my collarbone.

It was a brilliant night but maybe I didn't pay as much attention as I normally would have done because of the pain I was in. I travelled over with the lads for the return game in Milan and watched it from the stands in the San Siro. I didn't think we'd get out of there alive.

Their supporters were vicious and violent. They even attacked the coach. It was a nightmare.

OFF TO A FLIER

The record books show that I scored Liverpool's first ever goal at Anfield in European football when we had played Reykjavik but to be honest I don't remember it.

I do remember flying to Reykjavik for our first ever game in Europe.

I think we flew on a Dakota or something like that. It was definitely a small plane.

On one of the European away trips we visited a Nazi death camp before the game. I can't remember which country we were in - possibly Czechoslovakia - and they showed us round this camp. The Germans had completely obliterated the village during the War and, with the exception of one or two who had escaped, had killed everybody.

They'd wiped the whole place out and looking around there sticks in my mind.

One of the first games we ever flew to in England was down at Southampton and that was a bit of a nightmare.

I think we flew in a Dakota and we ended up

GERRY BYRNE

landing on a grass runway. That was a bit hairy!

Looking back on my days at Liverpool I've got a lot of fond memories. We had a lot of good lads there and, apart from the Scots, most of us were local.

When I was a kid growing up, Liverpool always had Scottish players and Everton always had Irish players. That's the way it was. The derbies were always something special to play in.

I forget the year now but Shanks was quoted in a tribute to me saying that he'd never seen a display from a full-back in a Merseyside derby like the one I'd put in at Goodison.

We actually played Everton in the Charity Shield at Goodison in 1966. We had won the league and Everton the FA Cup the previous season. It was also memorable because four of us - Roger Hunt, Cally, myself and Everton's Ray Wilson had been in England's World Cup winning squad.

They paid tribute to us that day and the four of us all received a tankard from the City of Liverpool.

EURO DISAPPOINTMENT BUT I'VE GOT NO REGRETS

Before the World Cup I played in the 1996 European Cup Winners Cup final against Borussia Dortmund at Hampden Park.

We lost the game 2-1 but we didn't deserve to get beat. Their winner was lucky. It went in off Ron Yeats. It was exciting to play in a European final but disappointing to lose the game.

We had a rematch with the Dortmund team years after the game. We went over to Germany to play them in a friendly but I was only fit enough to play for 10 minutes and I can't remember if we beat them.

I'd say that 1964/65 and 1965/66 were the two best seasons of my career.

I started the 1966/67 season by injuring my knee in the first game of the campaign against Leicester at Anfield. That injury started me on the road to retirement and my last game for Liverpool was in 1969.

I spent 14 years of my life at the club and I had some great, great times.

'MY DIGS WERE GREAT BUT I COULDN'T STOP FEELING HOMESICK – SO MY DAD SAID: 'JUST DON'T COME HOME!''

1979/80 – 1993/94
MIDFIELDER

RONNIE WHELAN

Before I signed for Liverpool I was playing for Home Farm back in Ireland and then Dundalk asked me to go to them but I said no as I wanted to move to England and go professional.

It was the Dundalk manager Jim McLoughlin who got in touch with Liverpool and said they should have a look at me. I came over for a two-week trial in the pre-season of 1979 and was offered a contract in the September.

Because I had been at Liverpool on trial I knew it was a big, big club. I'd followed football since I was a kid so knew the name of Liverpool anyway but it did open my eyes when I moved and saw the facilities at the training ground. Okay, it is nothing like it is now but it was top class then, the pitches were very good and Anfield has always been impressive.

My dad got a couple of caps for the Republic of Ireland in early '60s. He played for St Patrick's and Drogheda back home but there was never any pressure on me to follow him into football. He never pushed me into it and I am sure he would have wanted me to stay at home but he knew professional football was in England and that is where I wanted to go. He was always there when I needed him.

My main problem was that I travelled home too much in the early days. The more I went back, the more homesick I got and was finding it difficult to settle back down again.

It was always Sundays that were the hardest as nothing was happening and it was my dad who eventually said to me 'You're gonna have to stick it

out for a few months son and get to know people there. Just don't come home.'

Diggin' it down Annie Road

When I arrived in Liverpool I stayed just down the road from the Shankly Gates in digs on Anfield Road.

I stayed with Mrs Pyke there who looked after me and then moved down the road with Mrs Edwards who also had Kevin Sheedy and had looked after Alan Hansen before that.

Alan moved out so I moved in to Mrs Edwards' where Kevin was.

They were great, great women who really looked after us. Okay, it's never the same as home, but they did their best to try and make you feel as comfortable as possible. It was as close as it could get.

They looked after all the lads they had and really were good women.

The strong, silent type

It's difficult to explain how good Bob (Paisley) was.

I look back on it and can't really remember him shouting or screaming. That was left to Ronnie (Moran) and Joe (Fagan).

Bob picked the team and made decisions and they just seemed to be the right ones all the time. He picked good players and set them into a team pattern.

They had a good working relationship, Bob, Joe and Ronnie. They all knew which way they wanted to go and which players they wanted.

Bob was just nice and quiet but once he made a decision that was it. That's what made him such a

RONNIE WHELAN

> great manager. He made the right decisions at the right time, even with substitutions. It usually paid off.

Up for the cup(s)

Two of Liverpool's cup wins stand out for me for different reasons.

The first, for professional reasons, has to be the European Cup. It is the pinnacle of club football and winning it in Rome in 1984 when nobody gave us a chance was marvellous.

We won one and then lost at Heysel and didn't play in Europe again. That was a huge disappointment for me. When we got back in under Souey I hardly played.

I will always remember lifting the FA Cup in 1989 after Hillsborough. I was captain that day and it is something you dream of as a kid don't you?

You watch it every Saturday when the FA Cup is on – well I did anyway – and you think: 'One day I would love to walk up those steps'. That day I led them up, so on a personal note that was a special one for me.

We had some great, great players in the team at that point but I had kept the captaincy as Al (Hansen) had been injured most of the season. When he came back Kenny said to me I could keep it until the end of the season. This was 10 years after I had joined the club and I'd never been captain until then and was privileged to captain a club like Liverpool for a season.

Unfortunately we just couldn't win the double that year. We had a couple of slip-ups at the last minute. We had a chance to win three doubles in four years but just slipped up.

One of the big league games that stands out for me was when we beat Southampton 3-2 in 1982.

They were up at the top of league and had the likes of Keegan, Channon and Ball (not to be confused with Cannon and Ball) all playing for them. They scored goal of the season against us that day but I scored two to help us win. That was special as it more or less clinched us the league title, which was the first one for me.

We always saw the League Cup as a way into Europe by March.

The League Cup probably had a bit more prestige back in the '80s and so we would rarely play a weakened side, but priorities have changed in football.

We knew if we won it we could play out the

rest of the season with a bit more confidence as we were already in Europe.

It has been undervalued a bit these days, with clubs talking about rotation. I don't understand why only Frank Lampard can play all the games but nobody else can!

It was always a big day out at Wembley for us and the fans as well.

Best of the rest

You do look back at our success and think 'Yes, that was us'. Especially if you look at the teams now like Man Utd and Arsenal who have been doing it for the last decade. We never took it for granted at the time.

You just never wanted to lose. People were always waiting there to knock us, finish us.

It was great doing it but, at times, it would become a bit of a bind having to keep it up week in week out, month after month. It brought a lot of pressure.

I was lucky, though, in that I played for three great teams throughout the '80s. Early on it was with Kenny, Souey and Jocky and that. Then it was the team that won the double with Big Jan and Rushie. Then the last one was with Kenny again, Beardsley, Barnes and Aldo, Ray Houghton and Steve Mac and all them.

I was lucky to play in these three teams during that time but would have to say the best one was ▷

'WE HAD SOME **GREAT PLAYERS** BUT I HAD KEPT THE **CAPTAINCY** AS AL (HANSEN) HAD BEEN **INJURED.** WHEN HE CAME BACK **KENNY SAID** I COULD KEEP IT UNTIL THE **END OF THE SEASON'**

probably the early one with Dalglish, Hansen, Souey and Phil Neal all in their prime. That was a very, very difficult team to beat. I know some people will say the best they saw was Barnes and Beardsley, that team, but I think the earlier one was very strong, mentally and physically and the best I played in.

FILLING RAY'S BOOTS

I wasn't expected to get into the side as soon as I did mainly because 'Sheeds' (Kevin Sheedy) was there. Everyone just thought 'Sheeds' would follow Ray Kennedy into the left midfield role but then Bob decided to play me. I had never played in that position before and had always been a central midfielder but, yeah, it was a big boost to fill Ray's position.

You just have to do it, though, fill in and play to the best of your ability. Then Ray went not long after I got in the team so it was between me and Sheeds. He went to Everton, so that left me to play at left midfield.

I enjoyed it much more in the centre of midfield, but playing on the left meant playing week in, week out so I was more than happy.

When Kenny took over he bought Barnesie and Ray Houghton, two out-and-out wingers. I moved inside then alongside Macca and there was Spackers (Nigel Spackman) and Jan as well as Kev Mac who could come in.

RUSHIE GETS PUT THROUGH THE MANGLE

I roomed with Rushie quite a lot and remember one away trip when he woke up in the middle of the night, screaming in the bed.

He was hanging out the bottom of the bed screaming and shouting at the top of his voice and I was trying to wake him up.

When I eventually did he said he was having a dream where he was falling into a mangle and I was trying to pull him out. That must have been me trying to wake him up. That was a frightening night. I've never heard screams like it!

RONNIE WHELAN

'IT'S NOT THE FOOD IN YOUR STOMACH BUT THE FIRE IN YOUR BELLY'

Throughout the '80s was just a good time. People say we won things and all that but we had a great time every day. It was always fun in training and we did our serious bits when we had to.

I can still see Ronnie Moran in pre-season shouting when we were doing '880s' and '440s' runs. He'd be shouting 'don't be drinking water'. We weren't allowed to drink water! You look back at it now and think 'why not?'

Everybody drinks water now and are told to get fluid on board all the time but we weren't allowed it then. We weren't allowed bread rolls but we could have toast. There were so many little things that went on and we look back now and ask: 'Why could we not do those things?'

But then again, we were winning every week so we must have been doing something right.

That was the way things were. It was a case of 'this is what we've done all along'. Even when things went wrong in a game or we lost, they would look back in the book - they had a book with everything written in it - to see what we had or hadn't done in training. Then they would change little things accordingly to try and get back to winning again.

I'm sure it all went back to Shankly. As far as I know the book was Shanks' idea. They probably don't still do it now because everyone has gone. But Bob, Joe and Kenny all had this book that they would add to after training each day and would look back in it every now and again if things were going badly. It was a legacy of the famous old boot room and went on and on. I'm not sure if Roy (Evans) carried it on as I had left by then but things changed a little bit under Souey who had been away in Italy and Scotland for some time before he came back.

We have had unbelievable changes in the game nowadays with all the dieticians and nutritionists but I recall a famous quote from Shanks when he said: 'It's not the food in your stomach but the fire in your belly.'

'STEVIE, THE GREAT SCOTS

I guess you're always nervous when you join a new club, but walking into the Liverpool dressing room was a quite intimidating experience. I'd moved from a massive club in Scotland in Celtic, a team with a massive reputation, but here I was joining another one.

It was a new experience and totally alien surroundings for me coming from north of the border. I think what helped me settle was the fact that I was desperate for success and I walked into a dressing room where every single other person shared that same hunger.

The lads I met for the first time on my first day at Melwood were as good as gold. There were players there with big, big reputations - most of

AND **COOKING UP** SUCCESS'

them international players at the peak of their powers. I was replacing a fans' favourite in Kevin Keegan but everyone was brilliant to me in those early days. Without that, I probably wouldn't have settled into life in Liverpool as easily as I did.

I'd actually been down to Liverpool before I signed, as a 15-year-old kid. Even then I

remember everyone being extremely friendly towards me - a young, shy lad from Glasgow.

It was the little things they did that really mattered. Like my first night in a hotel in Liverpool city centre after I'd signed. It was after training and I was just settling myself in my room before going for a bite to eat. There was a knock on my room door and I ▷

remember wondering who it could be. It turned out to be Emlyn Hughes, who was the skipper at the time. He had just popped round to see if everything was ok and to check I was relaxed and comfortable. Little gestures like that may not sound like a lot but they made a real difference to the acclimatisation process for me when I was settling in.

ROOM-MATES AND TEAM-MATES

I only ever roomed with Alan Hansen once in my time at Liverpool, so far as I remember. People are always surprised by that because we were such close mates but I roomed with Graeme Souness for pretty much my entire time as a player.

We roomed together on international trips too and it just seemed natural. We were great friends on and off the pitch and we just sort of fell into a routine that suited us both perfectly.

We had developed this Scottish thing by then at Liverpool where myself, Alan and Graeme would insist that we were the master race. We had our facts and figures to back it all up - Scots invented

anaesthetic, televisions, telephones and even postage stamps.

We kept the same mantras going on and on until people actually started believing what we were telling them and the arguments from the English lads were becoming less regular.

Then Steve Nicol arrived.

I have tremendous respect for him as a player and as a person and he's still a good friend to this day but he utterly destroyed our sense of superiority within literally five minutes of signing for the club.

That was how long it took the photographers to get him into a Tammy hat and a silly Liverpool scarf. The silly grin he wore to accompany the silly scarf was the final nail in the coffin.

He was a lovely lad but he wasn't half the butt of everyone's jokes. To be fair the banter used to really fly around the dressing room - it just seemed that it always ended at Stevie. Some of the Steve Nicol stories are the stuff of legend. Alan Hansen used to get stuck into him every single day. It was part of his routine.

KENNY DALGLISH

MERSEYSIDE'S
WINNING TEAM

Get up, have breakfast, wind up Steve. It was a regular, everyday occurrence.

A favourite story of mine was when Alan left a note at the reception at Melwood for Steve. We knew someone owed him money so the note read that if Steve could get to Burtonwood Service Station at such and such a time then he'd get his money back. I think it was a Sunday morning he was supposed to go and meet the guy but we forgot all about it at the time.

The next time we heard about it, it was from Steve himself on the training pitch when he claimed he'd known it was a set-up all along. Big Alan didn't let on and claimed he didn't know what Steve was talking about.

He came up later on that day and said that he'd only waited there for an hour - with his wife in tow! But he was a warm, caring guy and always really popular with everyone else in the team. That's just part and parcel of the dressing room culture. Everyone takes it on the chin from someone.

TAKING STICK JUST MEANT YOU WERE ONE OF US

Ian Rush found life difficult at Liverpool early on in his playing days. He didn't find his best form in the very beginning and found life generally quite tough.

I didn't know at the time what I know now but he was very close to leaving the club before he had ever really got going. The reason, he told me, was because of all the stick he was taking off the other lads in the dressing room.

He wasn't scoring goals and he wasn't really clicking yet but the lads could see it was going to come.

You knew the first time you saw Rushie that he was going to be a player. What he didn't realise was that the ribbing he was taking in the dressing room was acceptance.

In our dressing room you only worried when the joking at your expense stopped. He simply wasn't used to that level of banter - but that all changed later. ▷

KENNY DALGLISH

▶ **BREAKFAST IN BED BEHIND THE DREADED IRON CURTAIN**

European trips with Liverpool were normally uneventful - because of the careful planning that went into the preparation. It was almost like a military operation.

The worst place you could be drawn was behind the Iron Curtain where you were leaving western civilisation. Some clubs that went over there didn't take their own food and their own chefs but Liverpool made sure they did.

If you're ever watching a video of a Liverpool team on an away European night and you see three or four unfamiliar faces lurking on the bench, or behind it, then those will be our chefs.

It was great. We would be in Russia, or Poland or Bulgaria or somewhere like that and there we were being fed breakfast in bed. Alan Glynn, Harry White and Jack Ferguson from the Holiday Inn oversaw every step of our meals. They cooked, or stood watch, as every meal was prepared.

It was little details like that which contributed greatly to our success. We would always stay in Liverpool until as late as possible. Normally, for a game on a Wednesday night, we'd train at home on the Tuesday morning, have something to eat

and then head straight for the airport.

We'd arrive, go to the ground there and then and have a light session before hitting the sack at a reasonable time. We never went too early, because often your sleep was disturbed. You could cope for one night but too many nights like that would have ultimately started to tire you out.

SCOUSE FASHIONS

It was strange going into a dressing room where players were so conscious of how they looked - it was not what I was used to. There were mirrors and hairdryers everywhere at Melwood whereas I washed

'IF YOU'RE EVER WATCHING A VIDEO OF LIVERPOOL ON AN AWAY EUROPEAN NIGHT AND YOU SEE UNFAMILIAR FACES ON THE BENCH, THOSE WILL BE OUR CHEFS'

KENNY DALGLISH

my hair and left it to dry on its own.

A lot of the lads had moustaches when I arrived but I could never grow one. The only way I could have got one like Terry Mac's or Graeme's would have been to go to a shop and get one of those fake ones.

I never ever fancied a Phil Thompson perm either.

FROM ONE OF THE BOYS TO THE BOSS

I look back on the time I took over as manager now and I think it must have been so much more difficult for the players when my role changed. Back then I found it difficult to draw back from the banter and the dressing room stick that I loved so much but I had made my decision and I was going to give it everything.

I would walk into the dressing room sometimes

'BACK THEN I FOUND IT **DIFFICULT** TO DRAW BACK FROM THE BANTER AND **DRESSING ROOM STICK** I LOVED SO MUCH BUT I HAD MADE **MY DECISION'**

and the conversation would just dry up. The lads didn't know whether to keep going or drop it but I'd just turn on my heels and leave them to it for five or so minutes before going back. There was an invisible barrier there sometimes but that was only natural.

The boys were fantastic with me. Everyone was pleased and I'd like to think I carried on the traditions of the club that I had learned from Shankly, Paisley and Fagan. But I could still socialise with my team-mates on a Saturday night - just as I had always done. I really, really appreciated that. It might sound like nothing but it was significant and showed exactly the bond that existed during those fantastically successful years.

We played together, we socialised together but most importantly we won together.

Members of the Liverpool Family who will never be forgotten

Jack Anderson (62)
Colin Mark Ashcroft (19)
James Gary Aspinall (18)
Kester Roger Marcus Ball (16)
Gerard Baron Snr (67)
Simon Bell (17)
Barry Bennett (26)
David John Benson (22)
David William Birtle (22)
Tony Bland (22)
Paul David Brady (21)
Andrew Mark Brookes (26)
Carl Brown (18)
Steven Brown (25)
Henry Thomas Burke (47)
Peter Andrew Burkett (24)
Paul William Carlile (19)
Raymond Thomas Chapman (50)
Gary Christopher Church (19)
Joseph Clark 'Oey (29)
Paul Clark (18)
Gary Collins (22)
Stephen Paul Copoc (20)
Tracey Elizabeth Cox (23)
James Philip Delaney (19)
Christopher Barry Devonside (18)
Chris Edwards (29)
Vincent Michael Fitzsimmons (34)
Steve Fox (21)
Jon-Paul Gilhooley (10)
Barry Glover (27)
Ian Thomas Glover (20)
Derrick George Godwin (24)
Roy Hamilton (34)
Philip Hammond (14)
Eric Hankin (33)
Gary Harrison (27)
Stephen Francis Harrison (31)
Peter Andrew Harrison (15)
Dave Hawley (39)
James Robert 'Jimmy' Hennessy (29)
Paul Anthony Hewitson (26)
Carl Hewitt (17)
Nick Hewitt (16)
Sarah Louise Hicks (19)
Victoria Jane Hicks (15)
Gordon Horn 'Goffer' (20)
Arthur Horrocks (41)

Thomas Howard (39)
Tommy Anthony Howard (14)
Eric George Hughes (42)
Alan Johnston (29)
Christine Anne Jones (27)
Gary Philip Jones (18)
Richard Jones Bsc (25)
Nicholas Peter Joynes (27)
Anthony P Kelly (29)
Michael Kelly (38)
Carl David Lewis (18)
David William Mather (19)
Brian Christopher Matthews (38)
Francis Joseph McAllister (27)
John McBrien (18)
Marian Hazel McCabe (21)
Joe McCarthy (21)
Peter McDonnell (21)
Alan McGlone 'Gloney' (28)
Keith McGrath (17)
Paul Brian Murray (14)
Lee Nicol (14)
Stephen Francis O'Neill (17)
Jonathon Owens (18)
William Roy Pemberton (23)
Carl Rimmer (21)
Dave Rimmer (38)
Graham John Roberts HND (24)
Steven Robinson (17)
Henry Charles Rogers (17)
Andrew Sefton (23)
Inger Shah (38)
Paula Ann Smith (26)
Adam Edward Spearritt (14)
Philip John Steele (15)
David Leonard Thomas (23)
Pat Thompson (35)
Peter Reuben Thompson (30)
Stuart Thompson (17)
Peter F Tootle (21)
Christopher James Traynor (26)
Martin Kevin Traynor (16)
Kevin Tyrrell (15)
Colin Wafer (19)
Ian 'Ronnie' Whelan (19)
Mr. Martin Kenneth Wild (29)
Kevin Daniel Williams (15)
Graham John Wright (17)

PICTURE INDEX

DAVID FAIRCLOUGH:

Page 17 – Press-ups during training at Melwood; page 18 – signing autographs for fans; page 19 – lifting the European Cup with Phil Neal on a tour of the city; page 20 – a Milk Cup goal against Norwich City at Anfield in 1982; page 21 – off to conquer Europe at Liverpool Airport with David Johnson; with Ray Kennedy and Kevin Keegan after the St Etienne game at Anfield.

NIGEL SPACKMAN:

Page 22/23 – a diving header against Wimbledon at Anfield in March, 1988; page 24 – signed by Kenny Dalglish – a dream come true; page 25 – celebrating with Peter Beardsley and Craig Johnston; page 26/27 – meeting the fan club. Attending a bingo session during an Anfield Tea Dance in October, 1988.

TOMMY SMITH:

Page 29 – muddied but unbowed: a word of consolation in the dressing room from chairman H.E Roberts in May, 1972; page 30 – with a fan at the launch of a Kop Choir record in the 1970s; lifted by Ronnie Moran after the Reds' first European Cup win in 1977; page 31 – 'smile please' for a pre-season photo-shoot in the '60s; page 32/33 – a wet day on the training ground with Gerry Byrne, Emlyn Hughes, Roger Hunt, Chris Lawler, Geoff Strong and Ian Callaghan; page 35 – get in there! A penalty finds the net against West Brom at Anfield in April, 1972.

JIMMY CASE:

Page 36/37 – a typical Case rocket finds the net against West Brom in August, 1977; page 38 – pointing the way to Rome with Phil Neal in 1977; page 39 – this Case goal in the 1977 FA Cup final against Manchester United couldn't prevent a 2-1 defeat; fans hail the 'Bionic Boot' in 1978; page 40 – celebrating in the bath with David Johnson, Phil Neal, Terry McDermott and Ray Kennedy; fending off Arsenal's Willie Young at Anfield in 1977; arms aloft after another Case goal; page 41 – wearing the famous Hitachi top.

JAN MOLBY:

Page 43 – celebrating the 1992 FA Cup at Wembley with Bruce Grobbelaar; page 44/45 – Liverpool's penalty king versus Charlton at Anfield in September, 1986; page 46 – on the spot again 'for a fiver'; celebrating with Craig Johnston; page 47 – all white now: Ronnie Whelan joins in another goal celebration in 1986/87.

RON YEATS:

Page 49 – cheers to the 1965 FA Cup – the first in Liverpool's history; page 50/51 – training at Melwood on a chilly day in January, 1965; page 52 – climbing high to clear the danger at Stoke in 1968; page 53 – heading off to Italy for a European Cup Winners Cup tie against Juventus in 1965; page 54/55 – the 'Colossus' takes flight at Anfield.

JOHN ALDRIDGE:

Page 56 – a happy feeling holding the 1988 league championship trophy; page 57 – signing in at Anfield; page 58/59 – a fans' hero at Charlton in August 1988; making himself at home in the dressing room after arriving; page 60 – with Peter Beardsley and Ronnie Whelan after scoring in the 1989 FA Cup semi-final against Nottingham Forest; page 61 – with daughter Joanne at Anfield after the Hillsborough tragedy; two of a kind – with Rushie on a bus tour after the '89 FA Cup win.

JOEY JONES:

Page 62/63 – with Kop fan Phil Downey, one of the creators of the famous 'Frogs Legs' banner; page 65 – a cult hero, with the fans; in aerial action at Anfield in 1977; in relaxed mood; page 66 – a Joey Jones fan following the Reds in Europe; page 67 – training ground laughs with Phil Thompson; a view to a thrill – taking time out with Steve Heighway, Ray Clemence and David Fairclough.

MICHAEL THOMAS

Page 69 – having a laugh with Ian Rush on the tour of the city after the 1992 FA Cup triumph; page 70/71 – scoring at Wembley against Sunderland in the '92 final; page 73 – Wright on! Celebrating a goal at Anfield in 1997 with Mark Wright, Dominic Matteo and Paul Ince.

BRIAN HALL:

Page 74/75 – all together as a squad as Shanks gives Tommy Smith a 'player of the year' award as voted for by 'Inside Football' readers in 1970/71; page 76 – on the wing against West Brom at Anfield; page 77 – a shot on goal against Spurs in March, 1971; page 78 – home are the heroes – fans salute the 1974 FA Cup winners; page 79 – a smile for Steve Heighway, a scorer in the 1974 FA Cup final against Newcastle.

PHIL NEAL:

Page 96 – signing in for Liverpool with Bob Paisley; page 97 – cheers Bob! With the boss after another title is wrapped up at Anfield; page 98 – training ground instructions from Joe Fagan; jumping the final barrier with the European Cup at Wembley in 1978; page 100 – the magic of Rome; page 101 – a tale of two penalties. Top left at the Anfield Road end against Spurs and sealing Liverpool's first European Cup in Rome with the third goal in 1977.

PETER CORMACK:

Page 102/103 – a typically competitive game of five-a-side at Melwood with Bill Shankly and Bob Paisley;

page 104 – running out at Anfield in 1974; page 105 – a lonely training stint in 1976 and scoring against Birmingham thanks to a Kevin Keegan cross; page 106/107 – Newcastle were undressed! Looking on as Kevin Keegan scores Liverpool's famous third goal in the 1974 FA Cup final.

JIM BEGLIN:

Page 109 – hats off to the FA Cup heroes of 1986; page 110 – an infamous injury against Everton at Goodison in January, 1987; at Stamford Bridge for the famous title decider of 1986; page 113 – double up! Around the city streets with the '86 silverware.

ALAN A'COURT:

Page 114 – wearing the red shirt with pride in 1962; page 115 – the great man prepares for another day's training at Melwood; page 116/117 – hitting the wall. Ending up against the Kop wall as the fans look on during an Anfield cup tie against Southampton in 1960; page 118 – a big cheese! A business interest after football; page 119 – looking on as Tony Rowley gets his head to a corner in 1957.

IAN CALLAGHAN:

Page 121 – the two amigos. Wearing a sombrero with Tommy Smith on another foray into Europe; getting used to handling silverware with Shanks; page 122 – celebrating the '74 FA Cup triumph with Kevin Keegan; page 123 – on England duty with Gerry Byrne and Gordon Milne; page 124 – relaxing in May, 1978 with Tommy Smith after the Reds had retained the European Cup; page 125 – training at Melwood in July, 1976.

ALAN KENNEDY:

Page 126 – signing in with Bob Paisley, four hours late; page 127 – a magical feeling after beating Roma to lift the European Cup in 1984; page 128/129 – the fans monitor the action in April, 1985; page 131 – the winning spot-kick in the penalty shoot-out against Roma; a Real hero – scoring the 1981 European Cup final winner against Madrid in Paris.

DAVID JOHNSON:

Page 133 – enjoying a goal with Terry McDermott; page 135 – with a modest superstar. In the dressing room with Kevin Keegan and admiring the colourful Liverpool masses before the 1977 European Cup final; page 136 – sitting out the 1978 European Cup final against Bruges through injury; page 137 – savouring another Anfield strike.

PHIL THOMPSON

Page 138/139 – addressing the Liverpool faithful at a city centre reception after the 1974 FA Cup triumph; page 140 – a champagne moment in the Liverpool dressing room;

page 143 – weighing in for another heavyweight European challenge at Liverpool airport with Phil Neal and Terry McDermott; page 144/145 – training on a famous terrace in the '70s; page 146 – saluting the fans with Alan Hansen as another championship is clinched; with Sammy Lee, Patrice Bergues, Gerard Houllier and Joe Corrigan after the 2001 UEFA Cup win over Alaves in Dortmund; page 149 – in the hotseat. Taking charge of Liverpool in dramatic circumstances against Dynamo Kiev in 2001; page 150 – with Phil Boersma, Emlyn Hughes and Tommy Smith at the opening of a Walton hairdressing salon in 1973.

ALAN HANSEN:

Page 153 – in the bath with the European Cup, 1978; 154/155 – with team-mates at Anfield watching the famous Bruce Grobbelaar handstand in 1984; page 157 – on an away trip with the Bruce Grobbelaar in the '80s; waving to the Anfield crowd at a testimonial in August, 1988.

GERRY BYRNE:

Page 159 – trainer Bob Paisley examines the most famous broken collarbone in Liverpool history after the 1965 FA Cup final win over Leeds; page 160/161 – in action against at Anfield in the '60s as Tommy Leishman looks on; page 162 – on England duty, signing autographs with Ian Callaghan in 1966; page 163 – shaking hands with Ron Yeats on a snowy testimonial night as Tommy Lawrence and Ian Callaghan look on.

RONNIE WHELAN:

Page 165 – a young star eyeing up the silverware on arriving at Anfield in 1979; page 166/167 – enjoying a goal against Southampton in 1982; page 168 – hoping for good luck in the Milk Cup final against Manchester United with Ian Rush in March, 1983; page 169 – celebrating with John Aldridge after the opening goal of the dramatic 1989 FA Cup final against Everton.

KENNY DALGLISH:

Page 170/171 – with Jimmy Case, Phil Neal, David Fairclough, Alan Hansen, Emlyn Hughes and Ray Clemence celebrating the 1978 European Cup; page 172 – getting measured up for the FA Cup final in 1988; page 173 – double delight. With Steve McMahon, Steve Nicol and Craig Johnston showing off the 1986 championship trophy and FA Cup to fans in the city; page 174/175 – in action against Dinamo Bucharest in the semi-final of the European Cup in April, 1984; page 176 – scoring the only goal of the game against Bruges in the 1978 European Cup final at Wembley; training with room-mate Graeme Souness; page 177 – graduating to the Boot Room as Liverpool player-manager with Ronnie Moran, Bob Paisley and Roy Evans.

WALK ALONE

Trinity Mirror Sport Media

OTHER TITLES PRODUCED BY SPORT MEDIA:

'Oh . . . I Am A
Liverpudlian And I
Come From The
Spion Kop'

'The Kop
Annual 2005'

£20.00

£8.99

Both of these titles are available to order by calling
0845 143 0001 or by sending a cheque payable to
Sport Media to Sport Media Books, PO Box 48,
Old Hall Street, L69 3EB

(*d*) The annals of Great Britain, of the Venetian republic, of France, of the American federal union—together form a repertory and illustration of all methods of sovereignty. Dr. Whewell in his *Elements of Morality* analyses the normal tendencies to differing forms of government. I make a short extract :

" The natural tendency of the progress of time is to generate an " aristocracy ; but this tendency may be counteracted by the activity of " the democracy. Again, the democratic element may be so feeble that " the nation may be entirely governed by the past ;—by an ancient " aristocracy, or an ancient line of monarchs. Where freedom is thus " extinguished, the State answers its moral ends imperfectly. Again ; " the monarchical element may be enfeebled in various ways : as by " dividing the executive from the judicial character ; by presenting the " State itself, not the king, as the source of justice, and by distributing " the sovereign executive power. The executive power may be held but " for a short time, as by consuls or presidents for a year, or a few years. " By such means, democracy may be established, with very small evident " mixture, either of monarchy or aristocracy."

A recent traveller in Central Africa describes ' Abeokuta' as a federal republic under a perpetual president, and considers that people, whom he describes as " the remotest and most barbarous of African tribes," to be a living refutation of the opinion, that the Greeks invented federal government. BURTON, *Exploration &c.*

(*e*) " The fundamental regulation that determines the manner in " which the public authority is to be executed, is what forms the *Consti-* " *tution of the State.* In this is seen the form by which the nation acts " in quality of a body-politic : how and by whom the people ought to be " governed ; and what are the laws and duties of the governors. This " constitution is in fact nothing more, than the establishment of the " order in which a nation proposes to labour in common for obtaining " those advantages with a view to which the political society was estab- " lished. VATTEL

(*f*) "Public Law has for its object the State, that is, the organic " manifestation of the people : Private Law embraces the legal relations " between individuals, and is the rule or expression of those relations."

SAVIGNY (trans. by Sir G. Bowyer)

(*g*) *municipium,* a town, a civil community.

(*h*) "Criminal jurisdiction is the public power of taking cognizance of " crimes, and imposing punishments for the public welfare——civil juris- " diction is that which has for its object the application of laws not " intended for the punishment of offenders, but declaring, defining or " creating natural or civil, immutable or positive rights." BOWYER

SECTION IV.

The jurist has to do with the origin, analysis, definitions, composition, meaning, application, differences, of laws—of those rules of conduct and intercourse, which are at once the growth and the cement of civil society.

The necessity, and therefore the origin of Law, has been shown, *viz.* 1. natural or moral, as coeval with the human family, 2. civil—the growth of society, and medium of organised government.

So, the analysis, definition and composition of every civil law, are severally deducible from conclusions already arrived at; which may be thus summed up or epitomised.

All laws of conduct are based on or spring out of the one universal, immutable Law. Following, led by Reason to follow the mighty Lawgiver of the universe, men frame rules of conduct, which are not part of the general Law, inasmuch as they are not, nor are they intended to be, of universal force or application, but are subsidiary and supplemental—an adaptation and carrying out of the spirit of the general code or scheme of right and wrong, to suit the peculiar circumstances of a portion of the race of Man. All however, in all ages, and in all places, are bound by that general code: it follows that, the particular laws deduced from or added to it, should not infringe any part of that code, but, on the contrary, should harmonize and fall in with, although not of it.

Such was the doctrine of the great ethical and political philosopher already quoted :—

"Law, now, I understand," wrote Aristotle, in his *Rhetoric*, "to be either peculiar or universal; peculiar, "to be that which has been marked out by each peo-"ple in reference to itself, and that this is partly "unwritten, partly written. I call that Law universal, "which is conformable merely to dictates of nature; "for there does exist naturally an universal sense of "right and wrong, which, in a certain degree, all in-"tuitively divine, even' should no intercourse with "each other, nor any compact have existed—"

Thus, civil Law is a development of moral Law: breach of a civil law is a breach of duty, a moral transgression. It is, however, a breach which might not be possible at other than certain times, in other than certain places, between others than certain men. In respect therefore of their particularity, of their merely local or personal application, civil laws are properly said to be different from and beside the moral Law.

Yet, as has been demonstrated, the first element, the ground-work, the warrant, of every civil law must be, the moral Law.

But, the command, the mandatory dogma or rule in a particular civil law, may contain more than any moral law enjoins, *e. g.* a prohibition to kill wild animals (*feræ naturæ*) fit for man's food, as woodcocks, hares, snipe.; a prohibition to grow tobacco or opium,

to export or to import corn, wines, &c; a command
to build, to cultivate, even to wear clothes, after a prescribed mode. Such forms of legal restraint have
a merely relative and temporary value: they are,
in the main, purely arbitrary and speculative.[a] Yet
the circumstances of a particular State may render
such innovations upon or supplement to the moral
Law properly and morally expedient. This, then, is
a conventional or civil element; and it enters into the
composition of civil laws, generally and as a rule:
for, even those laws which sound as mere repetitions
of what the moral Law enjoins, e. g.—Slay not a man !
Take not that which is another's!—are, strictly, no
exceptions. ·Different codes of civil Law define differ-,
ently, according to the conventional opinions or the
necessities of each community—what is criminal homi-
cide, and its varying shades: so, the definition of
what is another's, also what constitutes a wrongful
appropriation, vary in different States.

The most distinctive and universal feature of
difference in the two codes, of Nature and of Man,
is, the arbitrary or civil sanction.

"Execution," pithily wrote the great English
lawyer, Coke, "is the life of the Law."

Execution, punishment, penalty, sentence—are
terms expressive of the vital action and force
of civil Law: when they cease to have meaning or
effect, Law has no civil or political existence; it is,
then, but a precept or dogmatical injunction.

"Justice," declares the *Dharma Sastra*, "was
"created by Brahma under the form of Punishment."

So then, every civil law is composed of a mandate (—a command, an injunction, an imperative proposition, a dogmatical precept, a warning, a prohibition or direction—) and a sanction; the mandatory part having a moral element and a conventional element.

The latter may be also called, the civil, the artificial, the mutable, the local, the arbitrary, the human —element, incident or quality; each epithet indicating a characteristic not included in the indispensable, universal, or moral element.

The nature of Man—his faculties and his propensities—must determine the scope and application of Law: in other words, the motive, subject, operation of rules of conduct must correspond with, be within Man's sphere of action—a dogma thus explained by Domat:

"We cannot take a more simple and surer way "for discovering the first principles of laws, than by "supposing two prime truths, which are only bare "definitions. One is, that the laws of Man are "nothing else but the rules of his conduct; and the "other, that the said conduct is nothing else but the "steps which a man makes towards his end."

To argue upon, and to explain the end of Man, the purpose of Man's existence, is, to lay bare the foundations, to develop the structure, to illustrate the necessity and application of Law. In Man's steps towards his end, we know must be found every intermediate object and aim which consist with the purpose and end of Man's being: and it is the observation of an old English moralist, that, whatever is directed

in the shortest way to that end, may be called
'right,' as a right line is the shortest of all.

To associate and to form communities, to erect
powers and principalities, to organise schemes of
political and social action, to possess, to enjoy, to
improve, to explore, to discover, to speculate—such are
human aims and occupations, all tending to the end:
for they are the natural results and promptings of
Man's wants, and of Man's Reason; that Reason
being influenced (not seldom clouded and impeded) by
a secondary power, Man's will—itself but a result of
motive forces.

Association—the union and concord of intentions, of
aims—must, in action or operation, restrain something
of the will of each individual in the union: hence,
civil Law itself has been defined, 'the deliberate reason
of all, governing the occasional will of each.' What
each one is to have, not to have, to do, to refrain
from, must be ascertained. To every grade and
form of association, this rule and necessity applies
and inherently belongs.

Political associations—primitive nationalities—are
formed gradually and variously, discordant wills give
way and combine, uniform action is authoritatively established, by degrees: that uniformity is civil Law,
the result of collective sentiments, habits, manners
—of convenience, of circumstances, in continued
association. (b)

LIBERTY: EQUALITY.

It follows from, and is indeed but a paraphrase of
the preceding sentences, that subjection to Law indi-

cates restraint and coercion—a uniform and compulsory progress, notwithstanding and in contrast with the ever-varying will: the Law's power is necessarily supreme and single, admitting of no rival, no interference.   It is a primary characteristic of all Law, to define as well as to enjoin restrictions—to define and circumscribe, for each member of a law-directed community, a range of action; thus to preserve and protect the *common* weal.   Without speculating upon the ideal (general and abstract) freedom or license of the human will, it is an obvious truth, that, the indulgence or exercise of that mysterious motive-power cannot, under any circumstances, have unlimited scope or range: its proper arena of action, as well as the faculties of its agents, must always be limited.

The terms 'liberty' 'freedom' represent a range of action, and have always a relative significance, *e. g.* in relation to the moral Law—to expediency or safety—to the economy and exigencies of civil society.   In this last relation, liberty has a juridical meaning and value, and may be defined 'the range of action of social Man.'

"In governments," wrote Montesquieu, "that is, "in societies directed by laws, liberty can consist only "in the power of doing what we ought to will, and "in not being constrained to do, what we ought not "to will." [c]

He is free, he enjoys liberty, who knows no other check or trammel, in the exercise of his will, than Law, moral or civil; nor without constant general forbearance, can there be particular or individual

F

liberty. Admirably is this truth at once expressed
and illustrated by Cicero,:—"For this it is we are
"servants of the Law, that we may be free men." [d]

Thus, Law confers as well as secures freedom of
action. That the security is but imperfect, must
follow from the impossibility of preventing (which is
something else than punishing for) results of the
errant will and ways of men. So is Man constituted
—the victim of his own mysterious and dangerous,
though valuable, ennobling prerogative, free-will!

It is in this definite and significant view of liberty,
that Kant defines *jus* (*i. e.* a juridical system of right),
to be, "the aggregate of conditions under which
"any one's freedom of choice (*arbitrium*) becomes
"compatible with the liberty of others; conforming
"to a general law of liberty." [e]

Man, the rational creature, has a conscious purpose,
an intent, whenever he exercises his faculties. His
own free-will, his own choice and option selects
and determines that purpose. Law—moral and civil—
may, indeed must, constrain his will, *i. e.* by the
threat of sanctions or (in exceptional cases) by pre-
ventive coercion. But, there is a constraint which
is a constant and normal infliction, leaving its victim
without any possibility of choice, any use of his
free-will, any discretion to do or not to do. One
so subject, has not liberty; his will's choice—his
arbitrium (a comprehensive name for all action of
free-will) is not limited merely, *i. e.* by any limit as
a result of some organised scheme of common subjection, voluntarily submitted to by moral agents—but

the domain of free-will is converted into a silent, barren waste : whilst Nature's privilege, to cultivate, to lay out, to improve that domain, is transferred (— control over that privilege is transferred), as an increment, to a particular external power, to a foreign *arbitrium*, whether of one or more—external, and therefore wholly irrespective of, needing no impulse from the rational or other motives of him upon whom it is thus brought to bear.   Such an one is, a slave—the mere instrument of another's will. Being divested of free-will, of the exercise of his Reason to shape his intents or his conduct—being, therefore, without moral responsibility (in respect of his involuntary progress), he has lost his human supremacy—his manhood, at all events its outward characteristic ; though, may-be, having the consciousness, as he undoubtedly holds the dormant prerogative, of a rational, morally independent, will.

Equality, in jurisprudence and in political science, means—the equal, unvarying protection of Law, to which each one is entitled.   Men have equal rights, but to unequal things.   The station, duties, possessions, condition, success, of individuals necessarily differ—a necessity as real and as rational, as the physical differences of stature, of colour, of temperament.   What rightfully belongs to each, should be equally secured to each, by Law. *(f)*

The measure of what should belong to any member of a civil society, is the result, in each case, of an aggregate of facts, which indicate the condition and claims of the individual.   Law does not create, but enquires of and marshals those facts, under the several heads—*status;* contract; wrong. As the incidents and accidents of each one's civil position, are, under those heads, found to be; so must follow his civil advantages and claims, created or recognised by each jural system of rights, wrongs, remedies, duties, as hereafter explained.

(*a*) In every such instance, the wisdom or the error of legislative intervention—whether or not the particular interdict be within the sphere of civil Law—is demonstrable, by means of that great effort of modern progress (vaguely foreshadowed by Aristotle), the science of Political Economy. The rules of this science furnish a formulary test of legislation, and are in aid of the application of laws: they reveal the practical working and intrinsic results—while jurisprudence traces and analyses the gradation and history—of a people's laws.

(*b*) This view, while it ignores deliberate, *a priori* construction of a primitive polity, does not touch any theory of motives or incentives that bring men together. Bacon defined the aim of legislation to be, "that the citizens may live happily."—and Aristotle insisted that civil society was founded, not that its members might *live,* but that they might *live well;* repudiating the notion, that a State is "an alliance "mutually to defend each other from injuries, or for a commercial inter-"course." Aristotle thought individual virtue to be the normal aim and purpose of statesmen and legislators. But little research or reflection is needed to discover, that, methodizing, even knowledge of the legitimate uses and modes of civil association, are efforts of a society when organised, not preceding or during its formation. Instinct (or natural human tendencies), necessity, wants, emergencies, produce arrangements and relations, which mental effort, philosophical and scientific enquiry, in time analyse, investigate, and mature. Legislation proper cannot be the origin either of a State or of laws.

(*c*) The latent force of that seemingly simple proposition discovers itself in the following philosophical dogma of Kant:

"Liberty, considered with reference to the mental legislation of "Reason [—the moral sense], is, in truth, but a faculty [—a range "of action]: the possibility of wandering from [the precepts of] that "legislation, is but defect of power."

If a road to a certain goal be along the edge of a precipice, the possible accident, that a way-farer may, carelessly, rashly, or ignorantly, step over the precipice, can scarcely be included in the idea or description of his liberty to travel to that goal or on that road. So, in the path of life, the will or the physical faculty to transgress, to go astray, to fall —is a weakness, a misfortune, a defect, not an extension or effort of liberty, in any significant or rational sense of that term.

(*d*) In this account of liberty, no provision is made for the unrighteousness of any law, such as may excuse or, in plain obedience to a paramount rule, even warrant disobedience. A law, which the subject can have any righteous option about obeying, is exceptional; it is not a juridical, but a political (also a moral) dilemma.

There is another, and perhaps the most popular application of the word liberty, in which sense or use it has ever been a very tocsin of dispute and strife, and in which it admits not of definition, *viz.* the position to which the subject, under every or any government, is entitled, as respects freedom of speech and of action, as respects also, voice, power or share in every or any function of government. This is a problem—a different one in each case—of legislation, and of speculative politics.

Bentham, commenting on the 2nd Article of the French Declaration of Rights, of 1791, wrote:—

"We know what it is for men to live without government, for we see "instances of such a way of life—we see it in many savage nations, "or rather races of mankind; for instance, among the savages of N. S. "Wales, whose way of living is so well known to us: no habit of ob- "dience, and thence no government—no government, and thence no "laws—no laws, and thence no such things as rights—no security— "no property:—liberty, as against regular control, the control of laws "and government—perfect; but as against all irregular control, the "mandates of stronger individuals, none." Bentham ignored 'natural rights,' even in the constitution of the family, except as a mere consequence or inference from brutal *i. e.* physical force; therefore, he ignored domestic government, as 'regular.' This dogmatic view (more formal than real) does not affect the force and truth of his illustration of so-called liberty in the absence of civil sanctions.

(*e*) This is not the place to discuss theories formed upon an absolute, single, yet undefined meaning of liberty, *viz.* co-extensive with the possible indulgence of an ideal will. Every law, in that view, however traced and whence-soever it emanates, infringes liberty. Theorists of that school, although strenuously ignoring a code of conduct antecedent to and irrespective of human systems, insist upon a 'natural' liberty; this really being, when analysed, an unnatural license. They cannot gainsay, that men have *not* liberty, as the feathered race have, to soar among the clouds, to ride aloft with the winds, nor yet to dwell with fishes in the deep waters—that men have *not* liberty to set at naught the universal *law*, that animal life needs for its support a constant, tedious process of eating and drinking: in this region, *viz.* of physics, a law is recognised—a natural law, one before and beyond human contrivances. But, that men are not naturally—irrespective of human devices, opinion, and prohibitions—*at liberty* to kill, to maim, to cheat their fellows, is, by the same school, considered an unwarranted and unphilosophical assumption!

The jurist regards only civil liberty, which does not need nor invite any speculative enquiry of a natural or præ-civil liberty.

(*f*) " It has been said, that *All men are born equal.* But it is " evident that this is not true as a fact. For not only are children, " for a long time after birth, necessarily in the power of parents and " others ; but the external conditions of the society in which a man " is born, as the laws of property and the like, determine his relation " to other men, during life. If it be said that these are extraneous and " accidental circumstances, not born with the man; we answer, that " if we reject from our consideration, as extraneous and accidental, all " such conditions, there remains nothing which we can call intrinsic " and necessary. but the material conditions of man's existence; and " if we were to adopt this view, the principle might more properly be " stated, *All men are equally born.* The relations of Family, Property, " and the like, are as essential to man's moral being, as Language, " without which his mind cannot be unfolded to the apprehension of " Rules, and the distinction of right and wrong. If therefore our " assumed equality rejects the former circumstance, it must reject the " latter." *Elements of Morality.*

SECTION V.

"THE *conceptions* of the fundamental Rights of "men are universal, and flow necessarily from the "moral nature of Man: the *definitions* of these "Rights are diverse, and are determined by the laws "of each State." [a]

"Private Right lies under the protection of public "laws; for Law guards the people, and magistrates "guard the laws." [b]

Whatsoever a man may claim protection for, to be protected in, by appeal to Law and to the sanctions of Law, is his Right—lawfully his own, under guarantee of Law; *e. g.* life, property. Liberty (as defined in SEC. IV.) is rightfully claimable; therefore liberty may be designated a Right. But liberty is more scientifically classed as the entire aggregate or sum of each one's Rights. For, Rights are powers, faculties of action or of enjoyment, marking out, constituting each man's range of action: each man's Rights therefore necessarily cover the area of his civil liberty. A Right is, essentially, an idea of the future, *viz.* the continuance of what is, or, the assured coming of what might or might not come to pass. [c]

The respect, restraint, conduct, imposed, by law, on every one, with regard, in relation to every Right of every other one, is, in each instance, an obligation. So that, each one's liberty is bounded and defined by a wall, a hedge-row of obligations; beyond and close

*

upon which, on all sides, are the several, separate do-
mains of others' Rights—all other areas of liberty.

The obligations of moral Law are called, as
such, emphatically, duties; being what is due to
Reason, to Nature, to God. Therefore, in so far
as any scheme of civil Law is, probably (though
perhaps not critically nor precisely) in consonance
with the universal code—in so far as obedience to
civil Law is an alternative refuge from confusion
and lawlessness—to such extent (at any rate), such
obedience is a paramount and moral duty.[d] The
word 'duty' is also used generally, as a synonyme of obligation; moral duties, legal duties.
However undefined, even vague or conjectural, the
ideas of mutual Right and obligation, in a primitive
polity; still, civil rules of Right and obligation
must always practically exist. Every emergency,
every phase of relation and of collision—whether
creating, exhibiting, or infringing Rights—is provided
for. Experience and civilization mature the rational
and skilled understanding, adoption, formation of a
scheme of Rights and of their infringement: but, as
the rudest polity must contain an adjudicating function—as no association, professedly (however rudely)
organised as a polity, can exclude any possible contingency that may call for a rule of decision upon
Right and obligation—as the occurrence and development of commerce, of modes of dealing, of oppres-
sions, of mutualities and antagonisms, depend not
upon Law or civil rules; but, as already explained,
Law is called into exercise in order to give those

inevitable results of Man's propensities and wants, scope, limit, or check, adapted to the exigencies of civil life—it follows, that, Rights and their correlative, obligations, are implied, to an indefinite extent, in every grade and kind of polity. It also follows, that the knowledge, the precise demarcation, the minute tracery (as it were in a network) of civil Rights, progresses with the progression of a people, in the arts and improvements—in the intellectual culture—in the combination and fixedness of purpose—that characterise, more or less, all civilly-social existence. With respect to formal or express legislation; it is clear, that definition of Right enters into every enactment or promulgated law. One object of every complete legislative act must be, to guard against the infraction of a Right; and, in so far it must, in some way, define, create, or affirm the Right treated of (*), determining, within the purview of that particular law and as the legislative judgment, the national conscience there wills, what is right and what is wrong.

No enquiry, then, can be more germane or more essential, in the study of jurisprudence, than, what are or may be Rights civilly protected—jural Rights, their qualities and incidents.

Every violation of a Right, is, a Wrong; and, being a negation of, or opposed to *jus*, it is an in-jury.

REMEDY.

Compensation for, reparation of the loss occasioned by, wrong and injury, is every man's Right.

G

"Now, since," wrote Heineccius, "whatsoever ren-
"ders another more unhappy, injures him; but he
"renders one most unhappy, who, having injured
"him, does not repair the damage; the consequence
"is, that he who does a person any injury, is obliged
"to make reparation to him; and that he who refuses
"to do it, does a fresh injury, and may be truly
"said to hurt him again."

This Right may be defined—restoration, actually
or virtually, to the state of things existing before
—rather, which would have been but for—a Wrong
done (i. e. to the *status quo*), as far as possible.
To protect, to enforce, when due, (thus giving
a value to) every civil Right, Law provides a
remedy—a method of pursuing the wrong-doer, of
verifying and of obtaining the Right. Hence, the
Law maxim, 'Every Right has a remedy'; Right and
remedy being cor-relative terms.[f] Thus, breach of
some law, infringement of some civil Right, necessarily precedes exercise or defined existence of the
Right of remedy; which, until such breach, is merely potential and contingent:[g] it is a Right that
accompanies or supplements every other civil Right.
Remedy is the indicator, the witness of Wrong;
it is the road or means of attaining to, as well as
a test of the particular sanction, which the Right,
the rule of Law violated demands. Pursuit of
remedy leads, in the first instance, to a new, defined
Right and legal claim, *viz.* adjudicated restoration
—which term includes the restorative equivalent,
compensation. If the payment or other act of repara-

tion decreed, be resisted, then the sanction applicable is enforced. [h]

Civil Law must always protect—guarantee immunity from harm to, the body, the person—each one's self. Detriment to, interference with, active assumption of power over the life, the physical or the mental condition of a fellow man—gratuitously and without necessity, moral or civil—is, universally, a Wrong.

Wounding, striking, unauthorised personal trespass or restraint of any sort, acts directly causing damage to health of mind[i] or of body, illegal meddling with mental or bodily action—such are infringements of personal integrity and security, the first of substantive Rights.[j]

Our Indian Penal Code protects all classes of subjects, whether Christian, Hindu, Mahommedan, Seikh, or of any other creed or denomination whatever, in rational exercise and expression of what each may hold to be—Religion; by punishing taunt and ridicule of religious feelings.[k]

By such treatment of intolerant and rude disregard of solemn and valued convictions—even, may-be, of popular credulity—the personal civil Right to independent thought, in a wide and most important (perhaps the highest) range of mental activity is recognised and vindicated.

All laws imposing restrictions upon expression or communication of thought (e. g. censorship of the Press), range under this head; inasmuch as they prescribe and define the subject's personal liberty in a particular field of thought and action.[l]

Nor, is State or jural protection confined to applying remedies and sanctions, in their ordinary acceptation, *i. e.* as a cure or consequence of wrong. The Law should prevent and resist evil, as well as repair and punish. A threat, accompanied or conveyed by attempt or gesture of violence, itself confers a Right adapted to the necessity of the case. Self-defence is that Right, as well as the expression of that necessity. The defender is, unavoidably, an instrument of the Law. The imminent danger of the aggression, which, if continued, may be irreparable, places the party attacked in an exceptional position; which releases him from his general obligation to respect every one's person and to abstain from personal violence. The immunity guaranteed by Law, is not to be converted into a weapon or opportunity of violence, nor a means to aid and promote violence; the attempt so to use it cancels, for the occasion, the violator's general Right: the shield or *ægis* of Law drops, vanishes.

The same rule and reasoning applies to protection of any Right, *e. g.* possession, wherever a similar necessity, *viz.* for the threatened party to act as an instrument of the Law, exists; the emergency precluding recourse to tribunals or public officers. Just as contract (it will be seen) creates an occasional law and obligation, *viz.* to observe the terms of the

contract ; so, violence or attempt of violence, in each
case, creates, gives birth to a new Right, of resistance, coercive repulsion, self-defence—a Right enforced, not through the active interference of Law,
but by an exceptional permission, by withdrawal of
a general prohibition.

These are not only juridical rules, but a part of
natural Law; contradiction of which would be an
act of oppression, not of Reason : for, State-coer-
cion is but a civil substitute of the inherent natural
Right, self-protection.

The aggression which warrants disregard of another's general Right of personal security, is not
confined to aggression upon oneself. Right of resistance must be co-extensive with the duty, the
obligation and the Right of protection; for, wherever Law declares any Right or imposes an obligation, all acts and power necessary for efficient exercise
and performance thereof are delegated, as of-course.
Moreover, wherever the public weal, the general
peace of the community, e. g. prevention of heinous
crime or of clearly wrongful violence, calls for private
interference ; there, such violence, such vindicatory
coercion as the occasion morally justifies, come under
this head of Right.

The English Courts have supported the Right of
protective coercion, in defence of a child, a wife, a
husband, a relative, a servant, an apprentice, a friend,
a neighbour.

This Right, has an obvious attendant risk, viz.
he who assumes to exercise it may mistake the occa-

"rights, capacities, and duties, or those incapacities
"and exemptions, are considered as forming or
"composing a single though complex being, and are
"bound into that complex One by the collective name
"'condition.'" Rights of status necessarily vary
and multiply with the social, commercial, official,
artificial relations, created or recognised by each
system; active disregard of which are, in that system,
civil personal wrongs. Depriving a father of his
child, a husband of his wife; injuring either father
or husband through personal injury to the child or
wife; illegally and maliciously alienating customers
from a tradesman, clients or patients from a lawyer
or medical practitioner—such are obvious instances
of injury to status.

With respect to the status, the relative rights,
created by State-offices, as of judge, magistrate,
military commander, &c; interference with those
rights—*i. e.* with execution of the duties assigned
to the offices respectively—although it must involve
personal indignity and cause for individual complaint,
is an affair of State, a crime; since, the
primary and most material injury is, to the public,
the nation, whose service and welfare is thereby
marred or trifled with. But, the officer may, by
some fraud or machination, lose his office, or his
hold upon the confidence of the public, the estimation
of his superiors. Here would be private and personal
wrong or damage, by means, through the channel
of his official status.

Most frequently in such cases, status and special

characteristics are rather a criterion of the amount of damage done, of loss to be compensated, than of a distinct injury: inasmuch as the wrong complained of is a violation of an absolute—of a direct, as well as of . an artificial or relative Right; *e. g.* defamation, illegal deprivation of property such as profits or income.

RIGHTS OF FAMILY.

The members, components, of a family, have reciprocal rights, as such—rights of that status, *viz.* of parentage, filiation, blood-relationship. The primitive, universal, and paramount character of this class of rights give them a special significance: they stand in relief among status-relations: they constitute primary society, the basis or commencement of all civil union. As the paternal typifies all dominical and imperial control; so is there found in the filial and fraternal ties, the type and precursor of civil subjection and of civil forms of fellowship. Civil Law often deals arbitrarily, at all events very variously, with the marital and the parental instances of this class of status-rights; in the character, and duration, and evidence, of paternal authority; in all incidents of the marriage tie—in its very idea and definition. The subject is treated at length in a separate section.

GOOD-NAME: SELF-RESPECT.

Reputation, character, is the life of life, at once the attractive and the repulsive medium of our social mingling—the lustre or the bane of each one's

H

social existence. It is the 'reflex sentiment' (so named by Dr. Whewell), consciousness of which determines the worth of all that life can give, to the large majority of mankind. It is a second self. Obviously then, to lessen, to lower, without warrant of Law, the reputation, character, existimation[r] of any-one among his fellows, must often be a serious social and civil grievance. Hence, laws of defamation, slander, libel.

Good-name is a moral reward, therefore a moral Right,. and, in one shape or another, always vindicated by civil Law. Like to sale-price of a marketable commodity, fair repute or good-name fluctuates, but it .is a normal result, and the integrity of the premises which produce that result (as with price) is of vital consequence to all. Therefore, Law provides, that the market be not tampered with.

But, in order to earn, to have a title to good name or repute, in other words, a claim to respect from others, there is one intrinsic motive and personal sentiment imperatively needed, viz. self-respect[s]; the integrity and preservation of which is therefore a Right, and, as an action of the mind, may range under the Right of security: yet, it is also in close alliance with the Right to good-name, whenever this is earned or sought.

To make an insulting speech, may—and that, merely in respect of personal dishonor, of wounded feelings,—infringe a civil Right: for, the sentiments, the manners, the civil content of a people, may require so nice an estimate of personal immunity. In the *Dharma Sastra;*

"If any give abusive words to a deformed or dis-"eased person, whether the words be true or untrue "or in the form of irony, he shall be fined—"

The Penal Code of British India treats as an intrinsic civil Right, the mental modesty—also the (oriental) seclusion of women: any violation of either is a crime.

History tells, how insults have been, Law approving, wiped out with blood. The historian of Sweden (Geijer) quotes an old law of those famous northern tribes,—"that, whosoever upbraided another, as not "being 'a man's match nor a man in his heart,' should "render himself to do battle with the man he had "insulted, at a spot where three ways met. If the "person against whom the words had been spoken "came not to the meeting, it is said, then must he "needs be such a one as he hath been called, and "can never again bear valid testimony, nor take oath. "If the person who spoke the words came not, he was "to be publicly proclaimed infamous (*niding*), and a "memorial of the fact must be erected at the spot."[t]

PROPERTY.

To have, to possess, to use—these are terms indicative of property, a natural institution, one of primary society, found in, because essential to every stage of society; however improved, modified, analysed and built upon by civil laws.

In the simplest association, if mankind but co-existed without associating, something or the use of something must be an individual's own, entirely or for a time: this is necessary to any enjoyment of life, to life itself—and this is 'property.'

What is one's own, the interference of every other is excluded from: this is the essential condition of ownership. Exclusion is then, the generic, the fundamental idea in property. Men are associated in order to enjoy the common birth-right of mankind, the Earth and the things of Earth. The Author of the Universe, by giving that birth-right and heritage in common, effectually decreed and compelled association: association necessitates rule and method and mutual forbearance *(supra* p. 32).

Its necessity being established, what is the medium or the criterion of appropriation, of property? The answer is,—occupation, labour. By 'occupation' [u] is meant, the act of a first taker, the effort to appropriate; which act and effort, if continuous and sustained (as must be assumed), include labour. [v] Eastern codes have expressly recognized industrial labour [w] as a basis of property :—

MANU—"Sages, who know former times—pronounce "cultivated land to be the property of him who cut "away the wood, or who cleared and tilled it." And from the *Sheraa*—"He who brings into life "land which was dead, he is the owner thereof."

Such is the character and origin of this Right, as a necessary mode of enjoyment or benefit. Its jural significance, its guarantee, must of course be from Law: and in this sense one may understand

Kant's dogma,—The notion of a 'mine and thine'
external to self can have no existence save in the
social condition, *i. e.* in civil society or union—not
as a confusion or identification of the primitive
'Right of all' with the distinctive idea of property.[x]

Regarding property as a rule of enjoyment—a pre-
ventive of, a safeguard against confusion and dispute
among men, it may well be contended, that, where
dispute is not physically possible (as, where duality of
claims cannot be), there, property is not possible,
at least in a civil sense.[y] Variety, modes, divisions,
disposal of proprietary rights—depend on the methods and policy of each scheme of civil laws: *e. g.*
feudal, zemindary, copyhold, labour-rights in land;
the several rights and modifications of property
as, hirer, pledgee, factor, custodian, general owner
where there is a pledge.

Grotius says—" Formerly, when concurrence of the
"entire race of men was practicable, partition was
"a mode of original acquisition—now, it can only
"be by occupation."—and elsewhere, " Thus we learn
"how *res* came under proprietorship : not by a
"mere act of the will; inasmuch as strangers could
"not know what any might desire to be theirs, so
"as not to meddle with that; moreover, many might
"have desired the same thing—but [property came]
"by pact of some sort, either express, as by parti-
"tion; or tacit, as by occupation. It is to be sup-
"posed that, when enjoyment in common became
"distasteful, but formal partition was not yet made,
"it must have been unanimously agreed among all

"that, whatever each one had occupied, he should
"have that as his own."

Purely original acquisition of property is, to the
jurist, a mere speculative enquiry; inasmuch as every
system of civil laws must apply positive rules to determine the ownership of all *res* (things) within their
dominion; even those seemingly derelict. If unappropriated land be without the territorial sovereignty of any State, the first efficient occupant, by his acts
of occupation, necessarily brings the new acquisition
under dominion of the laws of that State and
sovereign to whom he owes allegiance; and those laws
clothe the new territory with a definite character and
quality, as a subject of property.[e]

For, the political status of the acquirer invests him
with a representative character, whether he will or no:
he carries that status with him everywhere; nor
can he acquire, in any place, any rights, but in
subordination to the laws of that society of which he
is a unit. This is a necessary deduction from the
relation of sovereign and subject, *i. e.* political supremacy.

COMMON PROPERTY: PUBLIC PROPERTY.

It is obvious, that many things which are the
heritage of mankind, which Nature has spread and
preserves for Man's sustenance and enjoyment, are
incapable of specific appropriation.

For the same cause that many things, as, land
for habitation or cultivation, food for consumption,
must be divided and entirely appropriated, to be

of use to, to be available by individuals, *viz.* that no other mode will answer the end—for the same cause it is, that the air we breathe, the sea, the sea-shore,[aa] are obviously impossible of rationally exclusive appropriation; inasmuch as their very use, their advantage implies, that they are *general and common at all times to all mankind:* which condition itself specifies and defines the entire class of such things.[bb] Were it otherwise, the liberty to appropriate (where physically possible) in such cases once admitted, the appropriators must lose much more in what they are excluded from, in the deprivation consequent upon such liberty, than their own appropriation could possibly compensate. This truth is ratified by universal consent; it is a corollary to the juridical theory of liberty.

Just so, certain edifices, roads, &c. within the territorial limits of each particular State, are and must be, *common and public to all its subjects;* *e. g.* buildings for public worship, for public entertainment, highways (whether of land or water).[cc]

ACCESSION.

Property, besides its use and significance as a sharing, an apportionment, a plan for enjoyment of the estate of the human species, this Earth and the spontaneous gifts of Nature, applies also to the product of labour, (not the labour of occupation and appropriation merely, but) that which is fabricated by Man, the fruit of industry. Man cannot create, he can but improve, and extract utility from the works of Creation, by labour. Here is an indisputable basis of property, of exclusion, of preference in enjoyment. Difficulty however may occur with reference to the material upon which the industry, the skill is employed; *e. g.* agriculture and horticulture, architectural structures, sculpture, painting. If the labour and skill which have produced the cultured field or the work of art, be the property of A, but he has, wilfully or unwittingly, worked upon the soil, the marble, or the canvas of B; there is a confusion of rights: these must be disentangled and apportioned by positive conventional rules of civil Law. The dilemma has given occasion to casuistical ingenuity. Heineccius thought:

"Seeing a master has a right to exclude all from "the use of what is his, he has a right certainly "to hinder any thing from being joined to what "is his against his will. Wherefore, since what "is added to any thing of ours, either renders it "useless, or at least worse, or renders it more "valuable and better, because he who renders our "goods worse hurts us; the consequence is that he "who has rendered our goods either useless or worse "by an industrial accession, is obliged, taking the "spoilt goods, to repair our damage; and if he did it "by deceit, and with evil intention, he is likewise "liable to punishment. But, if our goods are ren-"dered better and more valuable by any artificial "accession, then there is a great difference when the "two things can be separated without any considerable "loss, and when they cannot. In the former case,

" since the master of each part hath a right to exclude
" all others from the use of what belongs to him;
" but that cannot now be done otherwise than by se-
" parating the two things; the consequence is, that,
" in this case, the things are to be immediately separat-
" ed, and to each is to be restored his own part. But,
" in the other case, the joined things ought to be
" adjudged to one or other of the two, the other
" being condemned to pay the value of what is not
" his, to the owner who is thus deprived of it; and,
" if there be any knavery in the matter, punishment
" is deserved."

The Mahommedan Law doctors, looking upon an
unlicensed industrial accession, *i. e.* such an one as
changes the character of a thing, as an ousting of
the owner—usurpation (*ghœsb*), assume, as a rule, a
change of property, and substitute the right of compensation: but they have among them much ingenious variety of opinion, and varying rules for
varying occurrences. [dd]

The Roman Digest teaches: "When one out of
" another's materials fashions something for himself,
" Nerva and Proculus are of opinion that the fashion-
" er is the owner, inasmuch as that which is fa-
" shioned, had not appertained to any one. Sabinus
" and Cassius think it more carrying out Nature's
" rule, that he who was owner of the material be also
" owner of what is fashioned from that material,
" inasmuch as without the material nothing could
" have been fashioned———But the opinion of
" right-thinkers is between those two, *viz.* if what is

I

" fashioned can be reduced again to the mere material,
" then what Sabinus and Cassius hold is the more
" correct doctrine; if it be not capable of such
" reduction, then the doctrine of Nerva and Proculus
" is more correct—"

The result, in principle, and as the solution of a
problem in jurisprudence, is, that the adjustment of
loss and gain from industrial accession, must be made
by each scheme of civil Law for itself, according to
the views and convenience of each particular people.

Natural accretions; as alluvial deposit from a
river, increase in growth or production—flowers,
fruits, offspring of animals—all such seem naturally
claimable, as necessarily and primarily acquired by
the proprietor of the principal land, trees, animals, &c.
of which they are severally the increment or product.
But this class of accessions also need to be ordered
and subdivided by artificial rule: e. g. the Roman
system was,—' If an island rise in a public river (not
in the sea, for then it belongs to the occupant), and
become fixed in the middle of a river, it is in
common to those who possess the land nearest to
the bank on each side of the stream, according to
the breadth and length of each frontage. If it lie
nearer to the frontage of one estate on either side
than to that of the other, that inheritance or
estate has as many more feet or yards in the island
as it is nearer to it. But if the whole island is
nearer to one estate than to the other, that estate
claims the whole. This is to be understood where
the lands on each side have not any certain limits

and bounds ; for if they have, there can be no claim or title to such an island, but it belongs to the occupant. If the river divide its course, and make an island of land by uniting its stream afterwards, or shall overflow a ground, that land does not belong to any occupant, or to the neighbouring estates, but to its first owner. An island rising in private rivers and lakes wholly belongs to the private persons who are owners of those lakes and rivers.'[ee]

RIGHTS WHICH ARE FRACTIONS OF PROPERTY: USE, SERVITUDES.

I have treated the Right called 'property,' broadly and simply, as a relation between a person and a thing—a power over and in respect of a thing— understanding by 'thing', whatever substance may be appropriated. But it is obvious, that the relation cannot be merely corporeal or material. All rights are jural ideas and dogmas. And these, when in- cluded in or a consequence of property, are in great part, as already observed, conventional civil crea- tions. But, however various in form and significance, the generic character of all rights whatsoever, that are incident to or growing out of property, admit of classification.

Austin defined ownership or property:—"the "right to use or deal with some given subject, in "a manner, or to an extent, which, though it is "not unlimited, is indefinite."

A nearer approach to an exhaustive description of personal dominion in and over the materiel and products of Earth, or whatever may be property, seems to be—'Full property, as a private civil Right, is; the union and aggregate of all civil rights in and over and in relation to a thing, excepting and exclusive of the State's Right.'

The exception refers to the *dominium eminens* (eminent domain), a paramount power in the sovereign, or collective political body—a power variously limited and defined, but inherent and indispensable —to interfere with or to supersede private Right, in protection or furtherance of the common weal; *e. g.* enforced purchase, for public purposes (as a road, a hospital), of a private estate. This public Right will be presently treated of.

There is another use of the terms, property, proprietor, owner, *dominus—viz.* with reference to a portion only of the rights of enjoyment and control included in either of the definitions given. Of those several *jura*, one only indicates or is typical of *dominium ;* and that is, what the Romans called *jus abutendi* (a Right to use up, to make away with), *i. e.* power to dispose of, as well as to alter the substance and identity of, the thing—to deal with it by jural transfer, or by destruction, change or conversion of the subject matter. This it is, which distinguishes the general owner from the owner of a fraction or an incident of property, *e. g.* a hirer. Terms signifying ownership are commonly applied to the relation indicated by a Right, however limited; as, the proprietor of a way, of a toll, of a fishery, of a Right of pasturage, of a license to kill game. Every relation between a person and a subject-thing is a mode of real Right or Right *in re,* and therefore, a mode of property, giving, to the extent and compass of the individual or determinate relation, a power to exclude. And jurists distinguish between a dealing with the actual subject itself, *e. g.* driving a horse, enjoying the shade of a tree, dwelling upon land—to which they confine the term 'use'—from profiting by what comes from, *i. e.* the produce of the subject, *e. g.* the horse's foal, the tree's fruit, corn or rice from the land: such profits are *fructus,* material products or gains—either civil and artificial, as money for hire of an animal—or natural, *viz.* the animal's offspring. The distinction is from Rome, and is an arbitrary limitation of the comprehensive *usus,* which means, colloquially and intrinsically, turning to account, having the advantages of, dealing with. *(ff)* In a kindred science, Political Economy, 'utility' has been defined, 'the capacity of a thing to satisfy a desire': 'to use,' 'using,' is, in that view—the satisfying a desire out of or by means of a thing. Merely looking at some things is using them, *e. g.* pictures and other similar works of art; but, to be seen, is the only advantage (or means of advantage) such can yield—the end therefore, primarily, of their formation and existence. Not so with what exists for more practical ends, and does not in any way exhaust its purpose by being seen, *e. g.* a steam-engine, a loaf of bread: and dealing with a thing, to be a jural use of it, must be an efficient dealing—a dealing which is, in itself, an end, something gained, not a mere inchoate and intrinsically ineffective proceeding, as taking a loaf in the hand before and in order to its being eaten.   If the loaf be restored to its place, put down again before any portion of it is eaten; the loaf has not, at all, been *used*.

The loaf belongs to a class of things which jurists call fungible, *i. e.* functionable; one loaf may, ordinarily, represent, do the function of any other loaf of the same sort.   And this must be so with whatever things are consumable, or got rid of by mere using; in other words, by applying them to their legitimate purpose, their being put to use: such are, each species of edible things, current coin. They have not, as a rule, individual significance, but are estimated in classes or species. It may be said generally of fungible things,—their use is their consumption, natural or civil, *viz.* food eaten, money spent.[gg]

A fructuary may be another than the usuary—the possessor or the usuary may have to surrender the whole or a portion of the *fructus*. This is the case with every subordinate or tenant-occupant of land who pays 'rent'—who, in other words, yields up a portion of the product or profits of cultivation to his landlord. Nor is a Right to use, identical with the possessory Right; the usuary holds, subject to his own special interest, for and as representing him who has the general possessory (holding) interest *extra* the separated use. And certainly, a fructuary is not necessarily either possessor or holder of that which yields his *fructus*.

The two rights joined, are usu-fruct, which must usually include the right to hold, as an incident or means of using, but does not signify nor indicate a larger possessory interest than belongs to him who uses. Other distinctions have been drawn of rights coming, generally, under the head of 'use.'

English Law has 'easement,' which is, some Right, some special enjoyment and comfort, conceded, to the Public generally, or to a neighbouring land-owner, as a burden upon the estate of him who makes the concession. He is therefore obviously curtailed, so far, in his ownership; for he is under jural compulsion to permit or to forbear from something—a permission or a forbearance inconsistent with that universal exclusion denoted by complete, unbroken property.

Thus, in Roman Law, easements and certain other powers in or over land, were called 'servitudes,' in token of the ownership or dominion being, to the extent of the outside Right, subservient to another than the general owner.

It appears, that property is not and cannot be an abstraction: it must be connected with possession or with use, mediately, contingently, potentially, or actually and directly. So may be said of all rights severed from the full dominical power (of using, fruition, disposition) which is expressed by 'property,' *dominium.* A Right to drive or to walk over a neighbour's field, a Right to pluck fruit from a neighbour's orchard, a Right to drain water from your own cultivation through your neighbour's—those valuable rights are, as rights, intangible: but, the Right of owning a house, a field, a horse, is, in like manner, intangible; it is an idea, a potentiality; differing from the three rights first named, in extent, in degree, not in kind. A juridical distinction has been adopted from the Roman jurists, who distinguished claims or rights over or in a subject of property, but which are severed from the larger Right of ownership—dominical title—also from Right of possession, as of a different class, 'incorporeal.' True it is, the one description of Right is not so substantially represented as the other; it lies, practically, in the conduct and forbearance of the (so-called) proprietor or possessor: but, this is a circumstance merely, accidental, not a jural difference, and affects, not the character of the Right, but the facility of its enjoyment or exercise. In each case, the *corpus*, the substance, the land which furnishes the Right, is the essential, the one indispensable element or incident; separating the entire class of such rights from a Right of conventional obligation, which is represented, solely, by the conscience, by the moral will of the person bound, and which therefore is an abstraction, something incorporeal.

It is certainly questionable, whether rights of property are scientifically distinguished, as to their character, extent or compass, by the limit of time —duration; which seems to be an accident,—an external or collateral circumstance—not a quality. An estate of which there is full power of enjoyment, for life or for years, is, intrinsically, complete, as an existing right of dominion, notwithstanding the apparent resolutory condition of time. If,

however, the limit of duration include a curtailment
of the powers of use, of taking the produce, of actual
disposition *(jus utendi, jus fruendi, jus abutendi)*,
then, the Right itself is, to that extent, curtailed ; but
not by reason of the restriction of time. The most
liberal transfer of mere usu-fruct must differ from
full property, from a purchase out and out, in this,
viz. the absence of a power of altering the substance
or of changing the mastery of the substance. So
that, the ordinary expression of a limited duration
(which, intrinsically and rationally, must be, in some
form, an inherent condition of all ownership), is
found, when analysed, to include and imply absence
of some portion of full dominical power. The most
absolute usufruct is but a 'servitude'; the most
unqualified *possessory* Right, is but a fragment
of 'dominion.'

On the other hand, the English 'fee-simple'
land-owner has full property ; and yet, his power of
posthumous disposition is limited—in other words,
the operation of his power of control is not perpetual. *(hh)*

POSSESSORY RIGHT.

It remains to speak of possession as a fraction of
proprietary dominion—as a Right, and a jural fact,
irrespective of the merely physical or material
relation which the term 'possession' colloquially indicates. "For what," asks Austin, "is possession (mean-
"ing legal possession) but the *exercise* of a Right ?"—
that Right being a jural relation, a cause of having.

K·

The etymology of possession has been variously
deduced, as, from *posse* (to be able, to have power),
from *positio* (placing, fixing); each origin leading to
the simple colloquial notion of, having or holding.
Kant repudiates the physical relation 'in space and
time' as having any thing to do with the juridical
idea of possession: *viz.* "A tract of land is
"not mine, as a thing external, because I occupy it
"with my body (for my liberty to occupy it is not
"here in question, but the internal conception of
"Right), but, if I remain the possessor of the land,
"when I move to a distance from it, then the sole
"question is the 'mine' of external right; and to
"argue that my constant presence on the spot is a
"condition of my ownership, is to maintain, either
"that it is not possible to have anything external as
"one's own, or that one must occupy two places at
"once!"

External rights may be relative and comparative;
juridical possession may exist against one, who
is under an obligation to recognise and respect it
as a Right, and not against another, whose servant or agent or deputy the holder, the ostensible (though vicarious) possessor may be. Moreover, physical possession or holding may be conten-
tious and contestable, juridically, in a two-fold sense.

If a wrongful holder do not set up right, but
might; if he ignore or defy the notion of any civil
appropriation having been made of what he holds;
asserting his own will or desire merely, for a cause
of possession—his only relation to the thing held,

consequently to *bonâ fide* claimants of the possession is, as violator of the Law; and he is pur-
suable as such.

But, if the holder, although wrongful, believe in
his own juridical claim, honestly (as far as appears)
contending, that he has a Right, of any kind, to
hold, either generally or against a particular adverse
claimant; then, his position deserves respect, however
fallacious his views and claim.   He is an honest possessor; the non-possessor must prove, as well as assert
in a juridical manner, his abstract Right, his 'title.'

Hence the popular adage, 'Possession is nine points
of the Law:' it is, however wrongful, a juridical fact,
and is protected by a Law dogma or postulate, which
identifies unquestioned possession with full property,
and, apparent possession with probable property.   The
wrong, if the fact of possession be one, concerns
only him whose Right is interfered with—a Right,
which the Law must undoubtedly vindicate, when informed, by proof which supersedes and outweighs
the apparent fact, the semblance, similitude of
Right, *viz.* mere possession, and displaces the inference—dissipates the false colour of ownership arising
from it.   To require such proof is the Right of the
actual present possessor.   Extent or character of
proof is a distinct question.   Adverse proof is a
contest of antagonist forces; as one position is lost,
new ground may be taken up: it is a matter of
procedure, of the logic and machinery of litigation.

EXAMPLES OF ANALYSIS OR RESOLUTION OF PROPERTY.

Such is an analysis of 'property,' which, generically, indicates and expresses adjustment and division in enjoyment of things. I have shewn it to be a concrete or compound idea, capable of resolution. Titius owns a horse: for one or two-hours of the twenty-four, Titius rides or drives the horse, which, for the remaining hours, is in the keeping of Marcus; who has contracted with Titius, to feed and lodge his horse—in consideration (*i. e.* taking as a remuneration) that Marcus is at liberty to employ the horse when not required by Titius: Quintus hires the horse from Titius, for a month, to ride and use, without disturbing the arrangement with Marcus: Titius sells the horse to Caius, to be delivered when the month of Quintus is expired. Now, after the sale, and during the month, no less than four men are separately and distinctly interested in, and have differing juridical relations with the horse, and with each other; each interest being an off-shoot or fraction of the ownership or *dominium*, which at first was simple and entire in Titius. Here we have,—present limited ownership and jural possession in Titius; deferred ownership in Caius: use in Quintus; custody and conditional use in Marcus.

Again; suppose the owner of sheep to have sold two shearings of their wool to A, and the product of two lambings to B, but to have let, in the meantime, the benefit of the flock's grazing (*i. e.* clearing the grass off and manuring a lawn) to C: here, the possession must be with C, who must permit A (proprietor of the wool) to shear, and must surrender the lambs to B; and *then* the owner may dispose of the sheep. C had a partial *jus utendi;* A and B certain *jura fruendi* (as to different products); the contingent *jus abutendi* remaining, as the badge of dominion. Sub-divisions of interest—of Right—may be multiplied, by continuing the resolutory process, the analysis and separation, the multiplication and dividing, of the attributes and advantages of complete, exclusive property, —entire, undivided dominion, over a thing.

The word 'interest' is a common indefinite term used in describing modes of right to possess or to enjoy ; 'possessory interest,' 'usufructuary interest,' 'proprietary interest,' 'disposable interest,' 'alienable interest,' 'hereditary interest'—all or either of which may or not be conjoined with the fact of holding ; a fact, in itself presumptive of every interest in the jural holder.

The thing or subject possessed is called 'a possession': so, the subject of property or proprietary interest, is called, 'a property ;' and, if in land, 'an estate'; the last term being also, and more correctly used as synonymous with 'interest,' *e. g.* hereditary estate, life-estate, estate for years.

SEIGNORY: EMINENT DOMAIN.

The notion of property altogether disconnected from present or future Right to possess or to use, has been a device of military or despotic rule; it is a refinement—the product of an artificial and non-natural state of society and manners.

Such ideal, detached, nude proprietary claim is, when analysed, rather a personal than a real relation, and may be described—a relative lordship, mastery, dominion over the owner of a thing, *in respect of his ownership*, where the claimant of the seignoral Right or relation has no Right or power whatever (usuary, possessory or otherwise)—nor expectation of any—in or over the thing itself.

We might suppose a patriarch thus portioning members of his family, and reserving some paramount power to interfere; while he separated and gave up the actual and beneficial enjoyment of landed or other family possessions.

The feudality of the middle ages of Europe, at the period when fiefs first became hereditary, affords an instance of this anomalous *quasi*-proprietary relation.[ii] When the relation includes or entitles to any substantive benefit, as, surrender of any produce, rent, perquisites (absolute or contingent); then seignory is but an ordinary property-right, an incident of status or of contract.

More practical and significant is the 'eminent domain' (alluded to *supra* p. 60), an imperial right or power, of which seignory would seem to be an offshoot or imitation.

"To kings belongs *potestas* [political dominion] "over all; to private men, property." "The country "is the State's; but, not the less, each one possesses "therein his own." [kk]

"Private property," wrote Kant, "can belong to the "subject people alone—and this, not collectively, but "distributively."·

'Eminent domain' is one of a class of juridical rules—political laws, designated, or included in the term, *imperium* (empire). [ll] It is that sovereign interference with, supervision and pre-eminence over mere individual rights, which, according to the policy and constitution of each State, attaches to its several governing branches : *e. g.* in England, the great and multifarious powers of the royal prerogative, the usages and privilege of parliament —in India, the universal and paramount pledge of private estates for revenue. The most ordinary and valuable private rights are thus seemingly infringed, *viz.* in lawful exercise of the *dominium eminens*—of the *imperium* vested, presumably for the good of all, in him or in those who represent State-power. The exercise of such public and paramount control, is therefore an exception to every private Right.

In States where the administrative function of Government as holder of the public purse, is not controlled by any direct representation of the possessors of private property, all taxation and revenue imposts may well be classed under the head 'eminent domain' ; for taxation has been correctly defined, in general, 'appropriation of private property for public ends.'

GOOD-FAITH: RIGHTS OF CONTRACT.

Need it be said, that good faith—truth, is the condition, the bond of human intercourse?

" Our intelligence being by no other way to be
" conveyed to one another but by speaking, who fal-
" sifies that, betrays public society ; 'tis the only way
" by which we communicate our thoughts and wills ;
" 'tis the interpreter of the soul ; and if it deceives
" us, we no longer know, nor have any other tie upon
" one another. If that deceive us, it breaks all our
" correspondence, and dissolves all the ties of govern-
" ment."(mm) Speech is the specially-human instrument ; but, every act, every mode of development
of will, every omission as well as commission that
may in any way affect a fellow-man, is good or bad,
right or wrong, in proportion as the will (the motive
power) is honest—is earnest in intent to do right.

Good faith, as generating and justifying mutual
confidence, is the basis and indispensable element
of all contract, convention, commerce: but the civil
import of good-faith, as an inherent social necessity,
generically and not merely in conventional dealings,
is much more wide and comprehensive ; that import
being, fidelity of purpose, circumspection, practical
sincerity, fair dealing, active right-mindedness in
every legal relation, in every jural act. To be treated in good faith, is therefore a substantive Right ;
and will be enlarged on, when I come to phases
of wrong, many of which are but a negation
of active good faith, of an honest and circum-

spect will.   A Right of contract means, a Right
to make or to enter into a contract; it also means,
a Right resulting from contract.   The two rights
differ as cause and effect—as a power, from its exercise: the one Right is potential and general—always
a part of the area of civil liberty—the second, a
positive result, a specific acquisition.

Convention, covenant, contract, compact—this is
the voluntary tie, the artificial *vinculum*, created
by private will—not by the will of the community, the Law.   When men come together, are
drawn together, in good faith, in order to carry
out their respective wills by combination and
co-operation, not infringing Law; they are said
to contract *(con* together, *tractus* drawn), to
covenant *(con, venio* to come), or, using the same
words substantively, to make a contract, to make
a covenant or convention. Their co-operation (*con,
opera* exertion) is manifested and carried out, either;
1. by something done at the moment, *e. g.* an
exchange of a horse for a book; or, 2. an asserted
resolve, on one or both sides, to do something
at a future time, as, to give the horse or the book
ten days hence—or, when some specified event shall
have come about.   Such asserted resolve is a promise, an undertaking.   In the words of Domat:

'The use of conventions is a natural consequence
of the order of civil society and of the ties
which God forms among men. For as He has
made the reciprocal use of their industry and
labour and the different commerce of things neces-

L

sary for supplying all their wants, it is mainly by
means of conventions that they make arrangements thereto. Thus, for the use of industry
and labour, men enter into partnership, hire themselves out, and in various ways act the one for
the other. Thus, for the use of things, when
they have occasion to purchase them, or a mind
to part with them, they traffic by sales and by
exchanges, and when they only want them for a
time, they either hire or borrow them ; and according to their other different wants, they apply to
them the different sorts of conventions.———
The subject matter of conventions is, the infinite
diversity of the voluntary ways by which men
regulate among themselves the communication and
commerce of their industry and labour and of all
things according to their wants. The commerce and
communications for the use of persons and things
are of four sorts; which make four species of
conventions. For those who treat together, either
give each other, reciprocally, one thing for another, as
in a sale, and in an exchange; or they do one
thing for another, as when they mutually undertake some business for each other; or otherwise one does something, and the other gives
something, as when a labourer gives his labour
for a certain hire; or lastly, one of them either
does or gives something, the other neither doing
nor giving any thing, as when a person undertakes
gratuitously the business of another, or that one
makes a gift out of sheer liberality.'

The four are, shortly; 1. gift for gift *(do ut des)*; 2. deed for deed *(facio ut facias)*; 3. deed for gift *(facio ut des)*; gift for deed *(do ut facias)*; 4. gratuitous: the three first are bilateral, reciprocal; the fourth, unilateral, in jural effect and significance.[nn]

Under the first head range, barter, exchange, sale: under the fourth, gift, as a pure benefaction. 'Exchange,' simply, and as usually understood, *viz.* as a present and complete occurrence, is undoubtedly a convention, a result of agreement, an act of commerce; but, so understood, it has no future, no element of suspense, no incidents calling for interposition of a law of contract. The same comment applies to gift, as a mere one-sided, actual transfer. Each is, *primâ facie*, a name for a past event—one not creative of personal obligations, nor in any wise subject to fluctuation of will; not therefore needing support of civil sanctions or remedies, as a contract. But, such views, however obvious, are not universal, nor free from exception. The translator of *Futawa Alumgeery* thus defines 'sale' in the code of the musulmans. 'Sale is the exchange of property for property, with mutual consent; and it is constituted by proposal and acceptance, or by reciprocal delivery.' In that Law, traffic of one definite substance *(ayn)* for another definite substance, is one of four modes or descriptions of the sale-contract; another mode being, where one of the articles of traffic is in any way indeterminate (although known and described), or is fungible, and is therefore a claim and right

merely (*deyn*), *e. g.* current coin. When the articles
on both sides are homogeneous as well as fungible,
as grain for grain, coin for coin, there, (because of
the prohibition of *reba*, usury) strict equality of
weight or measurement is required; and, in *surf*
sales (*i. e. deyn* for *deyn*), immediate actual transfer of the rights trafficked in is indispensable. So
that, with them, exchange and sale are in the same
category, as a contract. In the Roman system,
although 'exchange' strictly was no contract, yet,
whenever one party in a convention had actually
given over a subject of property (*res*) to another
because and on the faith of that other's undertaking to transfer something else to him, by way
of barter or exchange, then, the occurrence was
a 'real contract,' under which the return was compelled: but this had no relation with the contract of 'purchase and sale.' The laws of *Islam*
scarcely recognise pure benefaction, as either a
mode or a cause of jural transfer. In them, 'gift'
is regarded as a venture for an expected 'return,'
which establishes reciprocity. A saying of the
Prophet is recorded,—'A donor preserves a right
to his gift, so long as he does not obtain a return
for it' (see *Hedaya*)—hence, disability to retract
is exceptional. The same jural ideas are carried
out in the relations of the wife's right, *mihr* or
dower, with the marital power and privileges. In
another sense, it may well seem inconsistent and
illogical to describe 'gift' as a unilateral transaction. The part of the receiver is not onerous or

responsible; yet is his part not unimportant, since he must give accord; and, as must be assumed, he, by so doing, gratifies the giver of the gift, *viz.* by acceding to the latter's wishes and act. Benefaction however, real or ostensible, is the normal character of those human dealings and interchanges with which civil Law has to do. The donor or giver's self-satisfaction is no appreciable civil gain; the civil benefaction of a 'gift' is therefore one-sided. But, Justinian, sympathising with the feelings of indiscreetly liberal and ill-used donors, conferred on his subjects a general authority ('*generaliter sancimus*'), whatever the status of the parties or the circumstances of the gift, to recal liberality wasted upon the grossly ungrateful and undeserving: the license to revoke, not to descend to the donor's heir. The grounds of revocation mentioned in the 'constitution', are; *injuria atrox*, described to be, violence to the donor's person, or fraud in prejudice of his fortune, also non-fulfilment of any concurrent provision on the donor's part, whether with or without writing.

The invention of a representative medium, a type of value, *viz.* current coin, money—necessarily facilitated transfer of and traffic in every description of property, right, and advantage: that invention in some respect changed or added to the science of jural conventions. I translate from *The Digest* the words of the jurist Paulus:

'Buying and selling took its rise from exchanges. Since, in former times, there was not money, as now; nor was one commodity called *merx* (merchandise, goods), the other *pretium* (a price): but every one, according to the exigencies of the day and of circumstances, interchanged useless things for useful; seeing, it frequently happened that what was a superfluity with one was a want with another. But inasmuch as it did not always nor as a matter ofcourse come about, that, one man possessing what another coveted, the former should be willing to accept, in lieu, what the latter happened to have, therefore a substance was fixed upon, the acknowledged and permanent estimation of which should meet, by its uniformity of value, the difficulty of exchanges. That substance, being impressed with some public device, passes current as a medium of property, not so much in respect of intrinsic value, as a measure of quantity; henceforth, commodities interchanged were not both designated *merx*, but one was *pretium.*'

A notable change brought about by the invention of money, was, the relation of debtor and creditor, in the modern sense and as ordinarily understood, as distinct from the relation created by a deposit or bailment of what, in the language of Paulus, is properly called, *merx.*[oo] Loan of money is intrinsically different from the loan of what money may represent: the latter, if an infungible commodity, must be returned to the lender *in specie;* if fungible, must be precisely of the same nature, intrinsically. Money is always not merely fungible, but may intrinsically vary, as silver for gold, and has no other use or value than to be passed away, in exchange for *merx*, or what is saleable. The Roman *mutuum* embraced not merely money, but whatever was estimated in kind, by weight, number or measure. The characteristic of the *mutuum* is thus noted by Paulus;—'It is called giving a *mutuum* because from mine it becomes thine (*de meo, tuum*): insomuch that if it does not become thine, the obligation [of *mutuum*] does not arise.'

A simple and scientific, though not minute analysis of the advantages and obligations, generally, created or producible by contract, was in use with the Roman jurists, each word having a technical force, *viz. dare*, when the promise or contract is, to transfer property, in full Right; *præstare*, where it is, to afford and furnish some advantage, as use, hire, or other benefit whatsoever, not being a proprietary transfer; *facere*, where it is a personal service, or some act or conduct not included in the two preceding—some exertion or some forbearance.

There is a not unusual mode of contracting which includes imposition of a conventional penalty for violation or neglect of some contract-obligation; as, where a sale contract contains a clause to the effect—'If I fail to make delivery as herein agreed, then I shall forfeit and pay to you £100.' It is in form, an alternative, but, in substance, a remedy, with a defined result, as a contract-sanction agreed on for the occasion. This method may of-course be applied to support any manner of undertaking or stipulation.

The essentials and determinate incidents of every contract or jural convention are, 1. the parties to it, 2. the subject-matter, object of it, 3. its mode or form.

All persons having separate juridical existence, *i. e.* whose *status* does not involve a disability to speak and act for themselves, may contract: hence, children are partially, madmen entirely incapable.

The field for the matter and object of contracts, is, as already explained, the entire range of action permitted by the Law of the Land; interchange, modification, transfer, partition of rights, of property—whatever men may lawfully do or enjoy.

Such is the origin, the natural history, and general character of the class of jural obligations named 'contracts,' *i. e.* 'rights—therefore obligations—of contract'. Every scheme of civil laws recognises the inherent power and disposition of mankind, as well as their social need and advantage, to have dealings together, by interchange of rights, of properties,—by undertakings, by commerce of expectations. But, each scheme has its own requirements. For certain arrangements or bargains to have the character of contracts, one scheme requires that the matter agreed on be recorded in writing and be attested by the proper seals or signatures (or both,) of the persons contracting—the same or another scheme requires, that particular dealings, to be recognised as contracts, must find expression in a particular form of language, that no other words, however intelligible, will suffice—another demands that a specific public officer testify to the making and the terms of a contract —or, that a registry of the fact, with specific formalities, be made by a specified authority. Now, it is plain, that those several requirements are artificial and arbitrary—that they form no part of the natural incidents of human dealings ; nor is any one of them intrinsically essential—either to constitute or to shew a moral union of wills. It follows, that the moral fact, however obvious or unquestionable, of a particular conventional arrangement having been come to, upon any subject or of any kind, between members of any community, does not suffice as a manifestation of a contract ; treating this word, 'contract' as the name of a class or head of sanctioned (*i. e.* civil) obligations.

Hence one ground of significance in the third determinate incident above noted, *viz.* the 'mode or form.' Whatever the motive or ground of the jural, even the formal requirement,— whether certainty and preservation of proof, or prevention of deceit (and this either against contractors or with reference to some law, some State-prohibition), or what else—that special legal requirement it is, which, in each case, is the chief and essential material or substance of the 'contract'—the jural edifice—the structure—the web of obligations, which the parties are bent on giving birth to. [pp]

It has been wisely and beneficently said by an

M

English judge, from the Bench,—"Courts of Law "are never better employed than in supporting the "rules of morality:"[qq] yet, with strict, though with somewhat technical truth, lord chancellor Eldon declared—"deciding upon civil rights, I "have nothing to do with the morality." Where the Law does not annex an obligation to a particular engagement or undertaking, no moral considerations can entitle the judge to pronounce that engagement obligatory : for him to do so would be, plainly to contradict and to contravert the *jural* rules of which alone a civil judge is exponent and vindicator. The principle of this distinction is well exemplified in the instance of a suit being founded upon a document or an arrangement which, according to the Law of the country in which the tribunal sits, may produce valid contractual obligations, but which nevertheless cannot be enforced by that tribunal, because the Law of another country—*e. g.* where the alleged contract (whether proved by writing or otherwise) was made—does not annex any civil obligations to the same : the rules of private international Law and the *comitas gentium*—hereafter to be explained—frequently obliging the tribunals of a State to carry out, not the rules and obligations laid down for the observance of those who are subject to the laws of that State, but the rules and requirements of some other State's laws, under which the contract had its inception or was to be performed. "If a contract

"is to be performed partly in one country and
"partly in another, each portion is to be interpreted
"according to the laws of the country where it
"is to be performed."[rr]

As to mere ceremonial requirements, in contract;
from history we learn their meaning and their justification.

In the infancy (moral and civil) of a nation, all
organisation is in the rough—in out-line; the
cords of duty and of right, provided by the nation
to hold society together, are strong but few, and
of a coarse texture; ethical refinements and niceties
are unknown, or, if known and believed in, are
regarded as needing super-human effort to observe;
and, accordingly, they who do observe them are
admired as exceptional beings. Voluntary efforts
at right-doing which involve self-sacrifice or self-de-
nial,—i. e. without palpable appeal to self-love or to
fears, without appalling incident or superstitious
sanction—are, in those days, not looked for.

Thus, Herodotus narrates:—" the Lydians and
" Medes, on occasion of solemn compacts, were used
" each one to draw blood from his own arm, and
" each licked the other's blood" (bk. I, s. 74): "the
" Arabs used to make their covenants in this wise—
" a man stood between the contractants, made
" an incision in the palm of each with a sharp
" stone, and, taking a woof of each one's garment,
" smeared with the blood seven stones placed in
" the centre, invoking Bacchus and Urania"
(bk. III, s. 8): "the Scythians poured wine into

"a large earthen cup, mixing with it the blood
"of those who were entering into the compact; hav-
"ing pricked with a needle or slightly wounded with
"a sword some part of the body of each, they dipped
"in the cup a scymitar, some arrows, an axe and
"a javelin, then, after much invocation, the con-
"tracting parties and the most considerable of those
"present drank it up" (bk. IV, s. 69): "the Nasa-
"mones [an African tribe] made use of this form of
"faith-pledging; each one gave to the other to drink
"out of his hand; but, should there be no liquid
"to be had, they took up the dust of the ground
"and licked it" (bk. VI, s. 172).[*] Colonel Tod
describing Rajpoot records, political and domestic,
of remote antiquity, relates,—"Every subject com-
"mences with invoking the sun and moon as wit-
"nesses, and concludes with a denunciation of the
"severest penalties on those who break the spirit of
"the imperishable bond." The Swedish historian
says of the Scandinavians,—"The great yearly
"sacrifices assembled and united the people.—Under
"the shield of peace, the sacrifice, with the attendant
"banquet, was prepared; deliberations were held,
"sentence passed, and traffic conducted: for which
"reason *ting*, the old name of these conventions,
"means both sacrifice, banquet, diet, assize,
"and fair." In Sprenger's 'Life of Mohammad'
is an ancient musulman legend, of the first
man, Adam, breaking faith with the angel of
death; it concludes with this reflection or moral:—
"The father of mankind is the father of deception.

"God, therefore, ordered Man, through Seth, to make "engagements in writing, and to call witnesses, in "order that they may not be broken—" The scope and moral of the legend is, to typify and record the prevalence of bad faith, in all ages, and the need of legal precautions.[tt] With the growth of commerce, the necessity, the general need (and value therefore) of good-faith, inevitably becomes more apparent; as well as the inconvenience of cumbrous forms or of superstitious ceremonial, in the conduct of trade and traffic, *i. e.* in contracting. Gradually, as the intrinsic worth of the jural tie of contract—and of its essential basis, conventional good-faith—forces itself (from any cause) upon a people's notice and conscience, the extrinsic ceremonial, the unwieldy harness of form, vanishes, by little and little—drops off, leaving only such dress and form as may suffice to attest the abstract mental as well as verbal undertaking. The obligation of contract becomes then merely, to use a Roman term, consensual, *i. e.* valued and enforced because of the *consensus* (mutual understanding), without more.[uu]

(a) WHEWELL. This is a clearer enunciation of Aristotle's sentiment:—" all men have some natural inclination to justice, but they "proceed thereon only to a certain degree; nor can they universally "point out what is absolutely just." *Politics.*

(b) BACON

(c) All must acquiesce in the reasoning of Bentham, that the chief value of that security which the Law confers, *i. e.* of every Right, is, the justification which it affords to expectation; and expectation may be explained and amplified, as a confident assurance, that, in the veiled future, either present and actual enjoyment will be continued, or, coveted

enjoyment will be attained. Indeed, the Law creates the expectation.—
"The savage who has killed a deer may hope to keep it for himself, so
"long as his cave is undiscovered; so long as he watches to defend it,
"and is stronger than his rivals; but that is all. How miserable and
"precarious is such a possession! If we suppose the least agreement
"among savages to respect the acquisitions of each other, we see the
"introduction of a principle to which no name can be given but that of
"Law. A feeble and momentary expectation may result from time to
"time from circumstances purely physical; but a strong and permanent
"expectation can result only from Law. That which, in the natural
"state, was an almost invisible thread, in the social state becomes a
"cable."   *Theory of Legislation.*

Bentham's reasoning, proving, as it does, that the goal of civil society,
in a very early stage of human progress, is inevitable, scarcely serves for
a premiss (as intended and used by him,) to induce the conclusion, that
Man's laws alone produce either Rights or obligations. Whether called
the moral sense, or a sense of utility, or a mutual dread and sense of need
of mutual protection, or what else—a common impulse and necessity has
universally (in time and place) formed society, and civil sanctions,
and laws.

(*d*) To what extent or when the subject is *at liberty* to disregard
mandates of civil Law, is a question of casuistry. Dread of such disregard—of the influence of civil sanction succumbing to other moral
motives—is a powerful ground for and cause of legislation. It has been
wisely said:—"the constitution of every country has in it something
"which is suited to the national character and the result of the national
"history; and is therefore the best basis for political improvements.
"The constitution of the country has claims upon our fidelity, reverence
"and affection. It is a fit object of such sentiments, as being the na-
"tional constitution; but its claims may be neutralised by its defects
"as a constitution, and by the impossibility of producing a reform by
"constitutional means."   WHEWELL

(*e*) It may seem, that this cannot be predicated of *merely* penal
laws or positive civil prohibitions, *e. g.* customs laws, sumptuary laws,
restrictions of the Press; but, as every prohibition is built upon the idea
that it is needful for the welfare of the community, it is the Right of
every member that the prohibition be enforced—and this, irrespective
of the mode of reaching the sanction, whether through a civil or a criminal proceeding.

(*f*) To use the words of an English judge (Maule)—'When a statute
gives a Right, then, although in express terms it has not given a remedy,

the remedy which, by Law, is properly applicable to that Right, follows as an incident.'

Hence, practical Law, the essential knowledge of a law-practitioner, has come to be thought and treated as little more than an explanatory catalogue of remedies. One so qualified, is a law-druggist, in contrast with the jurist or physician.

(g) like to Right of contract before any contract made.

(h) Austin supports the view of the pursuit given by Law being itself a Right, although but a sequel of other Rights, *i. e.* conditioned upon infringement of some original, prior Right: *viz.* "It is impossible " to extricate the right of action itself from those subsidiary rights by " which it is enforced. And it is manifestly absurd to deny, that the " process involves right because the rights which it involves are instru- " ments for the attainment of another right." Austin, therefore, explains and analyses "rights and obligations which do *not* arise out of violations " and those which *do.*" This Right (of remedy) it is which gives value and reality to every Right, secures each correlative obligation, comes into existence in substitution of something lost—which cannot be said to be included, valuable and material as it is, in any description of original Rights, personal or external. It is an alternative enjoyment (when any Right or fruition of Right is lost or invaded), just as sanction is the alternative to obedience of the Law's mandate. The alternative is a distinct command, an infliction ; so, remedy (legal redress, right of action, being an inquisitorial attack upon the party amenable,) is dis- tinctly given, as an alternative or adjective Right. The very first of the Decemvirate laws declares or confirms this Right, in the rule of compulsory attendance before the dispenser of the Law, the summoning *(vocatio in jus);* and the obligation from delict, *i. e.* created by wrong *(ex ipso maleficio),* found in the Roman system, is but a correlative to the Right of remedy.

(i) " —We ought not to render any one more imperfect or unhappy "*i. e.* injure any one. And because to what constitutes our felicity "and perfection, belongs not only our *body,* but more especially our "*mind,* this precept must extend to both these parts, and an injury to "our mind must be as much greater than an injury to our bodily part, as "the mind is more excellent than the body." HEINECCIUS.

(j) A French jurist, M. Fritôt, thus classes and enumerates viola- tions of personal security and freedom :—

"1. to deprive of the use of. any member of the body, or of any "physical or mental faculty—even publication of thought ; saving legal "restraint from abuse of any faculty.

" 2. to subject to cruel treatment.

" 3. to force a distasteful marriage.

" 4. to deprive either spouse of the other.

" 5. to separate parents and children.

" 6. to impose forceably any civil calling, or to deprive of one; even " to force into a military career, unless in organised submission to a " public necessity.

" 7. to meddle with and to appropriate the efforts of industry.

" 8. to interfere with voluntary disposal of time and industrial effort.

" 9. to restrict free change of habitation ; to fix to the soil.

" 9. to invade the privacy of home : to force into exile or abandon- " ment of home.

" 10. to imprison, or detain arbitrarily."

The list is neither exhaustive, nor quite consistent; but it gives a comprehensive view of trespasses upon personal inviolability and freedom. All rights, inherent and adherent, which are irrespective of relation between persons and things—which are included within the sphere of self, and action of self, however civilly extended—may be considered as modes of personal freedom; but a large class are more conveniently classed under *status*. I have intended to confine the present head, to invasions of person which ignore or interfere with primary, positive, necessary rights inherent in the person.

(k) Sec. 298. " Whoever, with the deliberate intention of wounding " the religious feelings of any person, utters any word or makes any " sound in the hearing of that person, or makes any gesture in the sight " of that person, or places any object in the sight of that person, shall " be punished &c." This enactment evinces an anxious sense (justified by experience) of risks,—of need for unusual State interference and protection ; the risks and the need being produced by an exceptional and forced civil or political mingling of races. Students of His- tory will recognise the truth and force of Chancellor Kent's opinion; who having boasted that—"The free exercise and en- " joyment of religious profession and worship may be considered " as one of the absolute rights of individuals, recognized in our " American constitutions, and secured to them by Law"—proceeds— " Civil and religious liberty generally go hand in hand, and the sup- " pression of either of them, for any length of time, will terminate " the existence of the other."

Here the term 'civil' refers to all other description of free thought and action than what exclusively appertains to the indulgence and cul- tivation of Man's religious sense. But, the most entire liberty (—range of action) in adoption of religious opinion, permits of State-measures for supplying the religious needs of a people. Religious action, in some direction, of civilized men, is inevitable. To make that action consistent with and subservient to the general welfare—to prevent its being subversive of the polity itself—is clearly within the province of the secular arm, and no infringement of liberty: whilst, direction of religious opinion and dogmas is out of the sphere of civil laws.

(l) It has been maintained (and surely not without reason), that, under no theory or scheme of civil government, is it rationally or morally permitted to the subject, to yield up or to abdicate natural faculties, bodily or mental; and therefore, Man violates the paramount, the obvious, Reason-promulgated code of Nature, when he surrenders or even alienates, generally, his personal liberty of thought and of utterance of thought: in as much as, in those consists the very essence of Man's rationality and distinctive character. It may be, and without hyperbole, affirmed:—Man in vain assents to be less than Man!

(m) These sentences are from the *Encyclopædia Metropolitana* ('Law'); whence I extract a summary exposition of the Right treated of, *viz.*—

'The right of self-defence is more comprehensive in a state of nature than in civil society. In the former, every individual is the protector of his own rights, with respect to the future as well as to the present. But in civil society, private individuals are permitted, and that from unavoidable necessity, to use violence only in the immediate defence of their persons or property; all steps for their future security being reserved for the public authorities. With respect to *present* self-defence, which we have now to consider by itself, its just limits we conceive, whatever some writers may assert to the contrary, are precisely the same in civil society and in a natural state. This right, as Grotius observes, arises directly and immediately from the care of our own preservation, which nature recommends to every one, and not from the injustice or crime of the aggressor who may threaten our safety. So that if a person, involuntarily, or by mistake or accident assaults me or in any way places my life in imminent danger, I am not to be debarred, by the consideration of his innocence, from consulting my own safety, even at the expense of his life. The law of charity does not require me to have a *greater* regard for him than for myself. But on the other hand, the same law requires that I should not have a less. If, therefore, my own defence will probably do him a greater injury than he will do me, I should

N

submit to be the sufferer. This is the broad and intelligible rule. Jurists sometimes introduce other collateral or subordinate considerations, which we cannot here examine, to modify the right of self-defence under particular circumstances. Cases of this kind, where, without any blame attaching to either party, the sacrifice of one or other of them becomes unavoidable, are of rare occurrence, and fall more properly within the province of casuistry than of jurisprudence. The right of self-defence, as jurists commonly treat it, relates principally to the repelling of wilful and malicious assaults. Pufendorf, and others after him, contend, but assuredly with very inadequate notions of the obligations of humanity, that the unjust intention of the assailant, however slight an injury he may attempt, deprives him of *all* title to consideration; and that therefore although it may sometimes be more *prudent* for the party assailed to submit to a trivial wrong, than to avert it by the death, even, of the assailant, there can be no *obligation* upon him to that effect. Where then should the line be drawn? The limit of rightful self-defence is, we conceive, identified with the limit of just punishment; that is to say, whatever would be the utmost amount of punishment that could properly be inflicted for the crime apparently intended, supposing it to have been completed, to that length of harm, the right of self-defence may be justly carried; beyond it, the obligation of endurance begins. Such appears to be the principle recognized in the laws of most well-regulated communities, which rarely suffer with impunity any crime to be prevented by death, unless the same, if committed, would also be punished by death. And thus the defence of life, limb or chastity, has in all or most countries, been held a sufficient justification for the taking of life. But it must be understood that the party assailed is in no case privileged to proceed even to the length we have stated, unless it be absolutely necessary for his own immediate safety. It may be objected that the limit drawn is merely theoretical, because in the hurry, danger, and excitement of the moment and moreover where self is in question, it is rarely possible to weigh the matter very nicely. However we have only attempted to describe generally what is strictly and rigidly *justifiable.* Some excess must always be *excused,* provided it does not surpass the fair allowance claimable on the score of ordinary human infirmity, and become an act of cruelty; in which case the gross excess would be a just ground of punishment. It only remains to be observed that, as a general rule, whatever violence an individual may lawfully exert in his own defence, he may equally exert in defence of another person who stands in a near domestic relation to him.'

(n) Such maturity of body and mind, as presumptively indicates ability to perform the duties and to fill the relations of civil life, is a problem that receives generally an artificial solution, by fixing a precise age when the citizen can act with legal effect and complete responsibility. Mere years however do not always decide: the English criminal code acts on the maxim 'malice is a substitute for mature age' *(malitia supplet ætatem)* after the 8th year: the *Sheraa* terminates legal nonage as soon as signs of puberty appear, after the age of 12 in a male, and of 9 in a female. 'The old Roman religious system assumed the natural life of man to be 120 years, reduced into 90 by Fate, and divided into three equal periods of 30 years, whereof the first subdivision of 15 years represented boyhood. The practical view taken by Servius Tullius added two years to this for military service; hence, probably, the variations we find in the period of puberty, which varied between 14 and 18, that is to say, in the 14th or 18th year. A man might be potent in the 14th year, but not strong enough to bear arms.'

(From Colquhuon's Summary.)

(o) which (nor less where universal suffrage prevails) must be an indication of political power and, usually, of fitness for State office or dignity. Besides, whether regarded as a result or as a means, it represents vast resources, material and moral; its possessor is set on high, and he cannot but influence the fate of the community, individually and collectively.

(p) He may be an idler, a vagabond, a helpless and cureless dependent upon casual or upon public charity: he may devote his energies to scientific discovery, as Humphrey Davy, Csoma Koros, and a host of pioneers of human progress; or to moral teaching by life-like, deep-searching fiction, as Smollett, Goldsmith, Thackeray, Dickens; or to purely philanthropic labours, the friend of the friendless, as Howard, Elizabeth Fry, Florence Nightingale; to a benevolent ambition and self-denying intellectual labour, as a public reformer and teacher, as Bentham, Austin, as (with more limited means of moral power) the Calcutta journalist, Hurrischunder Mookerjea,—or, a self-denying teacher of religion, such as were Felix Neff, Henry Martin, and many like to them, or as the apostle of education for the Native Indian, David Hare: he may be a Garibaldi, a Kossuth, a Robert Burns, a Samuel Johnson: he may be a devotee at the shrine of a debasing self-indulgence, using his Reason to misapply and degrade gifts of Nature and of Fortune, the only use of such an one being, as conductor and scatterer of material wealth and an example to warn. The many modes indicated of spending and passing life, obviously, can seldom (nor can any mode) be destitute of jural significance, with reference to the place, the value, the functions and influence of a man among his fellow citizens.

(*q*) Women, from natural, social, and civil causes, must have a distinct civil position or status. The kind and degree of subordination, the extent of civil and political capacity, regulating or composing the female status, are accidents of policy, of national sentiment, of history.

(*r*) *Existimatio* with the Romans was the aggregate of qualities and conditions, whether legal, conventional and social, or moral, that went to make up and render perfect, the honour and respectability as well as the (strictly civil) *status* of a citizen.

(*s*) Something else than self-regard or self-love—a sentiment which I before treated, under the name of *amour-propre*, as a Right ; but self-love, so far as justifiable, is merely self-preservation.

Even a casual observer of life and conduct, must be soon convinced, how valued and how indispensable is that considerate regard (or semblance of regard) for the feelings—that tender forbearance towards the frailties—of each other, which obtain among the civilized (whether polished or rude) of mankind, and which, under varied circumstances or modifications, are termed and represented as, politeness, civility, courtesy, amiability, philanthropy,—some, or all combined, of those qualities of kindness, of pleasantness, in temperament—at least in demeanour. As a current coin, such consideration and forbearance are appreciated, and therefore accorded by the most self-regarding ; for the hypocritical or reluctant bestower is ever a willing recipient of what he would, if he could, reserve and monopolise.

I extract from a popular author a forcible description of the uses of a feeling or quality, which, although indicative of human frailty, seems to include much that one may class with self-respect:—it is the hope, the seeking for, the expectation, of deference, of sympathy, of approbation, of praise.

"Vanity is to a man what the oily secretion is to a bird, with which "it sleeks and adjusts the plumage ruffled, by whatever causes. Vani-"ty is not only instrumental in keeping a man alive and in heart, but, in "its lighter manifestations it is the great sweetener of social existence. "—It delights to bask in the sunshine of approbation.—An imaginative "man recognises at once a portion of himself in his fellow, and speaks "to that. To hurt you is to hurt himself. Much of the rudeness we "encounter in life cannot be properly set down to cruelty or badness

"of heart. The unimaginative man is callous, and although he hurts
" easily, he cannot be easily hurt in return."

(Alexander Smith's Dreamthorp.)

Montesquieu enlarges upon the uses of national vanity, as contrasted
with national pride. Bk. xix, ch. 9.

(t) To upbraid one who had an insult, personal or hereditary, to
avenge, was an offence punishable by the laws of Genoa.

(u.) The etymology of this word may be safely taken from classical
Roman literature, where we find it thus variously used :—
'sleep occupies his limbs ;' ' paleness occupies his face ;' ' the fame
of it occupies our ears ;' ' sturdily occupy the gate ;' ' Ennius was the
first who occupied [*i. e.* employed] that phrase.'

(v) Dr. Maine defines ' occupancy' to be, " the advised assumption
" of physical possession," and considers the term to be misapplied in
denoting the origin of property ; to the early history of which he
despairs of obtaining a complete clue. Possession by groups of mankind
i. e. families or their extension, as instanced in the Indian village communities, is noted by Dr. Maine as the earliest trace of an exclusive ownership. The organised civilization of our race in groups, has been the
rule : and Dr. Maine ably exposes the error of individualising men
in the progress to jural institutions : still, occupancy of particular
spots of Earth, by the family or tribe or horde must have occurred,
and that deliberately. Discovery of historical truth, as to the mode
in which our race have settled or grouped, scarcely tends to displace the juridical postulate, that distinct primary occupation (as
the word is explained in the text) of all unappropriated subjects of
possible property, must be the beginning of every external real
Right. Nor is any dilemma suggested in the supposition that, among
rude men and tribes, a weaker occupant will be molested and ousted
by a stronger. The observance of the rule may have grown up slowly
and amidst obstacles ; and artificial sanctions may have only gradually
been introduced, to protect the occupant tribe or family or individual.
Such probable difficulties of circumstance do not refute the position,
that all material property must have had a first occupant (whether
a person or a group), who exercised an *arbitrium* (will, desire), either
adversely or permissively. " Primitive acquisition" said Kant, " is
" one not derived from any other's ownership."

A recent publication of high literary merit (valuable also for more
solid qualities) uses phrases like the following.—" Mr. Jonas has
" proved by experience, that, in cultivating his great occupation, &c."
—" in England, it is deemed requisite that a tenant farmer, on renting an

"occupation, should have &c." Now, Englishmen say, 'he has 100 acres in his occupation' but not, 'he has an occupation of 100 acres.' Elihu Burritt, the American author of that work, was doubtless familiar with this use of the word—one, suggestive of power, of Right, perhaps of personal superintendance, rather than of any corporeal relation.

The terms occupy, occupier, occupation, have acquired technical meanings in municipal laws, *e. g.* in the law of English parliamentary elections, and in the Indian ryot's charter, Act X. of 1859. Under all circumstances, an occupier is, a holder—at one time perhaps, of an interest, at another of a substance, distinctively.

(*w*) Certainly something more than the labour of mere occupancy *i. e.* taking and holding. But, we can scarcely speculate either upon the degree or upon the kinds and mode of use—of turning to account, which archaic chiefs construed into proprietary taking, *i. e.* occupancy. The rule of decision probably differed, with place and circumstance : under a tropical sun or in hunting grounds, need of ground for rest and shade (both or either), without more, might have afforded even a righteous plea for exclusive occupancy, within a rational limit. Nor are early polities at all uniform in their modes of appropriation—in utilising their aggregate of *res.* Among that ancient, numerous and hardy people, the Suevi, as we learn from an eye-witness, Cæsar, in his Gallic campaigns, individual property in land was unknown, because disregarded. A depôt only tarried at home, and provided for the wants of all, by culture of the fields ; whilst the bulk of the nation sallied forth to the more congenial pursuit of arms. And, of the Germans, the same author says ; "—nor "has any one of them any defined or appropriated land ; but the "magistrates and chiefs assign yearly to the several tribes and "families, who meet together for that purpose, as much land, and "in such locality, as they think fit, and compel them, after a year, "to change their holdings." To the same effect wrote Tacitus, in his treatise of the manners of the Germans. How different the race, of whom an officially accredited traveller and historian, Colonel Tod, records :—"The love of Country and the passion for possessing "land are strong throughout Rajpootana : while there is a hope of "existence, the cultivator clings to the *bapota* [patrimony], and "in Harouti this *amor patriæ* is so invincible, that, to use their "homely phrase, 'he would rather fill his *pait* [belly] in slavery "there, than live in luxury abroad !—" The same writer relates, with reference to the land-occupant or ryot, in one district,—" If

"in exile, from whatever cause, he can assign his share to trustees;
"and the more strongly to mark his inalienable right in such a
"case, the trustees reserve on his account two seers on every
"maund of produce, which is emphatically termed, *huk bapatá cá*
"*bhom, i. e.* the dues of the patrimonial soil." A resident and
traveller among the tribes of Southern Africa (the Rev. E. Casalis)
says of the Basutos and other primitive agricultural non-nomadic
peoples:—" The sale - or transfer of land is unknown among these
"people. The country is understood to belong to the whole community,
"and no one has a right to dispose of the soil from which he
"derives his support. The sovereign chiefs assign to their vassals
"the parts they are to occupy; and these latter grant to every father
"of a family a portion of arable land proportionate to his wants.
"The land thus granted is insured to the cultivator as long as he
"does not change his locality. If he goes to settle elsewhere,
"he must restore the fields to the chief under whom he holds them,
"in order that the latter may dispose of them to some other
"person." The traveller Burton thus speaks of his experiences at
Abeokuta in Western Africa:—

"Whatever be the tenure of property in ground, it cannot perma-
"nently be given or sold. A chief will, for a quit-rent, permit any
"stranger to cultivate unreclaimed commons, but the bargain is purely
"personal. If the original tenant die, the heir or successor is expected
"by another 'dash' [something to be given] to obtain renewal of the
"lease, and his refusal would justify in the African mind, his ejection.
"On the other hand, if the chief attempt to raise his terms, the heir might
"insist upon not paying a sum higher than the original quit-rent, and
"amongst the more civilized tribes the voice of the people would be
"on his side."

With the early Romans, property (*mancipium, dominium ex jure
Quiritium*) had a technical and political character: subjects of property
were arbitrarily classed: modes of transfer were cumbrous and curiously artificial. Variable and numerous as the peals, the harmonies
and discords, which may be rung upon ranges or octaves of bells
(illustrative of the laws and modulation of sound), are the modes,
the changes, the application, under which varying circumstances
exhibit—no less in the primitive civilizations still being discovered or
becoming familiar to us, than in the past history of mankind—the
simple principles, the bases of general jurisprudence. Whether this
or that community, whether the earliest organised political bodies,
whether the majority, have or not appropriated their portions

of the estate of mankind, or any subjects of property whatever, collectively, in groups, or individually, whether in simple and absolute dominion, or temporarily, for unlimited use or as partial usufructuaries,—whether with as little ceremony and method as do the feathered architects who, with unconscious and unerring skill, select sites for nest-building, the bees for their hive, the beavers for their elaborate and city-like structures; or, whether with Quirital formalities—are alternatives, questions and differences, not indicating any variation, or new principle of jurisprudence, but, all carrying out the simplest principles, each and all illustrating the same inevitable truths, the philosophy of the Law of property. The variations of circumstance and of rule, constituting the idiosyncrasy of each people's ways, wants and wishes, are phenomena, but not of the science of Law.

(x) A further extract from the same accurate and severe analyst of principles makes this more clear:—"At first, all men are in "common possession of the estate of the whole Earth, and desiring "(as all naturally must do) to gather the produce of that common estate. "This feeling of desire, however, by reason of the rivalry, natural "and inevitable, between individual wills, would go to preclude en- "joyment of that estate by any one; did it not also embody a law "of order for the will itself, according to which a separate posses- "sion in the common estate is capable of allotment to each indivi- "dual. But a distributive law of 'meum and tuum' for each, in "the common estate, after the axiom of an 'external liberty,' can "only result from a common desire, primitive and *a priori*—a desire "not implying any juridical act of association. It [such distributive law] "can not therefore exist save in a state of civil society; wherein "alone may be fashioned definitions of Right, of what is juridical, "of what is lawful." KANT

(y) As, suppose a single man happen to be in possession of an island, without interference or claim by any other,—can it be said that he is proprietor of the land, trees, fruits, animals and other *res* or productions which he enjoys? He can have no relation with any creature in his territory—no civil obligation, therefore no civil right. He is without society, therefore without rival or possible co-owner.

(z) It may be objected, that the illustration here contradicts the proposition; inasmuch as original property thus continues to be acquired.—The answer is; national acquisition as against other nations, comes under a different category, *vis.* international Law.

(aa) I include, as a matter of general jurisprudence, and irrespective of international rules, the shores of the ocean among *res* common to mankind—as only *quodammodo* (qualifiedly) appropriable. In practice, if the buildings or occupied lands of a town abut on the sea (as Madras, Brest, Naples, Brighton, Macao), it is too much to say, that the land, at least at high-water mark, is common to the world and beyond the State's laws—scarcely can it be said, that it is (to use a Roman phrase) extra-patrimonial. Sir Geo. Bowyer in his 'Commentaries on Universal Public Law' writes : "The shores of the sea incontestably belong to the nation that "possesses the country of which they are a part, and they belong "to the class of public things. If civilians have set them down as "things common to all mankind (*res communes*), it is only in regard "to their use ; and we are not thence to conclude that they considered "them as independent of the empire. The very contrary appears "from a great number of laws. Ports and harbours are manifestly "an appendage to and even a part of the country, and consequently "are the property of the nation. Whatever is said of the land "itself will equally apply to them, so far as respects the consequences "of the domain and of the empire."

The subject is somewhat differently treated by Lord Stair in his Institutions : "—so all nations have free passage by navigation through "the ocean, in bays and navigable rivers; and have also the benefit of "stations, or roads and harbours in the sea or rivers; and have the "common use of the shores for casting anchors, disloading of goods, "taking in of ballast, or water rising in fountains there, drying of "nets, erecting of tents, and the like. Yet doth the shore remain "proper, not only as to jurisdiction, but as to houses, or works "built thereupon; and as to minerals, coals, or the like found therein, "and so is not in whole common, but some uses thereof only. Nor "doth it follow, that these uses are not common to all men, because "they are denied to enemies; for, as for these, as we may take "away that which is in their power, in some cases; so much more "may we detain from them that which is our own; and as we "pursue their persons and goods in their own bounds, much more "in ours. The shore in the civil-law is defined to be, so far as "the greatest winter tides do run, which must be understood of "ordinary tides, and not of extraordinary spring tides. But the use "of the banks of the sea or rivers, to cast anchors or lay goods "thereon, or to tie cables to trees growing thereon, or the use of "ports, which are industrial, or stations made by art, or fortified for "security, are not common to all men, but public to their own

o

" people, or allowed freely to others for commerce, or in some cases are
" granted for a reasonable•satisfaction of anchorage, portage, or
" shore-dues, which oft-times belong to private persons, by their proper
" right, or by custom, or by public grant; but stations in these rivers,
" by casting of anchor, remain common, and ought not to be
" burdened."

(bb) Wild animals although certainly valuable to mankind, and
among the earliest of appropriated goods (by the chase), are not
in the class of common things; nor are the most formidable of brute
creatures beyond Man's dominant prerogative : they are, as land,
or fruit, or aught else appropriable, property, when and whilst
occupied. What is special with regard to this sort of *res* is, the
extra labour and skill to take them—to effect their capture and
detention.

(cc) The *res publicæ* of the Roman system included but a portion
of what is intended to be here classed; the distinction with them
having reference to local and national views. Whatever, for the
public benefit, is withdrawn from commerce, from individual appropriation, is, in a general and purely juridical sense, public.

(dd) " Whenever an article usurped is altered in consequence of an
" act of the usurper, in such a manner that it loses both its name and
" its original purpose, it is then separated from the right of the pro-
" prietor, and becomes responsible for it; but he is not entitled to
" derive any advantage from it until he pay the compensation. An
" example of this occurs where a person usurps a goat, kills it, and
" afterwards roasts or boils it; or usurps wheat, and afterwards grinds
" it into flour; or usurps iron, and makes a sword from it ;—or
" usurps clay, and makes a vessel from it. What is here advanced is
" according to our doctors. Shafei maintains that, after the alteration
" in the article, the right of the proprietor to it is not extinguished,
" but he is entitled to take from the usurper the flour of his wheat.
" There is also a report from Aboo Yoosaf to the same effect. He,
" however, maintains that in case the proprietor choose to take the
" flour of the wheat, he is not entitled to a compensation for the
" damage, as that would induce usury; whereas Shafei holds that he
" is entitled to a compensation from the usurper for the damage. It
" is also related, as an opinion of Aboo Yoosaf, that the right of
" property with respect to an usurped article which has been altered
" ceases in the proprietor, but that it may be sold to answer the debt
" due to him (*viz.* the compensation,) and that, in case of the death
" of the usurper, he has a preferable claim to the other creditors with

"respect to the article in question. The reasoning of Shafei is,
"that the substance of the thing being extant, notwithstanding it
"have undergone an alteration, it follows that the right of property
"still remains in the proprietor, since the quality is merely a dependant
"on the substance;—as where, for instance, the wind blows wheat
"into the mill of another person, and it is ground into flour; in which
"case it continues the property of the original proprietor of the
"wheat; and so also in the case in question. With respect to the
"act of the usurper by which the thing is altered, it is not to be
"regarded, since it is an unlawful act, and consequently incapable
"of becoming the cause of property,—as has been explained in its
"proper place. The case is therefore the same as if the act had
"never existed;—in the same manner as holds where an usurper kills
"an usurped goat, and tears the skin of it in pieces. The argument of
"our doctor is, that in the case in question the usurper has performed
"an operation which bears a value, and has therefore destroyed the
"right of the proprietor in one respect, inasmuch as the appearance
"is no longer the same, whence it is that the name is changed, and
"many of the original purposes of the article defeated; as grains of
"wheat, for instance, which are fit for being sown or roasted, but
"after being converted into flour are no longer fit for these purposes.
"In short, by the alteration of an article usurped the right of the
"proprietor is destroyed in one shape, and that of the usurper with
"respect to the qualities is established in every shape; and hence
"the right of the usurper has a superiority with respect to the
"original of that thing which has been in one shape destroyed."
Again:

"If a person usurp gold or silver, and convert it into *dirms*
"or *deenars*, or makes a vessel from it, such silver or gold does not
"separate from the property of the proprietor, according to Haneefa,
"—whence he is entitled to take it from the usurper without giving
"him any compensation. The two disciples maintain that the us-
"urper, in such case, acquires a property in the metal, and owes
"a compensation of a similar quantity of gold or silver to the original
"proprietor; because he has performed a valuable operation upon
"the metal, which in one shape destroys the right of the proprietor,
"since in so doing he has broken it down so as to destroy its
"original purposes, inasmuch as bullion is unfit to become the
"stock in a contract of *mozaribat*, or of partnership, whereas
"coined money has this fitness. The reasoning of Haneefa is, that
"in the case in question the substance of the thing usurped is ex-

"tant in every respect, insomuch that it still preserves its name:
"and the purposes to which gold and silver relate, such as price and
"weight, are also extant, insomuch that usury by weight takes place
"in them when coined, in the same manner as before coinage." And,
"If a person usurp the cloth of another and then dye it red, or
"the flour of another and then mix it with oil, in that case the
"proprietor has the option of taking from the usurper a compensa-
"tion equal to the value of the white cloth, or an equal quantity
"of flour, giving the red cloth or the mixed flour to the usurper,—
"or, of taking the red cloth or the mixed flour, giving to the us-
"urper a compensation equal to the additional value these articles
"may have acquired from the red dye, or the mixture of oil. Shafei
"maintains that in the case of dyed cloth the proprietor of it has
"a right to take it, and then to tell the usurper to separate and
"take, to the utmost of his power, his dye from it; for he holds
"this case to be analogous to that of a plot of ground; (in other
"words, if a person usurp a piece of ground belonging to another,
"and afterwards erect a building upon it, the proprietor is entitled
"to take the ground, desiring the usurper to dig up and carry away
"his building;) because the separation of a dye from stained cloth
"is equally practicable with the removal of a building from the
"ground on which it stands. It is otherwise in the case of oil mixed
"in flour, because the separation of the oil is then impracticable."

Hedaya.

(*ee*) From Dr. Colquhuon's Summary.

(*f*) The English 'use' originally denoted beneficial enjoyment,
having the benefit of, being analogous to the Prœtorian *in bonis* of
the Roman Law: it grew into a merely technical and auxiliary mode
of property.

(*gg*) The distinction is thus illustrated by Dr. Taylor—If I treat for
a slave, a house, or a horse; or, if a slave, &c. be left me by will,—that
specific slave or horse is due to me, *quia functionem in suo corpore
recipiunt* [because each respectively does its own work in its own
individuality]; and if I am creditor for one of these, my debtor
cannot force upon me one of another sort, though a better in value.
But such things as consist in number, weight, and measure, *non
specificam functionem sed generalem recipiunt* [have not any individual
function, but work in the general—interchangeably]: a legacy of £20 is
as lawfully paid in one legal coin as another; and, if I borrow a measure
of wheat, I am not expected to return the same grains, but am to
pay it in the same quantity, of equal goodness.

(hh) The distinction is very marked in the English system, between dominical and subordinate property, *viz.* 'the fee,' 'freehold,' 'realty,'— and 'chattel-real,' 'personal property in land,' 'leasehold interest (though for a thousand years).' The terms, freehold, realty, are certainly applicable to property which does not devolve on the proprietor's heir, (in which, therefore, he has not complete *jus abutendi*) : but a life-estate is incomparably more important than an estate for a term of years ; even though the term be such as must, physically, include scores of lives. The Roman *emphyteusis*, in its most valuable form, after the reign of Zeno, is a remarkable instance of *quasi*-dominical property (see Colquhuon 'Summary of the R. C. L.' § 169, &c.) : the anomalous interest of a Hindu widow heir is another instance, perhaps a closer approach to *dominium*—limited, but undefinable in words.

(ii) Butler in his celebrated Note (on Feuds) to *Co. Lit.*, remarks of the relation, at that period ;—"Though in point of dignity, of rank, "and of honor, the lord, according to the ideas of those times, enjoyed "a splendid pre-eminence over his vassals, his power over them was, com- "paratively speaking, extremely small.——The fruits and incidents of "the feudal tenure, in the original simplicity of the feud, were reducible "to two: on the part of the lord, to the obligation of warranty, that is, "to defend the title of his tenant against all others ; on the part of the "tenant, to an obligation of giving his lord his aid, that is, his military "assistance and service in defence of the feud." It is true, that the feudal estate lapsed to the lord upon failure of heirs, *i. e.* in such case, the lord came in place of the king or of the State : but this contingency is not any 'property' or jural interest in the land. "Government succeeds" wrote chancellor Kent, "as ofcourse, to the "personal and real estate of the intestate, when he has no heirs or "next of kin to appear and claim it ; but this is for the sake of order "and good policy—"

(kk) Grotius quotes those two sentences ; the first from Seneca, the other from Dion Prusæensis. Lordship over land was the sovereignty of the middle ages : subjection to power, when not simply military nor simply servile, was territorial : hence the nude superiority of feudalism. But seignory or *seigneurie* is used to designate a more tangible and usual mode of property; *e. g.* Hind, in his 'Labrador Exploration' narrates:

"As we sailed before a gentle breeze through the clustered Mingan islands in "1861, it suddenly occurred to me that exactly 200 years ago, namely, 1661, François "Bissot had been invested with the rights of *seigneur* of Mingan. For 200 years "these rights have endured ; but the owners are now dispersed far and wide in "both continents. Sailing amidst these remote islands, looking so fair and beauti-

"ful as we drifted lazily along before the dying breeze, I could not but think it
"both unjust and unpatriotic that abused and misapplied seignorial rights, conveying
"many million acres to single individuals, 200 years ago, should now exercise a potent
"influence in arresting the progress of settlement on the north of the gulf, in
"sight of the finest fishing ground in the world, and including the best parts for
"settlement. Yet such is even now the case; and many years ago many settlements
"would have been established on the Labrador shores, if seignorial rights had
"not frightened away hundreds who were disposed to establish a home there."

(*ll*) I am not sure that this view will be generally acquiesced in
by publicists; as *imperium* has had a more confined signification
given to it: but what is here laid down is consistent with the
teachings of Grotius and of Heineccius, as well as supportable in
principle.

(*mm*) MONTAIGNE. The moral sentiment is eloquently expanded
and enforced by Massillon, bishop of Clermont:—"We do not owe
"to all men the same cares, civilities, and attentions; but to all we
"owe 'the truth.' The different situation that rank and birth give us
"in the world, diversify our duties with regard to each other. That
"of truth is in all situations the same. We owe it to the rich as
"well as to the poor; to our inferiors, as well as to our masters;
"to those who hate it, as well as to those who love it, and to those
"who will use it against us, as well as to those who will use it for
"themselves. There are times, when prudence permits us to dissi-
"mulate or hide the love we have for our brethren; but there are
"none, in which we are permitted to conceal 'the truth.' In fact, the
"truth is not ours; we are but its witnesses, defenders and deposi-
"taries. It is the light of God in man, which ought to illuminate
"the whole world—"

(*nn*) Kant thus classed definable conventions:
"—the purpose of every contractor is, either—1. a unilateral acquisi-
"tion (this is the gratuitous contract), or, 2. a bi-lateral acquisition (this
"is the onerous contract), or, 3. guarantee of what is already his,
"without acquisition (a guarantee which may be, at the same time,
"gratuitous for one, and yet onerous for the other).
    "The gratuitous contract is;
    "*a.* keeping something entrusted (*depositum*);
    "*b.* loan of a thing (*commodatum*);
    "*c.* gift (*donatio*).
    "The onerous contract is;
    "*a.* exchange, in the widest sense, subdivided into
        "I. goods for goods, exchange;
        "II. goods for money, purchase and sale;

"III. loan for consumption (*mutuum*), alienation of a thing on "condition of getting it back some day *in specie* (as, corn for corn, "money for money).

"*b.* , the contract of letting (*locatio-conductio*), subdivided into,

"I. letting out a thing to one, for such use as he can get out of "it (*locatio rei*). If the restoration of the thing is to be *in specie* "only, 'interest' may be added as an onerous pact (*pactum "usurarium*).

"II. the letting out of labour (*locatio operæ*), that is to say, grant "of the use of my strength to another for a settled price (*merces*). "The labourer, in virtue of the contract, is the mercenary.

"III. the contract of mandate ; procuration for and in name of "another. If the procuration be effected by simple substitution "for another, without use of the person's name whose place is taken, "it is a mere conduct of affairs (*gestio negotii*). If the procuration "be carried out in the name of the other, the principal, it is a man-"date. Here, as in letting, the contract is onerous (*mandatum "onerosum.*

"*c.* the contract of security ;

"I. pledge with undertaking, simultaneous (*pignus*) ;

"II. suretyship, a promise given in support of a contractor's "promise (*fidejussio*) ;

"III. bail or hostage."

The juridical metaphysician has, in his instances of classification, availed himself of the Roman Law, the universal European model for illustration of jural science.

(*oo*) The distinct signification of this term is well indicated by its derivative compound, com-merce. A subject of commerce must have a price set on it—be appreciated, in the market. *Merx* was not applied to landed estate.

(*pp*) The nice requirements of 'consideration,' in the English simple-contract ; the strict requisites in the *obligatio verbis* of ancient Rome ; the precautions enforced in contracts relating to property of a British ship, in contracts protected by the English Statute of Frauds : these are familiar instances.

A passage in Professor Bell's 'Principles of the Law of Scotland,' under the head, 'conventional obligations,' exemplifies the arbitrary differences in different systems,—"The Law of Scotland does not "follow the Roman Law of *nudum pactum* on the one hand ; nor "recognise the subtilties of the English Law on the other."

(*qq*) Justice Park in *Britten* v. *Hughes* 5 Bing.

The speech of Lord Eldon, which follows, is to be found in the case *Bromley* v. *Holland*, 7 Ves.

Lord Loughborough, when deciding that a contract to succeed another in a public office was void (because impolitic), said—" This agree-" ment, resting on private contract and honor, may perhaps be fit to be "executed by the parties, but can only be enforced by considerations "which apply to their feelings, and is not the subject of an action. "The Law encourages no man to be unfaithful to his promise; but "legal obligations are, from their nature, more circumscribed than "moral duties."

(*rr*) See Kent's Commentaries (10th edit.) 2nd vol. p. 620, no. 1.

(*ss*) These several passages are somewhat differently rendered by Lord Kaimes, who quotes them in a note to his 'Law Tracts.'

(*tt*) To many the distich of Saadi will occur:

یا وفا خود نبود در عالم   یا مگر کسی درین زمانه نکرد

'Either real *wufah* (good faith) never was in this world, or, at least, no one now-a-days observes it.'

(*uu*) Thus it was in Rome. Beginning with the starch and tedious, but yet universal *nexus per æs et libram* (' bond by the brass and scales'), —which had no character of grossness, if rude; it rather indicated the rarity and little value of what was typified, to the 'men of the lance,'— and gradually fining down until the express abolition of 'law-formularies' A. U. C. 1095. The intermediate resolution of the Prætor, in the famous edict ('*Pacta conventa——servabo*'), was a virtual abolition of quirital despotism in matters of contract; thenceforth, the moral tie of good-faith in admission or observance of conventions was no longer totally alien from the jural ground of obligation.

The significance of contract-formalities will be further enlarged on under the head of 'alienation.'

SECTION VI.

THE FAMILY, NATURAL AND CIVIL: CIVIL SUBSTITUTES OR COPIES OF FAMILY RELATIONSHIP.

From those familiar and uniform relations which constitute primary society, which are the basis and type of (foreshadowing) civil or political society, necessarily arise civil modes of Right and obligation, *i. e.* civil status: nor is any chapter of a nation's Law more characteristic of national bent or more likely to exemplify the standard of a nation's conscience.

'The family' is a concrete name for the class or aggregate of relations now referred to. The family is not a civil creation, nor, in its main incidents, even exclusively human. But, civil laws, building upon the ordinance of Nature, construct and organise status relations, which represent and constitute the family.

Each civil system differs, more or less, from the prototype: either, deepening and extending (while following) the simple lines tracked out by Nature, or, diverging and deviating into artificial ways; at times so diverging and deviating as virtually to supersede (never obliterating) Nature's track.[a]

Family status is essentially one, in character as in origin: each subdivision or branch however, each instance or phase of the relation, has, in every system, its several incidents and properties, although growing from one root, attached and supplemental to one stem, *viz.* the marriage tie.

P

MARRIAGE.

Marriage, matrimony, wedlock, is, the coming together of the sexes, under a contract or legal *vinculum*, for procreation and nurture of children.

Being a contract, all general rules of contract (noted in the last Section) are applicable to this 'coming together'—con-vention.

Therefore, the views, the formalities prescribed and adopted in each civil system, determine what is and what is not a legal marriage. In one place, at one time, a particular religious form, or a technical ceremony is insisted on; elsewhere or in another epoch special publication or registry; it has occurred and does occur, that form and ceremony are dispensed with, the substance and intrinsic meaning of the marriage connection being alone regarded. [b]

In so far then, the jural tie of marriage, the proceeding, the union of wills accomplished in the marriage status, is strictly identical with 'contract'. In regard however to its universality and necessity, to its being but a reduction into order and adaptation to circumstance, of Nature's impulses, marriage bears a close analogy to 'property'—and this, without reference to marital domination.

As Reason modifies, extends, refines upon the general rule, the indefinite necessity of property; so do we find the simple primary idea of marriage modified and adapted to the wants, the temptations, the habits of various races, in varying schemes of civil Law.

The two institutions combined, may well be supposed to embrace all ordinary social requirements.

"The component parts of a house (*oikos*) are a "man and property.—But as to man, the first "object of his care should be respecting a wife."

So Aristotle; who quotes the old poet Hesiod,

"first house, then wife, then oxen for the plough."

and he admirably (for his Time remarkably) treats of marriage and its duties as of a condition, towards which mankind are "divinely predisposed." —"For the sexes are at once divided, in that "neither of them have powers adequate for all "purposes, nay, in some respects even opposite to "each other, though they tend to the same end. "For nature has made the one sex stronger and "the other weaker, that the one by reason of "fear may be more adapted to preserve property, "while the other, by reason of its fortitude, may "be disposed to repel assaults; and that one may "provide things abroad, while the other preserves "them at home. And with respect to labour, "the one is by nature capable of attending to "domestic duties, but weak as to matters out of "doors; the other is ill adapted to works where "repose is necessary, but able to perform those "which demand exercise. And with respect to "children, the bearing of them belongs to one "sex, but the advantage of them is common to "both; for the one has to rear them, and the "other to educate them."

The marriage union, being, in its general scope,

*

a normal result of human desires and of human association, is, considered civilly, a plan of restraint, an orderly and decent method of observance in regard to the sexual instinct. It is the assertion of Reason's prerogative in control of animal appetite. Further, marriage is an ordinance and scheme for preservation of infant life, for education (in a comprehensive sense) of human progeny. Marriage has also special value in civil polity, as indicative of paternity. Montesquieu enlarges on this:

" Among civilized nations, the father is that person " on whom the laws, by the ceremony of marriage, " have fixed this duty; because they find in him " the man they want. Amongst brutes, this is an " obligation which the mother can generally perform; " but it is much more extensive amongst men. " Their children indeed have reason; but this comes " only by slow degrees. It is not sufficient to nourish " them; they can already live; but they cannot " govern themselves. Illicit conjunctions contribute " but little to the propagation of the species. The " father, who is under a natural obligation to nourish " and educate his children, is not then fixed; and " the mother, with whom the obligation remains, " finds a thousand obstacles, from shame, remorse, " the constraint of her sex and the rigour of laws; " and besides, she generally wants the means." (c)

As an improvement or orderly development of Nature's ordinance, marriage, how variously soever organised and regulated, has two aspects, several, though each and together tending to one end.

The first and obvious aspect is, the purely moral,

social and personal, *viz.* satisfaction of human craving for a specific sympathy, companionship, aid, comfort—such as can be no otherwise sufficiently or fairly met and satisfied than in orderly conjugal union.

Neither history nor observation furnishes a deduction, that, among mankind, conjugal society is urged by no other want than the 'lust of the flesh,' even combined with desire of progeny. Each undepraved, unspoilt man or woman, however simple and rude, ever seems conscious of a moral incompleteness, capable of being supplied by (therefore demanding) conjugal society; understanding by 'conjugal,' no mere casual nor temporary nor optional yoke or tie. [d]

The second aspect of the marriage institution is political. Under whatever conditions, however disguised, mistaken, or corrupted, the form in which the institution may appear among a people—whether under the polyandry of some few eccentric races, as the Moplas of Malabar; the more frequent phase of polygamy; even with the licensed though covert libertinism of ancient Sparta; [e] or, whether under the most rigid dogmatic enforcement of a monogamic regimen; [f] every State regards and uses the institution as an agent to carry out its own policy, to extend its rule, to continue (in a manner consonant to the religious, moral and intellectual attainments of that people) the community and its institutions to future times, reining or giving way to the instincts and passions of men just as the general feeling or the views of those in power may incline. [g]

With whatever artificial attributes the policy or requirements of particular civil communities may clothe family relations, it is undoubted, that the social conduct and duties of husbands, fathers, sons and brothers, as such, are invariably a part or enter into the spirit and composition of every system of laws, and are moreover always defined and interpreted in precise conformity with the estimate and ideas of each nation as to what that conduct ought, morally or religiously, to be. The precise acts required from or justified in a good father, in a good son, often differ with different people: but the quality of goodness, as of badness, is ever measured and ascertained, plainly, by the moral sense, without artificial element or bias—unless indeed the influence of religious or of *quasi*-religious dogmas be considered an artificial element. [h]

Jural obligations and rights incident or proper to marriage, range under three heads; 1. conjugal rights, *i. e.* the *consortium, concubitus,* personal communion, which is the primary condition and immediate purpose of the contract; 2. changes effected, in pre-existent or supervenient rights, *e. g.* of property; 3. personal obligations other than the *consortium,* but collateral to or consequent upon it. [i]

It may be considered as a general and primary quality or incident of the married status, that each associate (spouse) has a right, a *jus* (bearing some analogy to *jura utendi, fruendi,)* in the person and

to the society of the other one—a right significant
of something less free or optional (as to the person
bound) than mere alliance or co-partnery, yet nowise
akin to a claim of servile subjection; it is a right
that betokens, as it demands, a real subserviency,
or at least adaptation, of will, of act, of mind—
such as is proper and incident to this status—
specially adapted to the objects, and growing from
the intrinsic character of marriage.[j]

Jural or civil manifestations which cover essential
incidents of the marriage contract and status, are
variously expressed in varying civil schemes.

By the *Sheraa*, "—the husband has no power
"to restrain his wife from going on a journey, or
"from going abroad, or visiting her friends, until
"such time as he shall have discharged the whole
"of the *muhr modjil* or prompt dower; because a
"husband's right to confine his wife at home is
"solely for the sake of securing to himself the en-
"joyment of her person, and his right to such
"enjoyment does not exist until after the payment
"of the return for it." [k]

Al Korân.—"Ye may divorce your wives twice;
"and then either retain them with humanity, or dis-
"miss them with kindness.—But if the husband
"divorce her a third time, she shall not be lawful
"for him again, until she marry another husband.
"But if he also divorce her, it shall be no crime in
"them, if they return to each other.—If ye be de-
"sirous to exchange a wife for another wife, and ye
"have already given one of them a talent, take not
"away any thing therefrom—"

In the *Dharma Sastra* it is declared,

" Him to whom a woman's father has given her,
" or her brother with paternal assent, let her ob-
" sequiously honour, while he lives; and when he
" dies, let her never neglect him." and,

" Though unobservant of approved usages, or
" enamoured of another woman, or devoid of good
" qualities, yet a husband must constantly be re-
" vered as a god by a virtuous wife."

" Married women must be honoured and adorned
" by their fathers and brethren, by their husbands,
" and by the brethren of their husband—"

" Neither by sale nor desertion can a wife be
" released from her husband." " Let mutual fidelity
" continue till death: this, in few words, may be
" considered as the supreme law between husband
" and wife."

" No atonement is ordained for that man who
" forsakes his own wife, through delusion of mind,
" deserting her illegally—" [1]

In the *Code Napoleon*,

" The spouses have the reciprocal duty of
" fidelity, relief, co-operation (*fidelité, secours, assist-*
" *ance*). The husband owes protection to his wife,
" the wife obedience to her husband. The wife
" is bound to live with the husband, and to
" follow him wherever he may think proper to
" dwell: the husband is bound to receive her,
" and to furnish her with everything necessary for
" the purposes of life, according to his means and
" condition."

Retributive vengeance—private sanction—accorded

or permitted against the accomplice in conjugal infidelity; judicial compensation to either spouse,
against the stranger to whom is imputable deprivation of conjugal society; remedial restoration of
that society, wrongfully withheld by either spouse,
or, the alternative penalties for abandonment—
by such indications, civil laws assert (different systems more or less determinately, and in various
modes) the *quasi*-real right of a spouse in the
other's person.[m]

Civil laws, as a rule, follow the suggestions of
Nature in allotting to the male partner protection
and superiority. "Moreover, it is manifest" wrote
Heineccius, "that this society would be very im-
"perfect, if it were equal in such a manner that
"neither had the faculty of deciding in any com-
"mon dispute; because it may happen, in many
"cases, that the two may differ in their opinions
"about the choice of means, and between two, in
"such cases, the dispute would be endless: where-
"fore, though the prudentest counsel ought to be
"preferred, yet, because it would often be contro-
"vertible which of the two parties in this society
"was in the right, there is reason to approve the
"common practice in this matter, and so to give
"a certain prerogative to the husband about affairs
"belonging to the common safety or advantage
"of the society."

Al Korân.—"Men shall have the pre-eminence
"above women, because of those advantages wherein
"God hath caused the one of them to excel the

Q

" other, and for that which they expend of their
" substance in maintaining their wives. Wives
" ought to be obedient, and keep . the secrets of
" their husbands, because that Heaven hath en-
" trusted them to their care." (a)

Such a view must usually lead to a right of
control, if not ownership, in the husband, of the
material wealth or property of the married pair.
This incident of the status was well expressed in
the ancient Roman system by the terms *manus*
and *potestas* ('hand' and 'power'); all claims and
material benefits of the wife, as an individual,
being at that epoch, as was her person, in subjection to the lord of her 'family' and 'house.'

So the English Common Law quaintly signifies,
in its old Norman jargon, the relative position of
the spouses, by the phrases 'baron' and 'feme-
covert' (*i. e.* under cover or shelter of her lord).
In these several systems the woman is civilly
absorbed, her personality is transferred—for the
purpose of outside civil dealings between the body
politic and social, the 'man and wife', and their
fellow citizens or others—to him who is alone
civilly responsible for her acts, as he is, for the
most part, owner of what would be hers, were she
unmarried.

The English *feme-covert* or wife has lost her individuality : "all that she owns, all that comes to
her, all that she earns, passes to the husband. (b
She cannot contract, save as his representative.
He is lord of his wife's lands or realty (without

disposing power) during the marriage, *viz.* their joint lives, and on birth of issue, becomes a life-tenant, should he survive, *viz.* 'tenant by the curtesy of England.'

In Scottish Law, the wife's personality is not so completely absorbed. By equitable evasion in the English Law, and directly in other systems, a separate and peculiar class of property may always be secured to the wife, in respect of which she is regarded as free from the status and bond of marriage. Such is the Hindu *stri-dhana*. But, "A husband need not return to his wife *stri-* "*dhana* appropriated by him during a famine, or in "order to perform sacred rites, or when suffering "from disease, or when in prison." *(p)*

The laws of France admit great latitude in the marriage contract as to the effect of the union upon the proprietary rights of the husband and wife respectively; but prohibit any stipulations that may "derogate either from the rights resulting from "the power of the husband over the person of his "wife and children, or those which appertain to "the husband as head—" *(q)*

With the Musulmans, union or confusion of property is no incident of marriage; which is, itself, but a *quasi* sale of the wife's person—the mere *jus concubitûs.*

Different systems provide differently for reciprocal contributions and joint responsibilities in respect of the common burdens of married life. The Roman *dos* was the contribution on the woman's side: in the English and Scottish laws, the same word, or 'dower,' is also used to denote the converse interest, *viz.* what the man must or may relinquish to his partner. (r)

Where the civil scheme of marriage status admits of the spouses having several interests in property, so that each may exercise his or her individual will in its disposition, we sometimes find rules of protection against irrational or improvident bounty between themselves. (s)

Nature dictates the relations of the married pair to their offspring, and the several rights or offices of nurture, education and guardianship which each respectively should accord to the other. How civil systems have dealt with this class of conjugal rights, may be conveniently adverted to under the next division of family status.

MANU.—"The production of children, nurture of "them when produced, and the daily superinten-"dance of domestic affairs are peculiar to the wife.".

PARENTAGE: THE FILIAL TIE.

The relation indicated by this double title, is, in its inception and full development, the end or purpose, natural and political, for which marriage is the instrument; as is apparent from the definition (above given) of marriage.

Offspring are either regarded and treated as the property of progenitors—virtually and *quodammodo,* if not absolutely—or, as wards entrusted to their charge, or, in a manner partaking of each of those modes of relation and custody.

Further, the period of parental domination may terminate when or shortly after the child becomes adult; or, it may last indefinitely, even during the parent's life, as with the ancient Romans and with all patriarchal tribes. The terrors of the Jewish code for filial rebellion were not restricted to childhood; they were a portion of the general penal system, binding all: nor is it to children or minors only that the less severe penalties but equally imperative injunctions of China are addressed.[t] So may be said in regard to the Hindu, practically, though perhaps rather in an ethical than a jural sense. [u]

Of the ancient peoples of Scandinavia, the historian Geijer writes:

"The father of a family, on the pillars surround-
"ing whose high seat were carved the images of
"the gods, was called himself, like the prince,
"*Drott*, and was priest, judge, and leader for his
"household.—As with the Greeks and Romans,
"and among all pagans, the father was free either
"to expose or bring up a new-born child; in the
"latter case he raised it from the earth in his
"arms, and had it sprinkled with water and named
"in the presence of his chief kinsmen."

Here is indicated proprietary dominion over the newly-born—an act, allowably, of passion or of caprice. But this dreadful option (of passive infanticide) does not itself prove, nor do I know of

any recorded proof, that with the earliest Roman,
any more than the Israelite father, the most practically cruel tyranny (over a child once under
nurture, and of which parental charge had been
accepted) was avowed to be less or other than a
quasi-judgment—a result of Law (not of caprice),
a punishment or an ostensible necessity, the decree
of a governor—if in theory autocratic, yet not
wholly irresponsible. (*)

The most rational, the most practical, the most
humane (and, in modern civilization, most admitted)
construction of the paternal office, is, as of a domestic, a special magistrate—the type, the representative, the necessary supplement, of civil or political
magistracy—entrusted with the charge, supervision,
government of the future man and citizen, of whose
existence he is the immediate cause. Well observed
Bentham—"The domestic governor may protect
"those subject to his authority from knowledge
"which may do them harm; he can watch over
"their social intercourse and their studies; he can
"accelerate or retard the progress of their enlight-
"enment, according to circumstances. This con-
"tinual exercise of power, which would be liable
"to so many abuses in a State, is much less so in
"a family; for the father and mother have a na-
"tural affection for their children, far stronger
"than that of the civil magistrate for those whom
"he governs. On their part, indulgence is gene-
"rally the prompting of nature, while severity
"is the effect of reflection. Domestic govern-

"ment can employ punishments in many cases
"where the civil authority cannot; for the head
"of a family deals with individuals, while the
"legislator can only act upon classes. The one
"proceeds upon certainties, the other upon pre-
"sumptions. A certain astronomer may be capa-
"ble, perhaps, of resolving the problem of longitude,
"but can the civil magistrate know it? Can he
"command this discovery, and punish him for not
"making it? But a particular instructor will be
"likely to know whether a given problem of ele-
"mentary geometry is level to the capacity of his
"pupil. Though idleness assume the mask of in-
"capacity, the instructor will hardly be deceived;
"in such cases the magistrate is sure to be deceived.
"It is the same with most of the vices. The
"public magistrate cannot repress them, because
"if he attempted it he must have spies in every
"family. The private magistrate, having under
"his eye and his immediate control those with
"whose conduct he is charged, can arrest the be-
"ginning of those vices of which the laws can
"punish only the last excesses."

In Pufendorf's treatise, we find the ingenious
(and not far-fetched) theory, that, like as the
beneficial conduct of an absent friend's affairs without his knowledge, imposes upon him obligations,
and, as it cannot but be presumed that, were
infants or children capable of judgment, they
would assent to parental care and control; so, the
very absence of personal capability and the need

of government, supplies—is an efficient substitute
for—consensual reciprocity. 'The presumption of
rational assent avails as express *consensus.*' 'For,'
also says Pufendorf, 'these notions have no repug-
nancy, *viz.* that an obligation should owe its
origin, at once, to a precept of natural Law and
to a tacit consent.' [w]

The extent of dominical discretion—the degree
of power, both to adjudicate, and to inflict sanctions,
confided or left to the domestic and social governor, must vary with the activity and character
of State-interference, of State-care, in educating
the rising generation of citizens. In the artificial
polity of Lycurgus, all training of youth was
usurped by the political parent, the State; so that
the functions of natural paternity could exist but
in name. [w] Usually, State-power comes in to su-
pervise and support, not to supersede the office
of a father. Even to inflict the ultimate penalty,
a Jewish parent but referred to civil authority, in
order to execute his self-adjudicated sentence.

"If a man have a stubborn and rebellious son,
"which will not obey the voice of his father or
"the voice of his mother, and that, when they
"have chastened him will not hearken unto them;
"then shall his father and his mother lay hold
"on him and bring him out unto the elders of
"his city, and unto the gate of his place; and
"they shall say unto the elders of his city, this
"our son is stubborn and rebellious, he will not
"obey our voice, he is a glutton and a drunkard;

"and all the men of his city shall stone him with "stones, that he die." [z]

In the French system, a father desirous of imprisoning a refractory child under the age of 15 years, and who is in no way emancipated from his care, has but to demand a warrant of detention from judicial authority, without any exposition of his motives or his ground of complaint.

Nor can it be said, that a rule of government or the conduct of a political executive in this respect, is any measure of political progress, of backward or advanced civilisation: it evinces merely the cast and policy of the particular system.

Courts, Legislatures, and Public Authorities, as a rule, in these days, decline all needless interference with morally defined family functions.

It scarcely need be noted, that, to provide his children with sustenance, at least during childhood and personal incapacity, is a civil obligation of the parent.

To lead on the mind in its early efforts, to train it, and if possible to wean it from the ever-ready guidance of ignorance and false impulses—is the special privilege and the highest duty of parents. Obviously, fulfilment of this duty concerns the welfare and must be of vital importance to the very being of a State: inasmuch as instruction and the discipline fitted for childhood, are direct means to forestal the action of penal laws, indeed 'of all' jural sanctions; while neglect or absence of those means must have, normally, a

R

converse operation. This duty is occasionally, as in Prussia (—at least, co-operation with State-efforts—) directly enforced : more usually, it is urged and invited, actively encouraged and assisted. (v)

Parental duties are mutual, joint, alternative : as a rule, they are conjugal, i. e. incumbent on the pair, not peculiar to either parent—except, indeed, for convenience and in respect of physical capabilities. The duties of nurture, sustenance, provision, bringing up, cannot be shifted from one to the other, as duties; though the mode and means of performance may differ with each. Nature has endowed the female with a rich aliment for her babe, with special adaptations for its tender care, with a finer sympathy for its little wants (perceptible only to the maternal sense); she has fitted the male to protect, to represent the home, to labour, to devise schemes of family provision, to preside over and to guide. From these general rules of natural provision arises a facility for division of labour, rather than any distinct separation of parental obligations.

Civil laws recognise, sometimes allot the fitting position of each parent; according to the social policy of each system.

MANU—"Let the father alone support his son—"

Until very lately, the English rule was severely strict; the mother could not, under any circumstances, assert a claim of custody or control (except where very tender infancy created a physical necessity), not even of society, but with assent and by indulgence of the father, in whom was the exclusive parental right. And, in an American case, the rule was held, as between husband and wife, to be so imperative, that the husband could not, by agreement with the wife, alienate to her his right to the custody of their children, and that such agreement was void.

This severity has been materially qualified by a statute of the present reign, which, in effect, deprives a father of the power, tyrannously to ignore the natural right of his children's mother to their society.——" When" said the Lord Chancellor, in a case where the provisions of that law were enforced, " the Court sees, that the maternal " feelings are tortured for the purpose of obtain- " ing anything like an unjust advantage over " the mother, that is a case in which it ought to " interfere."

By the Law of Massachusetts, the rule is, that the happiness and welfare of the children is to determine the custody in which they shall be placed, and the respective rights of the parents shall, in the absence of misconduct, be regarded as equal.

The French code gives exclusive rule and responsibility to the father, while present; in his absence, the parental function vests in the mother, but, for its exercise, she has occasionally to call in aid a council of paternal relatives. (s)

The English peremptory remedy in vindication of personal liberty, viz. the habeas corpus writ, is available on behalf of a child, to try the legality of the child's detention, by any one—as well as on behalf of a parent or other person, who may claim to resume, or be entitled to, the custody. The question for the tribunal before whom the child is brought by that legal process, is one of discretion and equity: an intelligent child's inclinations are consulted; there is every consideration of what is expedient, as well as of the mere jural right.

The power left to, or conferred upon sons to have and to deal with property, to contract, to act in any respect as citizens *sui juris*, must be (as in case of the wife) a question of special civil regulation; combining the policy of parental power, with the general question of civil minority and the protection thrown around those really or presumptively incapable of self-guidance.

The growth of the *peculium* or exceptional property of sons with the Romans, is one of the many proofs, to be found in all formal jurisprudence, of the inevitable relaxation in practice to which rules of policy and Law are subjected, with the growth of social exigencies and varying manners. Habit and social progress are stronger than the fetters of jural formality: they are powerful elements of heat and expansion, which loosen and permeate all artificial schemes of life and conduct.

Where children result from a union which is not 'marriage', in other words, are procreated under conditions which the Law (to which the parents

are subject) declares illegal, they are 'illegitimate,'
'natural' (as opposed to 'civil')—in Roman phrase,
not *justi liberi*. The status of such children is
governed, in each jural system, by two principles
or requirements, 1. ascertainment of the person
or persons clothed with the parental obligations,
2. discouragement of irregular and illegal sexual
concourse.

Illegitimate sons, in Athens, were excluded from
the paternal *phratria* (social class and rank), and
from succession to property; but they might be
legitimized by a kind of adoption, and thus admitted to all rights political and social, "at least"
writes Hermann, "when the father had not other
"strictly legitimate children."

So, later Roman jurisprudence, as well as modern
systems avowedly based on the *Jus Civile*, have
permitted an amelioration of the birth-status of those
who derive from their parents a lower civil and
social position than is held by their fellow citizens
of the same class who are born in wedlock. Their
original illegitimacy may be cured by 'legitimation.'
In Scotland, " A lawful child is one born in wed-
"lock, or within a certain time after the dissolution
"of the marriage; or born of parents who, at the
"conception, were under no impediment to marry,
"and have since intermarried." *(aa)*

The peculiarity of the English Common Law
in this respect, *viz.* in denying complete allevia-
tion for the birth-wrong of illegitimacy, may
be considered an historical accident, caused by

jealousy of Romish ecclesiastical domination or interference. [bb]

The technical brand (descended from Rome, but misapplied or wrongly generalised in modern jural language,) of, 'no man's son,' and 'son of the people,' is now seldom applied to the child of unlicensed birth. Supported by the dogmatic morality of the middle ages, such needless, cruel and very impolitic harshness of (what may be termed) jural ethics, has disappeared before the practical conscience, the safer and less fettered jurisprudence of modern Europe. "With the exception" writes Kent, "of the right of inheritance and succession, "bastards, by the English law, as well as by the "law of France, Spain, and Italy, are put upon "an equal footing with their fellow-subjects; and "in this country [America] we have made very "considerable advances towards giving them also "the capacity to inherit, by admitting them to "possess heritable blood." [cc]

ADOPTION.

Nature only can make a parent; and impotency or accident may disappoint those anxious to become parents, or, it may happen that a parent is disappointed by the uniformity of sex among his (perhaps numerous) progeny. It may almost be said, that Nature dictates an obvious remedy and consolation for every such disappointment, viz. transfer of the parental relation.

"Adoption," says Hermann, of the Athenians,

"was not considered as a mere right, but as a
"duty which, if omitted by the childless person,
"was usually performed after his death by his
"nearest relatives, lest his race, and its peculiar
"*sacra* should become extinct, a circumstance to
"which the State itself was by no means indiffer-
"ent."

By *adoptio* the Roman accepted a subjection to
or transfer of family dominion, in order to preserve his lineage and family-rites (*gens et · sacra
privata*). A father might even thus take to himself his own emancipated child. 'Dost desire that
Publius Fonteius have life and death *potestas*
over thee, as a son?'—is the recorded official
interrogatory put to one about to be 'arroga-
ted' by (*i. e.* one *sui juris* about to become as
a son to)—say, P. Fonteius. The transfer from
one *paterfamilias* to another, of son or daughter,
grandson or grand-daughter, was effected as a transfer of proprietary right. Although but an artificial and civil agnation was produced, fitness of
things was considered; for instance, a born eunuch
could not adopt, inasmuch as the relation simulated
could not possibly have been real.

The most artificial, as it is the most significant
and mystical, system of civil filiation, is that of
the Hindu Sastras. "Filial relation" says the
author of *Dattaka Chandrika*, "proceeds from ini-
"tiatory rites—" and, "Neither can it be said, that
"paternal right proceeds alone, from the relation, as
"natural father—" Yet, "the relation, as *sapindá*;

"of sons given, purchased, and the rest, to the
"natural parent, continues; by gift and so forth
"even, that does not fail; for, by reason of con-
"sisting in connection through containing portions
"of the natural father, it is not possibly to be
"removed while the body lasts." [dd] Thus, as with
the Romans, some sort of (though here, not a
well-defined) distinction is admitted between filiation
of blood, and a civil or ceremonial filiation. The
Sastras, however, recognize consanguinity of an indirect kind, viz. son of the wife or widow by an appointed relative, wife's son by one unknown, damsel's
son, son by the widow's second marriage. Here was [ee]
cognate sonship without either procreation or formal
adoption. The gift-son, &c. are substituted sons,
so made by adoptive rites.

With Hindus, impotency, so far from being an
objection to the adoptive act or power, is a special
ground and necessity—a doctrine that exemplifies
the distinction between their mystical sonship and
the merely civil substitution of western codes. [ff]

The 'son of two fathers' of hinduism bears
some analogy to the adoption introduced by Justinian, whereby a son given to a stranger, whilst
incurring new civil relationship did not forfeit that
of birth.

Artificial filiation is unknown to English jurisprudence; but is admitted in France, under
peculiar modifications; viz.

Art. 343, "Adoption is not permitted but to
"persons of either sex, upwards of fifty years of

" age, who shall not have, at the time of adoption,
" legitimate children, or descendants, and who shall
" be at least fifteen years older than the persons
" whom they propose to adopt."

Art. 345. " The power of adopting can be
" exercised only in favor of an individual to whom,
" during his minority and for six years at the least,
" the party adopting shall have furnished assistance
" and bestowed unremitting care, or in favor of one
" who shall have saved the life of the adopter, either
" in battle, or by rescuing him from the flames or
" the waters. In this second instance, it suffices,
" that the adopter have attained majority, be older
" than the adopted, without legitimate children or
" descendants, and, if married, that his wife consent
" to the adoption."

Art. 364. " In no case can adoption take place
" before the adopted has attained majority.—"

TUTELAGE: WARDSHIP.

This too is a jural relation of which paternity
is the prototype and original. Children and others
may need, that the State, the political, supervising
parent of an entire people, furnish a substitute for
natural paternity. An able exposition of 'The
sphere and duties of Government' thus deals with
this function of State:—

" To whose care the superintendence of the chil-
" dren's training must fall, after the death of the
" parents, is not so clearly determined by the princi-
" ples of natural right. Thence, it becomes the duty

s

" of the State to decide distinctly on which of the
" kinsmen the guardianship is to devolve ; or, if none
" of these should be in a condition to undertake
" the discharge of this duty, to declare how one of
" the other citizens may be chosen for the trust.   It
" must likewise determine what are the necessary
" qualifications for guardianship.   Since the guar-
" dians appointed undertake all the duties which
" belonged to the parents, they also enter on all
" their accompanying rights; but as, in any case,
" they do not stand in so close a relationship to
" their wards, they cannot lay claim to an equal
" degree of confidence, and the State must therefore
" double its vigilance with regard to the performance
" of their duties.————What we have here observed
" respecting minors, applies also to the provisions to
" be made in the case of idiots and madmen.   The
" difference chiefly consists in this, that these do
" not require education and training (unless we
" apply this name to the efforts made to restore
" them to the use of their Reason), but only care
" and supervision ; that in their case, moreover, it
" is principally the injury they might do to others
" which is to be prevented, and that they are gener-
" ally in a condition which forbids the enjoyment
" either of their personal powers or fortunes.   It is
" only necessary to observe, with regard to these,
" that as the return to Reason is yet possible, the
" temporary exercise of their rights is all that should
" be taken from them, and not those rights them-
" selves." (gg)

Females have been often, merely because of sex, classed among the helpless (or, may be, the un-safe,) who need tutelage, guardianship. This is emphatically so with the Hindus:—

MANU—"In childhood must a female be dependent "on her father; in youth on her husband; her lord "being dead, on her sons; if she have no sons, on "the near kinsmen of her husband; if he left no "kinsmen, on those of her father: if she have no "paternal kinsmen, on the sovereign: a woman must "never seek independence."

Among the Athenians, "Women were, in fact, "throughout their life in a state of nonage, and "could not be parties to any act of importance with-"out the concurrence of their guardians, whose "place the husband naturally supplied during his "life-time." (hh)

With the earliest Romans, women were under perpetual domination or tutelage: not so in the latter days even of the Republic; (ii) and a Constitution of the emperor Constantine expressly equalised the sexes, in exercise of private civil rights, with however one exception. (kk)

Social usage must always limit feminine members of the community to a narrower—at least a differ-ing—range of action and duties from those of men. This difference is most marked in the exclusion (as a rule) of the former from military, priestly, and political or governing functions. But, in modern jurisprudence, the civil rights of a woman, as such (without reference to marriage), e. g. to

hold, to alienate and deal with property, are in
no wise crippled, nor lower than they would be in
a man of the same position and under the same
circumstances. A sane, adult, single woman is her
own guardian, and unshackled.

'Tutelage' is derived from *tueor*, to preserve,
to guard: the term has special and primary reference to personal, even moral guidance—seconda-
rily, to charge of the pupil's or ward's. external
rights and property. The technical significance of
tutela in the *Jus Civile* is indicated by the name
given to a tutor's action or aid, *viz. auctoritas*
(from *augeo*, to increase, add to); inasmuch as
what the minor or pupil could do or attempt,
being augmented by the tutor's supplementary act
and confirmation, the two together constituted a
complete civil act.

Fathers are permitted to delegate their Right of
guardianship, wholly or partially, during their own
lives or when death has bereft their children of
natural protection; always however under State
supervision and the control of civil rules.

XII Tables—" As the father has ordained [by
" last will] concerning—the *tutela* of what belongs
" to him; so let the law be! If he die without
" disposition, and there be no [adult] son, let the
" next civil relative take the *familia!*"

In the French code: " when a minor, not eman-
" cipated, is without father or mother, and no tutor
" has been selected by his parents, and he has no
" elder relatives in the male line—he is to be

"provided, on the nomination of a family council,
"with a tutor."

Al Korán—"Examine the orphans until they
"attain the age of marriage: but if ye perceive
"they are able to manage their affairs well, de-
"liver their substance unto them; and waste it
"not extravagantly or hastily, because they grow
"up." [ll]

MANU—"The property of a student and of an
"infant, whether by descent or otherwise, let the
"monarch hold in his custody, until the owner
"shall have ended his studentship, or until his
"infancy shall have ceased." So that, by the letter
of the Sastras, guardianship of minors is a State
nomination in each case. [mm]

Law should and usually does protect and aid,
within rational limits, the infirm of mind and purpose, the silly, the weak and demoralised, from
obvious dangers that beset them (and beset those
having to do with them) in social and civil intercourse. But, one appointed to supply the care and
capability needed for charge and use of property
owned by the insane or the incompetent, is in
a different class or category from the protector of
the infant or the minor.

XII Tables—"If there be a madman or a
"squanderer, who is not in charge of any one let
"authority over him and over his goods be with
"his nearest relatives!"

Roman Prætor's injunction to prodigal heir:—
"Since, by vicious courses, thou art wasting thy

"patrimony and ancestral possessions, and bringest
"thy children to want; therefore I interdict thee
"from use of money and from business!"—and a
curator was accordingly appointed.

Al Korán—"And give not unto those who are
"weak of understanding the substance which God
"hath appointed you to preserve for them; but
"maintain them thereout and clothe them, and
"speak kindly unto them!"—a text seemingly of
general application. (**)

(a) *e. g.* the Roman *familia*, where all social and natural feeling,
ostensibly and for civil uses, succumbed to the *potestas.*

(b) The application and significance of form or ceremonial in marriage was exhaustively treated by Lord Stowell in the leading case of
Dalrymple v. *Dalrymple.* I extract some sentences of the judgment.

"Marriage in its origin is a contract of natural Law; it may
"exist between two individuals of different sexes, although no
"third person existed in the world, as happened in the case of
"the common ancestors of mankind: it is the parent, not the
"child, of civil society, *Principium urbis et quasi seminarium*
"*reipublicæ.* In civil society it becomes a civil contract, regulated
"and prescribed by Law, and endowed with civil consequences. In
"civilized countries, acting under a sense of the force of sacred
"obligations, it has had the sanctions of religion superadded.
"It then becomes a religious, as well as a natural, and civil contract ;
"for it is a great mistake to suppose that, because it is the one,
"therefore it may not likewise be the other. Heaven itself is
"made a party to the contract, and the consent of the individuals,
"pledged to each other, is ratified and consecrated by a vow
"to God. It was natural enough that such a contract should, under
"the religious system which prevailed in Europe, fall under eccle-
"siastical notice and cognizance, with respect both to its theolo-
"gical and its legal constitution ; though it is not unworthy of
"remark that, amidst the manifold ritual provisions made by
"the Divine Lawgiver of the Jews, for various offices and trans-
"actions of life, there is no ceremony prescribed for the celebration
"of marriage. In the Christian church, marriage was elevated

"in a later age to the dignity of a sacrament, in consequence of
"its divine institution, and of some expressions of high and mys-
"terious import respecting it contained in the sacred writings."

On the same occasion Lord Stowell remarked,—"It depends
"entirely upon the Law of the country, whether it is justly to be
"styled an irregular marriage. In some countries only one form
"of contracting marriage is acknowledged, as in our own, with
"the exception of particular indulgences to persons of certain
"religious persuasions : saving those exceptions, all marriages not
"celebrated according to the prescribed form, are mere nullities;
"there is and can be no such thing in this country as an irregular
"marriage. In some other countries, all modes of exchanging
"consent being equally legal, all marriages are on that account
"equally regular. In other countries, a form is recommended and
"sanctioned, but with a toleration and acknowledgment of other
"more private modes of effecting the same purpose, though
"under some discountenance of the Law, on account of the non-
"conformity to the order that is established."

The normal modes of marriage in ancient Rome, were three;
vis. by religious ceremonial *(confarreatio);* commercially, as an
alienation, the wife being treated as a thing bought *(coemptio);* and
3dly by mere prescriptive use of the woman, as of an ordinary
subject of property. Each of those modes brought the wife permanent-
ly under the *manus* of the husband, and conferred the *patria
potestas.* But marital domination declined even during the
republic; and the old forms fell into desuetude (leaving merely the
real contract, implied in *ducere uxorem*), not as a reform, but with the
growth of licentious habits. Rituals and *usus* gave place to mere property arrangements and festive celebration. Hence Juvenal suggests to
the husband likely to be dissatisfied with her "irrevocably joined
"to him by formal legal instruments *(legitimis tabellis)"*

> "Why wed at all? why waste the wine and cakes
> "The queasy-stomach'd guest at parting takes?
> "And the rich present, which the bridal right
> "Claims———?"   (*Gifford*)

There was, under the empire, another customary, recognised
mode of union of the sexes, having no civil or political significance, therefore less honorable, but neither illegal nor immoral,
and so far supported, *vis. concubinatus.* The specialty of the marriage called 'morganatic' and 'left-handed' among feudal nations,
consisted rather in the rank of the wife and the claims of herself
and children upon the husband's property, than in any want of

binding force or other character of the union. The foreign term etymologically signifies, morning-gift, *i. e.* after consummation.

Among Hindus, the necessity of following minute directions of the *Dharma-Sastras*, as to domestic and social conduct; the sacred duty for each male to found a family—being dogmas or imperative precepts, of paramount and supernatural authority—invest the status of marriage with a special character unknown to other peoples.

"To be mothers, were women created; to be fathers, men." (MANU)

This, in object and character, is analogous to the primitive Divine invitation of the Bible, 'Be fruitful and multiply and replenish the Earth!'; but to the Hindu it is one of a class of warnings and injunctions under imperative and terrific sanction. In effect, in influence, the denunciation of the *Rishis* has been and is infinitely more effective than was the famous *lex Papia Poppæa* with its varied civil penalties and privileges.

The *Sastras* ingeniously adapt requirement to circumstances: *bráhma, prájápatya* or *káya,* and *daiva,* are simple though solemn modes of receiving a bride from her father, the latter through the intervention of a priest and religious forms; *ársha* where gift of the damsel is preceded by a certain offering to the father, *viz.* a pair of kine; *ásura,* where the father and relatives of the bride are conciliated by considerable presents, in proportion to the bridegroom's means; *gándharva,* when the union is what in Europe is called, a love-match; *rákshasa,* capture of a maiden in war; *paisácha,* where a man by stratagem succeeds in possessing himself of the person of the woman of his choice. These are described, "eight "forms of the nuptial ceremony used by the four classes, some good "and some bad in this world and in the next." and, "—the "ceremonies of *paisácha* and *ásura* must never be performed." and, "Some consider the four first only as approved in the case "of a priest; one *rákshasa,* as peculiar to a soldier; and that of "*ásura,* to a mercantile and servile man." (MANU.)

The *Sastras* give no general license of polygamy. Supersession of a wife (by infliction of a rival) is resorted to with reluctance and as a duty, exceptionally: see Manu, ch. ix. śl. 80, &c.

As to satisfying the scruples and dogmatic persuasions of men, learned or simple, by any merely civil rules—inasmuch as under the same civil sway sectarian variety of opinion must usually prevail—it is a futile attempt and expectation. Of this, an accurate and amusing illustration is given by Galt in his *Ayrshire legatees,* where, the Rev. Zachariah Pringle thus communicates to his Scottish correspondent a marriage, in the heterodox English capital, of one of his presbyterian flock :—

"Anent the marriage of Rachel Pringle, it may be needful in me "to state, for the satisfaction of my people, that although by stress "of law we were obligated to conform to the practice of the epis- "copalians, by taking out a bishop's license, and going to their church "and vowing, in a pagan fashion, before their altars, which are "abomination to the Lord; yet, when the young folk came home, "I made them stand up and be married again before me, according "to all regular marriages in our national church. For this I had two "reasons; first, to satisfy myself that there had been a true and "real marriage; and, secondly, to remove the doubt of the former "ceremony being sufficient; for marriage being of divine appoint- "ment, and the English form and ritual being a thing established "by Act of Parliament, which is of human ordination, I was not "sure that marriage performed according to a human enactment "could be a fulfilment of a divine ordinance."

(c) All history supports the traditional existence of the family, in the remotest—what, therefore, we may term the primitive—condition of our race. Now, there can be no 'family', not merely in a civil, but in any definite sense, where paternity is not recognised or specific. Pater- nity is the key-stone of patriarchal and primary society; and when the fact of paternity ceases, generally, to be a question or doubtful among a people, marriage is, by that fact, indicated, and has assumed the rank and importance of a status, natural, civil and political. For then we have, father, mother, child, and *res familiaris—oikos*: "then only" runs the precept of Hinduism, "is a man perfect, when he con- "sists of, his wife, himself and his son." (MANU.) Under such circum- stances, moreover, is seen the established idea and rule of female conti- nence, as incident to contractual—not merely sexual—union. The conclusion is inevitable, that, restricted and orderly indulgence of a natural appetite (implied in marriage) must have been, as organised pro- perty was, among the earliest, if not the earliest of the manifestations' or applied efforts of Reason. With this, however, consists the collateral and yet more patent truth, that, habitual and shameful varieties—often national—in sexual intercourse—in neglect or corrupt diversion of the marriage impulse—in promiscuous and indefinite procreations, have abounded. But little moral reasoning is needed to demonstrate, that such instances—however and wherever prevalent—are exceptional, in the record of Man's progress and tendencies.

T

(d) There is much in the private and personal aspect of marriage-union which is and must be a mere matter of conscience, i. e. irrespective of civil laws as of conventional modes. This view is supported by the fact of the deference paid by the Law of every people, in the regulation of marriage, (e. g. as to conditions of the contract and what is seemly in conduct,) to religious convictions, both dogmatical and ethical. A man's religion must be, intrinsically and strictly, an individual consideration, actively urged through his conscience. What he deems a warrantable, a convenient and a rational method of satisfying the desire which may well be termed, marriage-impulse, is, to him, of deeper and wider significance than either political or social dictates. Thus it is we ever find, that, within the pale of each State's laws (occasionally even beyond that pale) unions of the sexes take place, scarcely to be classed as casual or undeliberate, which set at nought, no less jural *vincula* and jural modes, than they do the decrees of fashion and of social opinion. Such erratic instances are of necessity tolerated, while condemned. For their ethical character or excuse, no general rule or dogma can avail: each case has its idiosyncrasy. As to their reception in social circles, the least that can be said is—it is as though one were grossly to violate recognised modes of dress or of living, e. g. methodically devoting the night to the business and pleasures of life, and sleeping by day—or, going with bare limbs among a clothed and booted people—thus, or in any away repudiating the manners of one's nation and unfurling a standard of one's own. No one with impunity is singular, however conscientiously or even rationally: social despotism seldom allows a margin for corrective or conscientious irregularities.

(e) Heeren thus apologises for the loose conjugal morality of Lycurgus. "The complete organization of domestic society in "relation both to husband and wife, parents and children, which was "so framed as to further, even at the cost of morality, the grand "political object, the production of vigorous and healthy citizens."

(f) Or, may be, the unforced virtue of a people. Gilbert Stuart says of the ancient, the simple and warlike Germans;—"They "were unacquainted with that softer luxury which more delicious "climates introduce into society, and neither indulged a plurality of "wives, nor prohibited their women to attend them to the field, "to assist in their councils and to be useful and active in the "different occupations which employed them. For gallantry, accom-"modating every thing to the standard of pleasure, had not yet

"turned the sex from business, or made it the object of a criminal
"voluptuousness."

(g) It is no metaphor nor fanciful, to describe marriage, as having
for aim and object, the future, *viz.* an ultimate design, of which the
present is but a mean; for it is a foundation laid in the interest
and contemplation of a community that is to be, the now actors
forging, the while, links of a social and civil chain, to be continually added to, varied, renewed, under like conditions, by other
actors yet unborn—actors in successive marriage unions.

Several considerations germane to the topic of marriage here
present themselves, perhaps strictly belonging rather to the task
of legislation or artificial adaptation of laws to a people, than to
jurisprudence. Whether singleness and permanency are intrinsically
of the essence of marriage—or (which is virtually the same), whether, those qualities being so regarded by the majority of civilised
nationalities, excludes polygamists, as well as those temporarily (or for
such time as one or either spouse shall choose) mated with the
other sex, from the juridical class and status of the married, *viz.* on
the ground, that such associations are merely abnormal facts and
eccentric deviations from principles upon which (as those nations
hold) the universal science of Law is based—this paramount consideration is yet among the doubts of the politico-moralist of the
most advanced school. The judicial *dicta* following illustrate the
dilemma and the class of doubts to which this question belongs:—

Lord Brougham—"If there go two things under one and the same
"name in different countries—if that which is called marriage is of
"a different nature in each—there may be some room for holding
"that we are to consider the thing to which the parties have bound
"themselves according to its legal acceptance in the country
"where the obligation was contracted." and "—all that the Courts of
"one country have to determine is, whether or not the thing called
"marriage, that known relation of persons, that relation which those
"Courts are acquainted with, and know how to deal with, has been
"validly contracted in the other country where the parties professed
"to bind themselves." Ld. Robertson—"Although a marriage which
"is contracted according to the *lex loci*, will be valid all the
"world over, and although many of the obligations incident to it
"are left to be regulated solely by the agreement of the parties;
"yet many of the rights, duties, and obligations arising from it,
"are so important to the best interests of morality and good
"government, that the parties have no control over them; but they

" are regulated and enforced by the Public Law, which is imperative
" on all who are domiciled within its jurisdiction, and which
" cannot be controlled or affected by the circumstance, that the
" marriage was celebrated in a country where the Law is different."
" and "—a party who is domiciled here, cannot be permitted to
" import into this country a law peculiar to his own case, and which
" is in opposition to those great and important public laws which
" our legislature has held to be essentially connected with the best
" interests of society." The principle enunciated by this Scottish judge
applies to all obligations and jural results of the alleged marriage
status. In fine, this is one of that class of cases where the status
or condition of an individual, upon which his rights or immuni-
ties depend, is defined or arrived at differently in his foreign domicil
—according to which as a general rule, his personal condition would
be adjudicated, *viz.* by the comity of nations—from the mode
adopted in the country where the litigated question arises. The only
difficulty is, the admission or ascertainment of that status—and how
this is to be done, is regulated by the *lex fori* (the law of the tribunal, *e. g.* in an English Court, the English law). " We could
" not" observes an able living writer on subjects of Public Law
(Westlake), " recognize polygamy in christian Europe or America, on
" the ground that the plural marriages were contracted in Turkey and by
" Turks." Still, in British dependencies, personal laws which
happen to authorise polygamy, are of the *leges fori ;* upon which ground,
between certain British subjects, in those places, the condemned
anti-christian usage, being included and admissible under such
personal laws, is, by christian judges, daily sanctioned and supported. Were the question, however, recognition of slavery, or
of a right of infanticide, or of sanction to marriage between
uterine brother and sister, no construction of the *comitas gentium,*
nor even any general adoption of a class of laws, would effectually
impose those barbarous outrages of humanity, as jural usage, upon
the consciences of our judges. See remarks of an American Court,—
Story, *Conflict of Laws* § 116.

As to the grave and anxious consideration of forced continuance or indissolubility of the marriage bond—whether, like to the
status (usually) of a priest, of one initiated in the mysteries of
free-masonry, and other social or political orders, the seal of
marriage be set once and for ever—or, whether, and when, and
how it be soluble—the jurist can but regard such and analogous
alternatives as accidental results, as dependent upon national will,

juridically important rather as facts, than as they may involve moral (still less juridical) truth or error. The attention of the student is recommended to the comments and reasoning of Bentham, in the Section on 'Divorce' of his *Theory of Legislation*, published by M. Dumont (Hildreth's translation). Compare the musulman laws of divorce, quoted in the text (pa. 111.), with the Mosaic, in the 24th chapter of Deuteronomy.

Another, and certainly no minor consideration is, the disability to contract marriage arising from near consanguinity or of collateral family connection. Apart from any dogmatic view of the degree of nearness (which scarcely furnishes a principle), this is clearly a question of civilisation, *viz.* of physiology, of health, of manners, of domestic or social propriety and good taste ; moreover, as to all but the simplest and nearest blood relationship, it must be always matter of express and exceptional prohibition. More artificial bars to *connubium* (the Roman term for, capacity to marry) may exist, as, difference of race, of religion, of rank.

Other considerations there are ; such as the seat or partition of authority in the marriage union ; also, the age of competency in either sex ; also, the power of parents or superiors either to coerce into marriage or to prohibit any particular marriage, thus making the *consensus* not actual, but vicarious, else treating marriage as a paternal, as a dominical, or as a feudal property, in respect of the personal dependence of either or both of the contractants. It cannot be said, that these considerations necessarily evolve or appertain to any special rules of jural science. They are specific, depending for solution upon the facts and accidents of each people's ethical and intellectual condition ; and, when solved, ranging under general rules and conditions of contract.

Cicero's daughter, Tullia, was betrothed by her father before puberty, and at an earlier age than admitted of rational consent. And we know, that the peoples of Asia view the finding a husband for a female child as essentially a matter of paternal care and choice. That legislation is surely most to be commended, which limits coercive action to the negative prerogative of a *veto*, whilst the child is (even when marriageable) not *sui juris*, and which leaves the moral force of parental influence and filial affection to their natural course. Such rule is implied (even for a mature widow) in the remonstrance of Penelope's suitors :

"Send to her sire thy mother, to be assign'd
"To whoso *in his eyes and hers* shall favour find."

(*k*) It is not (as perhaps may seem) here intended to ignore the immoral and cruel despotism sometimes permitted to the head of a family; for indeed this historical truth supports the view in the text: the Roman *patria potestas*, in its most severe stage, was but an erroneous construction of the natural *imperium* or prerogative of paternity. So, every form of supremacy over the woman is justified by the religious and moral view of her conjugal position taken by any particular people or legislator.

(*i*) Lord Stair, expounding Scottish Law, thus classes "the "rights arising from marriage" *vis.* "1. the *jus mariti*, or conjugal "power of the husband over the wife, her person and goods, and "therewith by consequence the obligement [responsibility] for her "debts; 2. his power, and the wife's security, whereby during the "marriage she cannot oblige herself; 3. the husband's obligement "to entertain the wife, and provide for her after his death; 4. her "interest in his goods and moveable estate at the dissolution of "the marriage."

(*j*) The accidents of varying superstitions, dogmas of priestcraft, diseased fancies of the demoralised or ascetic brain, have often (and with but too much success) caused promulgation of views degrading half of our noble race to mere servitude, or, at best, mere instrumentality; thus ignoring the internal testimony, which each healthy-minded man has in himself, that woman is his helpmate —that, without his helpmate, he is morally crippled. Surely, review of nations and their history warrants our measuring the Reason, the refinement, the taste, the mental elevation of a people by their backward or ready recognition of this truth, of this feeling! Much more readily will it be admitted, that experience of individuals attests the elevation of character consequent upon a just appreciation of the marriage union, upon the subjection of physical to moral ends in the intercourse of man with woman. Well then, nor too emphatically concludes Dr. Whewell (*Elements of Morality*),— "there can be no peace, comfort, tranquillity, or order in a state "of society in which there are not permanent conjugal unions." Jural glossators, as well of the Roman Civil Law as of modern European Law, describe marriage,—'the lawful communion of a man and a woman, who unite themselves, by indissoluble bond, in order to perpetuate their species, for mutual aid in the task and burdens of life, and to share their lot in common.' This, if it be in some degree utopian, as an exclusive practical rule, is at least true and noble in conception, and (what is more to the purpose) it is by no means rarely exemplified, as all may testify—in spite of the universal obstacles, in our moral constitution, to permanent concert of minds and wills, in spite also of the inevitably large majority of ill-assorted conjugal unions.

(k) *Hedaya.*

(l) The first five quotations from Manu (ch. 5, 3, 9); the sixth from Devala.

(m) Mr. Spence narrates, that among the Visigoths,—" the mar-
"riage state was considered most sacred; the intruder on its rights,
"the offending wife and accomplices, might be put to death by
"the husband in the heat of his rage, with impunity, or
"they might be claimed by him as slaves; nor was the enticement
"of the wife any excuse for the adulterer. The Lombards even
"permitted a slave to take immediate vengeance on a freeman.
"The female who was willingly a party to the infidelity of a
"husband was delivered as a slave to the wife, and the suspicion
"of this detested crime authorised the liberal application of
"torture to the slaves who were supposed to have any knowledge
"of its commission." *(An inquiry into the origin of the laws and
political institutions of modern Europe)* See also Tacitus *de moribus
Germanorum*, sec. XVIII. &c. In the Nepalese remedial system,
among *Parbutteahs*, "If a female of the soldier tribes be seduced,
"the husband, with his own hand, kills the seducer, and cuts
"off the nose of the female, and expels her from his house." The
other inhabitants of Nepal "must seek redress from the Courts of
"justice; which, guiding themselves by the custom of these tribes
"prior to the conquest, award to the injured husband a small
"pecuniary compensation, which the injurer is compelled to pay."
(Journal R. As. Soc. vol. 1. Art IV.)

"If" explains Broom, in his English Law Commentaries, "the wife
"be assaulted, maliciously prosecuted, illegally imprisoned, or
"otherwise personally injured by a third party, our law in general
"gives an appropriate remedy to recover damages in the names of
"the husband and wife jointly; whereas, if the beating be so
"great or the injury sustained by the wife be such that the hus-
"band can allege and prove that thereby *consortium amisit* [he has
"lost the conjugal society], he will be entitled to a separate remedy
"against the wrong-doer in his own name."

The ecclesiastical remedy by suit for 'restitution of conjugal rights' is, in substance, a judicial enforcement of the *quasi*-real right described in the text.

(n) The mild tenets of Christianity fully enforce marital superiority, which is thus inculcated by the missionary Paul,—" wives, " submit yourselves unto your own husbands, as unto the Lord! " For the husband is the head of the wife, even as Christ is the " head of the church :—Therefore, as the church is subject unto " Christ, so let the wives be to their own husbands in every thing. " Husbands, love your wives—let every one of you in particular " so love his wife even as himself ; and the wife, see, that she " reverence her husband !"

(o) The feudal indulgence of dower, ' ad sustentationem uxoris et educationem liberorum' (for maintenance of the wife and education of the children)—the wife's 'equity to a settlement' (this being the price of a discretionary remedy), can, neither, be said to infringe the Common-law status of the wife. (The Right of dower may now be barred upon any acquisition of the husband.) The policy of English Equity is in aid and protection of the wife against an unreasonable exercise of marital power. But—" So com- " pletely is a feme-covert disabled from holding or recovering pro- " perty during coverture in her own right, that if a woman who pos- " sesses personal property, marries and settles it upon herself with- " out the intervention of a trustee, the husband is, in law, the " absolute owner of the property. So, the property in wearing " apparel, bought by the wife for herself whilst living with her " husband, out of money settled to her separate use before mar- " riage, and paid to her by the trustees of her settlement, vests " by law in the husband and is liable to be taken in execution " for his debts. And the savings of the wife, whilst separated by " agreement from her husband, out of a weekly sum allowed by " him for her support, may, after her death, be recovered, in an " action for money lent, at his suit, from one to whom, shortly " before her death, they had been disposed of by the wife by way " of gift." BROOM.

(p) YAJNAVALKYA.

(q) In the French Code, enjoyment and participation of rights of property consequent on marriage, vary, within a specified range, as the intending spouses pre-determine. If the 'regime of community' be preferred, no superiority or advantage, even in joint acquisitions, is incident to the marriage union, i. e. in respect of ownership, for the male partner has, as a rule, entire management and control of the common wealth (" le mari administre seul les biens de la " communauté—sans le concours de la femme.") Certain restrictions

are placed on his power of disposition. The widow, or, if the wife
predécease her husband, her legal representatives, may or not elect
to share the common property with its burdens.

This conjugal community or sharing may be modified in various
ways, never however derogating from the marital prerogative,
nor from the surviving wife's maternal tutelage. The French 'dotal
regime' is borrowed from Rome. *Dos* (dower) is the woman's contribution, on marriage, to the *ménage*. The marital stewardship
of this, is very qualified, and his interest is but usufructuary. He
is accountable for the *dos* as well as for all other property of his
wife whatsoever (embraced by the term *paraphernaux*) that may
come to his hands.

(*r*) I extract from the old Scottish Book of laws (*Regiam
Majestatem*) a portion of a curiously quaint exposition of
dowries :—

"This Latin word *Dos*, has twa significations; for it commonlie is called
"and signifies that, quhilk ane frieman gives to his spouse at the kirk-doore
"the time of the mariage. 2. Be the canon law, and civill law, all men
"are oblissed to indow and give ane dowrie to his wife, the time of the mar-
"iage. 3 Quhen ane man indows his wife, either he names the dowrie, or he
"names it nocht. 4. Gif he names it nocht; the third part of all his tenement
"and heritage perteining to him the time of the mariage, is understand to perteine
"to his wife as dowrie. 5. The reasonabill dowrie of ilk wife, is called tierce,
"or third part of the tenement perteining to her husband the time of the
"mariage; quherein he is vest and saised, as of fie and heritage. 6. Gif the
"husband names expreslie the dowrie, to be mair nor the third part of his
"heritage; the dowrie may nocht consist, nor stand in sa great ane quantitie, bot
"it sall be measured conforme to the third part, or les nor the third part. 7.
"Because ane man may give to his wife les then the third parte of his heritage;
"bot he may nocht give mair then the third, in name of dowrie. 8. It happins
"sometime, that ane man quha maries ane wife, hes littel heritage the time of
"the mariage, and thereafter is willing to augment the dowrie with lands con-
"quessed be him, conforme to ane third or les. 9. Bot gif na mention was made
"of conqueis the time quhen the dowrie was named, albeit the husband hes
"littel heritage, and hes conquessed thereafter many lands, the wife may clame
"na mair nor the third of the tenement quhilk perteined to her husband the
"time of the mariage; because she was first content therewith. 10. The samine
"is to be said, quhen ane man haveand na heritage, indowes his wife in silver,
"or other moveabill gudes, and thereafter he purchesses meikill land, or heritage;
"the wife may clame na parte of the saids lands as dowrie. 11. Because it
"is generallie trew, that how meikill it is that is named to ane woman for hir
"dowrie at the kirk-doore, and she be satisfied and stand content therewith; her
"dowrie may never be augmented thereafter, nor she may ever crave nor aske
"any greater dowrie. 12. It is to be understood, that the wife may make na disposi-

U

"tion anent her dowrie in the lifetime of her husband. 13. Because be the
"law, the woman is subject to the power and will of her husband, her dowrie,
"and all her gudes quhilks may perteine to her. 14. And therefore, ane man
"haveand ane wife, in his awin lifetime, may give, sell, or analie, in anie maner
"; as he pleases, his wife's dowrie. 15. And his wife is oblissed in this case, as
"in all other things quhilks are nocht against God, pleasantlie to obey him. 16.
"Moreover, the wife is bound to giue hir consent, and obey her husband, swa
"that gif he selles hir dowrie, and she consent thereto, after his deceis she may
"nocht repete the samine fra the buyer; gif she confes in judgement, or makes
"faith, or is convict that the samine was sauld be her husband, she makand na
"contradiction thereto. 17. After the deceis of the husband, the dowrie of his wife
"named be him, is vaicand, or nocht vaicand. 18. Gif it is vaicand, the wife may
"take possession thereof, and reteine her possession, with consent of the heire
"of the defunct husband. 19. Gif it is nocht vaicand, either ane part thereof
"is vaicand, and ane other parte thereof is nocht vaicand. 20. Gif ane parte
"is vaicand, the wife may take possession thereof in maner foresaid: and con-
"cerning the rest, quhilk is not vaicand, she sall raise a brieve of richt direct
"to hir warant to doe her richt, anent that towne, or plough of land, quhilk
"she clames to perteine to her, as her reasonabill dowrie."—"This Latin word, Dos,
"hes ane secund signification, conforme to the civill law of the Romans: And
"is called that quhilk is given be the woman's friends with her, to the hus-
"band, and commonlie is called *maritagium (or tocher)*."

(s) Thus, although when, in ancient Rome, the wife was allowed
exemption from the *quasi*-dominical control (the *manus*) which
absorbed her civil existence, there was no enacted prohibition to
her transferring, in an impulsive hour, all she had to her partner,
yet, wrote Ulpian—'It is a received observance (*moribus receptum*)
with us, that gifts between husband and wife have no validity.'
Certain exceptions were allowed, which, from their character, were
free from objection, as gift of a place of burial, of a slave in order
to manumission, &c. So, English Law has always protected the
woman, during coverture, against alienations of unsettled realty under
marital influence, and gives every encouragement to trusts having for
object protection of her separate estate against wasteful generosity.

(t) "All children and grand-children who are disobedient to the
"instructions and commands of their fathers, mothers, paternal
"grand-fathers and grand-mothers, or who do not adequately pro-
"vide for their support and sustenance, shall be punishable with
"100 blows. This law shall nevertheless only be understood to
"apply to cases of wilful disobedience of lawful instructions and
"commands, and to cases of wilful neglect of maintenance, on the
"part of such children and grand-children as have the means there-
"of." *Ta Tsing Leu Lee* (Staunton).

" The vital and universally operating principle of the Chinese
" government" (writes Sir Geo. Staunton) " is, the duty of submis-
" sion to parental authority, whether vested in the parents them-
" selves, or in their representatives ; and which, although usually
" described under the pleasing appellation of -filial piety, is much more
" properly to be considered as a general rule of action, than as the
" expression of any particular sentiment of affection. It may easily
" be traced even in the earliest of their records : it is inculcated
" with the greatest force in the writings of the first of their philo-
" sophers and legislators ; it has survived each successive dynasty,
" and all the various changes and revolutions which the State has
" undergone : and it continues to this day powerfully enforced, both
" by positive laws and by public opinion."

(u) Manu tells the *brahmachárí* or young brahman—" a natural
" father is the image of BRAHMA"—" that pain and care, which a
" mother and father undergo in producing and rearing children,
" cannot be compensated in an hundred years. Let every man
" constantly do what may please his parents, and on all occasions
" what may please his spiritual guide.—Due reverence to those
" three is considered as the highest devotion." " As long as those
" three live, so long he must perform no other duty for his own sake ;
" but, delighting in what may conciliate their affections and gratify
" their wishes, he must from day to day assiduously wait on them."
" —every other act is a subordinate duty."

(v) Ortolan apparently admits of no distinction between the
original Roman *potestas* and *dominium* : but he points out how natural
affection and national manners had, before any enactments, softened
and qualified the domestic tyranny. The imperial Constitutions
in the eighth book of the Code (Tit. 47), which are declaratory,
long preceded the legislation of Constantine defining the father's
crime who killed a son ; and they treat the *jus patriæ potestatis*
very much as it is to be found in the French Code.

With regard to the option of abandonment, it would seem that,
invaluable as the *aurasa* son is to a Hindu, there yet are conditions
under which one may be lawfully abandoned : see Colebrooke's anno-
tation *Mitakshara* § 20; also Vas'isht'ha quoted in the *Dattaka
Mimansa* (Sutherland) IV. § 14.

(w) Man is but the instrumental cause of his child's existence—
he exerts a power which he can neither explain, account for, limit,
or regulate. The helplessness of the human infant, the natural
storgē or parental instinct, and the character of aid needed—to

say nothing of the normal example of those beings whom we designate, the irrational creation—are circumstances, which leave but a narrow field for discussion or speculation upon the relation and duties of parentage. They indeed dictate the moral sense and reasonable theory—Nature's code—of parental conduct. Domat eloquently wrote : " The bond of marriage which unites the two " sexes, is followed by that of birth, which binds to the husband " and to the wife, the children who are born of their marriage. " To form this bond it is, God wills, that man shall receive life " from parents, in the lap of a mother, that his birth shall be " the fruit of that mother's suffering and labour, that he shall long " be in a state of weakness, such as needs the fostering aid of " parents, for his subsistence and bringing up. And, as God has made " that birth an instrument to kindle the mutual affection which " so closely unites *him* who begets and gives life to the similitude " of himself, with *him* who receives that life, it gives to parental " love a character graduated to the condition of the children, in " their birth, and in regard to all wants which are the fruits of " that life the parents have conferred, in order to incline them, " through that affection, to the duties of education, teaching, &c. " It gives also to the affection of children a character graduated " to the duties of subjection, of obedience, of gratitude, &c., in " which the boon of ,life involves them--a boon they in so far " hold from the parents, of whom God has willed they should be " born, as that it is certain, without the parents they should not " have had it—which binds the children to give parents all aid " and service in their needs, and above all in those needs attend- " ing the decline of life, and in regard to those weaknesses, infirmi- " ties, and necessities wherein children are able to render to parents " such offices as answer to the early benefits of which they were " recipients. It is in this order of things, from the birth of " children, giving rise to ties between them and the parents, that " lies the foundation of all their duties—duties, whose scope is easily " traceable in their various obligations. Moreover, upon the above " principles depends whatever civil laws may have laid down as to " what comes from the father's power, and as to the reciprocal " obligations of parents and children ; accordingly, these are munici- " pal matters, as are in like manner the rights which laws and " customs confer on fathers for the ruling of their children, for " celebration of their children's marriages, for administering and en- " joying their children's possessions, in respect of the revolt of

"children against what is due to parents, also injurious conduct of
"parents or of children in refusing sustenance, and the like."

A jural division of the period of filial relation into three portions, as we find in Grotius, is superfluous, perhaps fanciful. The
helplessness of childhood scarcely needs argument or illustration
to prove the necessity of dependence and obedience on one side
or of parental guardianship and control on the other. The second
stage—as it were, the twilight before the full dawn of early
manhood—is and must be one governed by purely civil and artificial rules of the parental function and its continuance, as a
safeguard, though not indispensable. In the third stage, *viz.* of
complete adult years, Reason suggests emancipation from the civil
bond of filial subjection, leaving entire, the piety and gratitude of
Nature's code.

(x) *Deuteronomy*, ch. xxi.

Referring to the subject condition of the most favored of sons,
the Christian apostle (a Jew) wrote: "—the heir as long as he is
"a child, differeth nothing from a servant, though he be lord of
"all; but is under tutors and governors, until the time appointed
"of the father."

Whether the accident of pre-existence, of itself, entitles to
pre-eminence, to superior place and respect, to power or influence,
irrespective of capability or intrinsic qualities such as, superior
knowledge, superior moral influence or mental endowment, or title
to gratitude for benefits conferred—is a question somewhat analogous, in character and significance, to one suggested by overween-
ing assumption on the part of those of our fellow men whose
claims to power, rank, or dignity are but civil accidents, *e. g.*
hereditary or sprung from the caprice of kings, &c. Worth is
not necessarily nor invariably denoted by length of life or hoary
experience; yet, Age is Nature's rank, aged men *should* have
earned respect during their passage through the trials of life.
It is no futile nor arbitrary presumption, then, that the fathers
of mankind may claim honor and reverence from their juniors
and successors. "Thou shalt rise up before the hoary head, and
"honour the face of the old man—" (*Leviticus.*)

Moreover, the sentiment is as universal as it is spontaneous.

(y) An able German publicist and Prussian statesman (W.
Humboldt) deprecates and argues against all direct State interference, further than to appoint guardians where parents are remiss,
and extend assistance when they are indigent. His argument

seemingly tends to prove, that children should not be brought up in groups or masses—that education should be individualised, have reference solely to the development of each child or each family and the circumstances surrounding each. See an interesting account of national provisions for education in the American States, and generally, by Kent, *Lec.* xxix. Shrewdly reflected Mr. Laing, when noting the prevalence of good manners among the French people—" It is but reading, writing, reckoning, and the catechism, " after all, that can be taught a people by the most perfect system " of national school education ; and those acquirements would be " dearly bought if they interfere with, or supersede family instruc-" tion and parental example, and admonition in the right and wrong, " in conduct, morals, and manners." (*Notes of a traveller &c.*)

(*z*) So by the *Sheraa*, if a widow have not contracted marriage with another than one nearly related to her first husband, she retains charge of his son, but only till the boy has attained seven years : at that age she must give him up to his appointed or his legal guardian, for education. A daughter is left with her mother until puberty. (See Macnaghten.)

(*aa*) Bell's Principles.

(*bb*) See Sir Edw. Coke's Commentary on the Statute of Merton.

(*cc*) The Mosaic law is :

" A bastard shall not enter into the congregation of the Lord ; " even to their tenth generation shall they not enter into the " congregation of the Lord." (*Deut.* xxiii, 2.)

One according to the dogmas of Hinduism misbegotten, *i. e.* whose conception was a crime in the parents, is thus described ; MANU—" A son begotten through lust on a *Súdrá* by a man of " the priestly class, is even as a corpse though alive, and is thence " called in law a living corpse."

(*dd*) " The word *pindá*" writes Sutherland (*Dattaka Mímánsá*, VI, 10, no.) " signifies either, ' the body', or a ' cake' or ' ball' of food " presented to the *manes* of the deceased: the word *sapindá* there-" fore, may denote either one consanguineally related, or one connected " through an oblation of such funeral cake." In Bengal, however, the latter is invariably the signification ; the double meaning is found in the *Mitakshara.*

(*ee*) ' was.' These modes of filiation are but antiquarian theories or traditional, being now forbidden as unfit for the present degenerate condition of mankind (*Dattaka Mimansa*, I, 64, &c.: see also ' General note' Haughton's edition of Sir William Jones' Manu);

but they illustrate Hindu idiosyncrasies of sonship. The raising up lineage by one of kin to the deceased husband was ordained by the Jewish Law (*Deut.* xxv, 5), and is exemplified in the tale of Boaz' marriage, as told in the book of *Ruth*.

It is the opinion of Biblical scholars, that adoption by the childless was a Jewish practice; *i. e.* taking a stranger into a family, in order to make him a part of it, acknowledging him as son and heir to the estate. (See Horne's *Compendious Introduction &c.*) With respect to the Arabs and to the Mahommedans, see Sale's Koran, ch. xxxiii. no. f.

(*f*) The *Mitakshara* ch. ii, s. 10, § 11, as translated by the learned Colebrooke, seemingly denies to the impotent the privilege or right of adopting: but I am well advised that the doctrine is unquestioned in practice, and that the received translation of the particular passage is rather an adaptation of the text. I annex an extract of a communication from the profound and trustworthy Eshwur Chundra Vidyasagara of Calcutta, *viz.* after acknowledging the general correctness of Colebrooke:

"I should think the following to be the correct rendering of "the passage: 'The specific mention of 'legitimate issue' and "'offspring of the wife' is intended for the exclusion of other "sons'—that is, if the disqualified persons have sons other than "the *aurasa* and *kshetraja*, they will not be entitled to inherit "or share the ancestral property; for, in the case of impotents, &c. "two kinds of sons alone are specified as entitled to allotments."

The learned pundit has also verbally explained to me, that the notion of inconsistency in adoption by an impotent is inapplicable to Hindus, inasmuch as this and all congenital defects are, with them, retribution for sins in a previous stage of existence, and in no wise forestal or remove the obligation of—male lineage ritually perfect. But the impotent's *dattaka* son is, like the father, entitled to maintenance only.

(*gg*) WILHELM VON HUMBOLDT (Coulthard).

(*hh*) HERMANN, *A Manual &c.* (Street).

(*ii*) M. Porcius Cato, addressing the Senate against repeal of the Oppian sumptuary law, said:

"Our ancestors willed that women should not act even in private "affairs but under guidance, that they should be under the *manus* "of parents, of brothers, of husbands. We, as it seems, suffer these "same women to meddle in public affairs, to be amongst us in the "*forum*, in public assemblies, in the *comitia!*" and, "Never with

"safety to our households may female dependence be done away
"with!" (Livii *Hist.* XXXIV, 2.)

The grounds of this distrust *(viz. levitas animi* and *sexûs infirmitas)*
show a similarity of opinion in this matter between the Hindu
Rishis and the early *Patres* of Rome.

(kk) "To females possessed of moral rectitude and mental ca-
"pacity, we grant, on completing 18 years, the capacity of adult
"age—so that they may enjoy, in all matters, precisely the same
"rights as males; provided, that they may not (unless permission
"be decreed) aliene landed estate." *Co.* II, 45, 2, § 1,)

(ll) A musulman can appoint a testamentary guardian. Matrimony and property are the two several purposes of guardianship:
for the first, the legal right, in absence of nomination, is with the
nearest paternal kindred; so, charge of the minor's property is
with the father's *wusee* or with the paternal grandfather or his
wusee, or with the magistrate, *viz.* the State nominee. (Macnaghten).

(mm) The old feudal wardship is not referred to; as it was a
merely arbitrary amd artificial institution. As observed by Chief
Baron Gilbert *(Common Pleas)* "—wardship in the feudal law was of
"another nature, for the guardian had the whole profits in the estate,
"and also the marriage of the infant, which was in order to bring
"him up to arms, and to marry such person, as they thought
"might continue the martial strain, that so the ward might subserve
"the original design of the tenure."

(nn) It follows an injunction to deal righteously with women,
in regard to marriage and dowry, and precedes one for treatment
of orphans quoted *supra* pa. 133.

SECTION VII.

HEIRSHIP, SUCCESSION; TESTAMENTS—*i. e.* JURAL DEVOLUTION OF RIGHTS AND JURAL REPRESENTATION, UPON DEATH: ORIGIN, NECESSITY, AND PROGRESS THEREOF, NATURAL AND CIVIL.

Each man having but a limited period (—the maximum is within easy calculation—) wherein all his bodily faculties and means of enjoying the things of Earth must be exhausted; it may seem idle to give him or suppose him to possess, never-ending relations with those things. It is, in truth, a supposition, a fiction, meaning something else than the words in which the idea is usually clothed may intrinsically convey.

The hereditary or substitutive element in that idea is a natural, a necessary incident or accessory of property, *i. e.* of complete appropriation; it is not merely civil or artificial: the power to transfer and aliene included in that idea, is but a development of the power to use and enjoy; 'disposition' being, as before explained, a mode of enjoyment, and has even been treated as a mode of putting to use.

"The uses of every possession," wrote Aristotle, "are two, both indeed essential, but not in the "same manner; for the one is strictly proper to the "thing, the other not; as a shoe, for instance, may "be either worn or exchanged for something else; "for both these are uses of the shoe; for he who "exchanges a shoe with some man who wants one, "for money, or provisions, uses the shoe as a shoe, "but not according to its proper use; for shoes

v

"are not made to be exchanged." And the illustration applies to every kind and form of disposal, as an exercise of dominion, whether qualified, contingent, gratuitous or otherwise. Still, a use which places the thing used, without at all consuming it, out of the owner's reach or further dealing with, even partially, is not properly so called; the term (or its equivalent) is metaphorically applied: for, it is the Right of property itself, *jus abutendi*—to make away with—the distinctive test of proprietary dominion, that is exercised or used, not the thing, the subject of the Right.

Succession to rights and property upon death, *i. e.* heirship, simply, is, substituted ownership—a substitution essentially distinct from 'alienation' or change in ownership; inasmuch as heirship is to fill up a vacancy, to supply *an* ownership: it imports (intrinsically and in the abstract) a necessary continuation of some personal Right of property, which, but for the scheme of heirship, would fail and lapse, leaving the subject of property, to the extent of the deceased owner's Right therein, derelict. This primary idea and basis of heirship is well illustrated by the familiar maxim in physics, that, Nature abhors a vacuum. In like manner, Law or civil order abhors *i. e.* does not admit of unowned *res* or subjects of property—in other words, does not admit the notion or possibility of 'things' having no relation with 'persons'—within the territorial limit of the State: ownership must be somewhere.

Here then we have the civil origin of heirship, as a general, indefinite necessity. The early development of the idea proceeds uniformly and naturally: as thus—the head of a family (the proprietor) dies—where else can we look for a substituted, a continuing owner, than among the family-group? whether it be, the elder member, or the aggregate of members, either males only, or otherwise. Some uniform contrivance of domestic stewardship or apportionment inevitably offers itself or is adopted. Further, and by an equally natural deduction, it may be said: the dependents upon the deceased citizen's bounty or labour have to be provided for. The relation of those dependents to—their claim upon the left estate of—their late supporter, their head, their cause (if a direct ancestor), could not but be acknowledged by the rudest healthy mind; because *felt* by every father, by every man not alienated from his kind. It is an inevitable adoption of the Law and suggestions of Nature, and is in close civil relationship with family-rights.[a]

MANU—"After the death of the father and the "mother, the brothers being assembled, may divide "among themselves the paternal estate—the eldest "brother may take entire possession of the patri- "mony; and the others may live under him, as "under their father—To the daughters let their "brothers give portions out of their own allotments "respectively—"

Al Korân—"Men ought to have a part of what

"parents and kindred leave—whether it be little
"or whether it be much—And when they who are
"of kin are present at the division, and also the
"orphans, and the poor; distribute thereof unto
"them. A male shall have as much as the share
"of two females—Moreover ye may claim half of
"what your wives shall leave, if they have no issue;
"but if they have issue, then ye shall have the
"fourth part—They also shall have the fourth part
"of what ye shall leave, in case ye have no issue;
"but if ye have issue, then they shall have the
"eighth part—"

"YAJNAVALKYA—"The heirs of a hermit, of a re-
"ligious ascetic, of a professed *brahmachári*, are
"successively, the preceptor, the disciple, and an
"associate dwelling in the same religious retreat."[b]

Genesis—"And Abram said, Lord God! what wilt
"thou give me, seeing I go childless, and the steward
"of my house is this Eliezer of Damascus?—
"Behold! to me thou hast given no seed: and
"lo! one born in my house [Eliezer] is mine heir."

Such is the recognised claim of the 'family,' whether natural *i. e.* of blood, merely social and civil,
or even what may be deemed accidental—of the
home-group, its branches and dependents.

Thus we have reached an important jural principle and landmark, *viz.* that the family, as a rule,
represent a departed owner. But, the details, the
apportioning of that representation, of its benefits
and burdens, scarcely admit of adjustment by any
general formula, nor of reduction to any fixed

standard as a jural principle. Certainly, direct descendants—offspring—have an obvious and (it may well be contended) a paramount claim. This is quaintly indicated in the Roman phrase *sui hæredes*, which may be rendered 'heirs of their own'; it marks an inevitable, inherent interest peculiar to one class of heirs, differing in kind —standing out in relief—from every other claim of succession, one born with the heir, and not an accident or a contingency in the sense that a remote or a collateral heirship is. Yet, that distinction and preference, if even itself definite or well-marked, leads but a short way in designating heirs or classes of heirs. Moreover, within the pale of the peculiar class are doubts and divisions. When, in the order of descent or representation, no *sui hæredes*, no inner and immediate circle of the family are present, where or how a successor is to be ascertained or sought, is not discoverable by the light of any jural dogma or of any general principle, but is a question whereof a solution must be sought—the answer and the fact is in each case a result to be found —in national idiosyncrasy, in the accidents of history (*i. e.* the influence and consequences of such accidents), in what may be termed the special proprietary policy current through any particular legal system. In the same wide field must a clue be sought to the selection or apportionment among immediate descendants that may obtain with any people, *i. e.* whether primogeniture, aggregate succession, exclusion or inferiority on account of sex or of any infirmity; also secondary representation, whether *per stirpes* or *per capita*; &c.—in each case, it is a special and particular, whether or no a purely civil, result.

These propositions are readily illustrated and confirmed by reference to the several sets of canons of inheritance, with their explanation and reasons, in several national codes or systems: the canons and their explanatory bases severally vary, internationally, precisely with the dogmas and moral accidents which in each case govern the national mind, and, therefore, the national legislation—more or less obvious and consistent, more or less in accordance with *a priori* conclusions of what is right and fitting, always a calculable result of manners and historical accident, as are all civil methods and rules.

GAUTAMA[c]—" Let kinsmen allied by the oblation " to ancestors, by family name, and by descent " from the same patriarch, share the heritage—" Such are the *sa-pinda* (same food-oblation) and *saman-odaca* (*samana* same, *udaka* water-oblation), the *sa-culya* (*kula* family or tribe, *ya* born of), and the *sa-gotra* (*gotra* race-founder or patriarch) of the Hindus.

YAJNAVALKYA—" An impotent, an outcast as well " as his son, a cripple, a madman, an idiot, one " blind, one miserably diseased, and such like, are " to be maintained, but do not share in the " inheritance." " The *stridhana* of a wife dying

"without issue, who has been married in one of
"the four forms of marriage called *brahma,* &c.
"belongs to the husband;—should she have been
"married in another form, then her *stridhana* goes
"to her parents."

"It was," writes Hermann, "a fundamental prin-
"ciple in Athenian Law, respecting the succession
"to persons dying intestate, that male descendants,
"or male relatives, always excluded the claims of
"females, who otherwise in point of relationship,
"had an equal or even a nearer right; and this
"was the case with descendants either in a direct
"or only collateral line, except that the right of
"collateral descendants ended with second cousins."

After the strict civil heirship of agnates (—of
which the test was, being traceable to one identical *patria potestas—)* in the *Jus Civile,* came
gentiles. These are described by Cicero: "*Gentiles*
"are, 'they' who have a common name': but not
"this only; 'they who have sprung from *ingenui*'[d]:
"nor does that suffice; 'none of whose ancestors
"have been servile':[d] one incident yet remains;
"'who are under no diminution of *caput*'—"

"By the Roman Law, as it was finally settled
"by the Novels, on the decease of an intestate,
"the descendants, of whatever degree, were called
"to the succession, in exclusion of all other re-
"lations whether ascendants or collaterals, and
"without regard to primogeniture, or preference
"to sex. Where the intestate left no descendants,
"such ascendants as were nearest in degree, male

" or female, paternal or maternal, succeeded to his
" estate, in exclusion of the remote heirs, and
" without any regard to representation; but with
" this exception, that, where the deceased left bro-
" thers and sisters of the whole blood, besides
" ascendants, all succeeded in equal portions *in*
" *capita*; and here, if, besides ascendants, the de-
" ceased left brothers' and sisters' children of the
" whole blood, the children succeeded to their pa-
" rent's share, by representation, *in stirpes*." And
with that system is contrasted the very different
scheme of feudal successions, *viz.*

" Originally fiefs were granted to be held at the
" will of the donor, and were, therefore, resumable
" at his pleasure; then, they were granted for a
" year certain; then, for the life of the grantee;
" then, to such of the sons of the grantee, as the
" donor should appoint, then, all the sons, and in
" default of sons, the grandsons were called to the
" succession of the fief: in the process of time, it
" was opened to the 4th, 5th, 6th, and 7th genera-
" tions, and afterwards, to all the male descendants,
" claiming through males, of the first grantee;
" and at last, was suffered to diverge generally to
" collaterals. But this, as to such collaterals as
" were not lineal heirs of the first donee, was
" effected through the medium of a fiction com-
" pletely and peculiarly feudal. When a person
" took by descent, his brothers, though in the
" collateral line of relationship to him, were in
" the direct course of lineal descent from the ances-

" tor. In proportion as the descent from the
" ancestor was removed, the number of persons
" thus claiming collaterally from the last, and
" lineally from the first taker, was proportionally
" multiplied. In the course of time, the first taking
" ancestor was forgot, and then, it was presumed,
" that, all who could claim collaterally from the
" person last in the seisin of the fee, were of the
" blood of the original donee."(e)

Civil Law invariably (because of necessity) provides for the vacancy caused by death of a citizen,
not merely in respect of his property-rights, but
in all his jural relations—that is, so far as the
necessity or significance of any relation survives
the individual actor. The removal by death of a
father or husband may not call for substitution in
relation to children or wife who are *sui juris;* but,
if the dead citizen were a magistrate, a land-holder,
a military commander, a guardian of minors, his
place, in all or any of those characters, has to be
supplied—here, the functions are the essential,
the individual an accident.

In respect to vacant ownership, it is provided
for in entirety; whether it devolve in the mass
(per universitatem), as it did upon the Roman
hæres; or in fractional proportions, as among Ma-
homedan sharers and residuaries; or, as to one
description, in the mass, and as to another in
fractional shares, as in the English 'real' and
'personal' successions.(f)

W

To be an heir, *i. e.* to be entitled to take and own the property of another when this other shall die, is a conditional Right. Heirship designates a status relation, that is, of family, and is a civil incident of such status. All succession to, or substitutive personation of the dead, other than what may result from family ties or from the disposing power of the late holder, is merely official or political: it is 'succession,' not 'heirship.' For instance, Law may provide for devolution of a crown, and of a dignity, for the permanence of a body-politic (as a college, a board of officials, a council of ministers), for the command of a regiment or of a ship—*i. e.* it may be part of the constitution and of the essence of those several functions and positions, that the contingency of an individual's death effects a specific change in the non-essential quality or accident of a particular individual or individuals being clothed with some duty or some privilege. This sort of functional and arbitrary replacing, obviously differs from descent or heirship of private rights and property, whether by Law, *i. e.* according to a general rule of Law, or, as in each instance planned by the late owner.

The only case in which the meaning and character of heirship could be merged in or confused with official succession, is, where family claims are displaced by universal communism, and where private property therefore, even when transferable *inter vivos*, is but a usufructuary Right, passing, upon death, to a State-nominee, unfettered by any natural obligations, any ties, or wishes of the departed holder. [g]

The power of posthumous alienation—exercised either, by designing a plan of succession to one's self, or, by abstracting something from the property to devolve upon a Law-named successor, for bounty or disposal not contemplated in the general provisions of Law—has been wholly or partially admitted, according as each civil system encouraged or interpreted the alienating and disposing attributes of proprietary dominion. An advanced stage of national progress, material and moral, suggests and justifies removal of all restraint, as affecting private interests, [h] i. e. an entire commercial license in rational disposition of property and rights, whether during the life of the owner or to take effect on death. This has come to be the case with the English. [i]

By the French code: "Acts of liberality, whe-"ther carried out between the living, or by last "will, cannot exceed the half of the donor's pro-"perty, should he leave at his death but one legiti-"mate child; the third, if he leave two children; "the quarter, if he have three or more."

Ancestral wealth is held by a Hindu with qualified ownership.

Mitakshara—"—the grandson has a right of pro-"hibition, if his unseparated father is making a "donation or a sale of effects inherited from the "grandfather—" [j]

The terms 'testament,' 'testamentary,' 'testator,' 'testacy,' 'testate,' 'in-testate,' signifying respectively, the instrument or act, its descriptive quality, the actor, and the condition, in regard to dispositions of property and rights to take effect after death of the disposer, are, like many other terms, in scientific no less than in colloquial language, legacies of Roman jural nomenclature: those terms refer (in the most obvious and reasonable construction of their etymology) to one circumstance and normal requirement of the Roman last will, which has been by no means always adopted in modern systems, viz. testes, attestation, witnessing. However arbitrary the use or application of those terms, they have obtained a recognised and well defined meaning in jural science.

Jurists have usually accounted for laws determining in-testate successions or heirship, by treating each method as a substitution for what the deceased would (normally) have devised as a fitting disposition of his proprietary relations and rights. One (nor the sole) objection to this theory, is, that testamentary devolution of property is not, either historically or by rationally conjectural inference, the precursor of Law-dictated devolution: the legal necessity and rule has always, and necessarily, preceded the arbitrary or discretionary power.

In the absence of any one possessing (according to any particular system) the status or claim of 'heirship,' the unowned res lapse as ofcourse to the common stock; i. e. the State cannot but be heir in the last resort (*ultimus hæres*). Class privileges, not strictly indicative of substitution or succession, may intervene between the two stages—*viz.* 1. private or family devolution, 2. public or State acquisition—where property has no hereditary owner, in the ordinary sense. The 'lord' of the feudal system, and brahmans (to the wealth of brahmans) among Hindus, severally furnish an instance of such intermediate class *quasi*-heirship.

(a) Two marked exemplifications of the views now offered are, the Roman and the Hindu plans of heirship, or devolution of property on death.

In the former polity, the Law designated the *hæres*, upon whom the *persona* should devolve. A provision of the XII. Tables introduced a practice (or gave it declaratory force as a jural faculty) to burden .the *hæres* with dispositions, legacies, as declared by the last will of the defunct citizen. Moreover, ingenious jural devices and legislation protected the natural dependents of a testator from cruel or manifestly unjust disappointment.

Spiritual or dogmatical obligations envelop and hem in the Hindu: they are due to the dead: the Law designates by whom and how they shall be fulfilled ; and, associated with the Right and duty to fulfil them, is, the devolution of ownership, burdened with those obligations, also burdened with the care of females and junior members of the family.

In each of those systems, but one definite juridical idea of succession is traceable, *viz.* that the ownership must be provided for, to the dead man's substance : but, the mode, in each, is governed, prescribed, by the paramount maxims, the dominant motives, the current and regulating principles of the particular social scheme : the variations or differences between one code and the other, are special characteristics of each people, not any variation of jural principles.

(b) It appears from Aulus Gellius, that the Roman Vestal could bequeath and could accept bequests, but could neither succeed as heir by Law nor could any (not appointed by the Vestal's testament) claim as legal heir to her : the public or State succeeded on intestacy. *(l.* 1, *c.* xii.)

(c) quoted in the *Mitakshara*. And MANU—"Now the relation
"of the *sapindas*, or men connected by the oblation cake, ceases
"with the seventh person (or in the sixth degree of ascent or
"descent), and that of *samánôdakas*, or those connected by an
"equal oblation of water, ends only when their births and family
"names are no longer known." In the *Mitakshara*,—"kinsmen sprung
"from a different family, but connected by oblations, are indicated
"by the term *bandhu* [connected, bound to]." *s. g.* sons of the
deceased's father's sister, &c.

(d) "For instance," writes Ortolan, "in determining succession
"to a *cliens* or to a freedman without agnates, resort must have
"been had to the *gens*, immemorially noble (*ingenua*), to which
"he [the *cliens* or the freedman] owed his origin, whose name
"and *sacra* his race had adopted: the nearest member of that
"*gens* was his heir."

(e) These two extracts, comparing the Roman and feudal plans
of succession, are from Butler's Note on Feuds, *Co. Lit.* 191 a.
Grotius remarks, that the various laws of succession, where there
are no children, may be all traced to two sources, *viz.* nearness
in degree of relationship, and reverting of property to the quarter
whence it was derived; and, as an instance of the latter rule, that
the father's wealth should go to the paternal branch, the mother's
to the maternal, *i. e.* on intestacy. He quotes Aristotle; "One
"should rather make suitable return to a benefactor, than bestow
"favors." also from a funeral oration of Lysias; "Return of favors
"received from the dead must be to their children, naturally, who are
"parcel of their parents, and whom the parents, if alive, would
"most desire to benefit." And with respect to self-acquired wealth,
Grotius gives the succession to him whom the deceased must be
supposed to have had most regard for, and whom he assumes to be
the nearest cognate.

(f) The modes and maxims of descent of lands in the English
Common Law are of that special character which arose in the mediæ-
val period of European history, as the last phase of the feudal system; primogeniture, early introduced when feudal sovereigns forbade
any division or splitting of fiefs; preference of males, because of
military services; exclusion of ascendants, as being incompatible
with the constitution of the feud. With respect to adoption of
any such rules in the inferior or agricultural tenures, Sir Martin
Wright (*Law of Tenures*) relates, that it was "in imitation of the
"more honorable tenures." Elsewhere we read, "The progress of

"the right of primogeniture in public, corresponds to the same "progress of it in private successions. Thus in the two first races " of the French monarchs, the succession to the kingdom was "divided among all the sons; and in the earlier periods of the " Saxon history, the same division of the kingdom is frequently observed " to take place."—And, as to collateral succession, "—by practice, with-" out a public ordonnance, it crept into the Law of Great Britain, as " well as into that of other European nations, that not only in "*feudis paternis,* but even in fiefs which a man had purchased him-" self, his collaterals *in infinitum,* as well as his descendants *in* "*infinitum* should -succeed." (DALRYMPLE, *An essay towards a general history of feudal property &c.*)

(*g*) For public policy may impose fetters, as in the English restrictions of, 'perpetuity,' 'superstitious uses,' incapacity of aliens; and the Roman prohibition of gifts between man and wife.

(*h*) This hypothesis supposes all property (not merely fiscal but dominical) to be in the State, either originally, as in the theory of Feuds, or by some accident, as among the Egyptians during the famine narrated *Genesis,* c. XLVII, v. 19 &c. It is related of the Samoans, a Polynesian tribe:

" The titles of the heads of families are not hereditary. The " son may succeed to the title which his father had, but it may "be given to an uncle, or a cousin, and sometimes the son is " passed over, and the title given, by common consent, to a per-" fect stranger, merely for the sake of drawing him in, to increase "the numerical strength of the family.—The land belonging to " each family is well known, and the person who, for the time " being, holds the title of the family head, has the right to " dispose of it. Although . the power of selling land, and doing " other things of importance affecting all the members of the fa-" mily, is vested in the titled head of the family, yet the said res-" ponsible party dare not do any thing without formally consulting " all concerned. Were he to persist in attempting to do otherwise, " they would take his title from him, and give it to another. The " members of a family can thus take the title from their head, and " heads of families can unite and take the title from their chief, " and give it to his brother, or .uncle, or some other member of the " chief family, who, they think, will act more in accordance with " their wishes." (TURNER, *Nineteen years in Polynesia*)

(*i*) From *Magna Charta* it is apparent, that English Common Law protected the claim of the widow and children to a 'reasonable portion' of personalty. And, accordingly, in the Register of old writs are found the king's writs (*i. e.* commands) on behalf of the widow and of the sons and daughters, against the executor of the proprietor's testament. This *was* the custom of the realm of England; one third only could pass under a last will.

In Scotland the '*jus relictæ*,' 'Dead's part,' and 'Legitim,' are (as much else in Scottish jurisprudence) a modernised edition of the great prototype born and matured on The Seven Hills.

Chief Baron Gilbert gives the following reasons why, under the original feudal law of England, landed estates did not ordinarily pass by last will—"A feud was at first no more than the Right "which the vassal had, to take the profits of his lord's lands, "rendering unto him such feudal duties and services as belong "to military tenure; so that the tenant had only the use of the "land, and the property (*dominium*) still continued in the lord—on "the death of the tenant, the land lay empty and fell into the "lord's hands, and the taking it out of the lord's hands was called "*relevium* [when it devolved upon the natural heir as the lord's "ward, and burdened with the widow's thirds or dower,] which "was in the nature of a new purchase——Besides, this way of "conveyance [by last will] wanted that solemnity, which the feu- "dists thought necessary to establish in transferring lands, that if "at any time a dispute should arise, it might be the easier deter- "mined by the *pares comitatûs* [tenants of the district], who were "witnesses to that notorious and public manner of conveying by "livery—"

(*j*) Latitude of construction among glossators and pundits, and the free commercial tendencies of English Law, have combined to weaken and modify (if not repeal) in Bengal, the doctrine, that, "—ownership "of father and son is co-equal in the acquisitions of the grand- "father—" (YAJNAVALKYA).

SECTION VIII.

'Title' *(titulus)* is a word used by jurists, somewhat ambiguously, as indicating the signs or evidence *(indicia)*, by or through which any of the jural faculties called 'rights' are known to exist, when to be presumed, when proved. A Right may be known and apparent in its exercise, or usually so; *i. e.* the fact that a particular jural power and faculty—one of the jural class, rights, is held by a particular man : but, should it be required to know, to ascertain, whether that man is the legal and the real as well as the *de facto* or the apparent holder of the faculty he is exercising and putting to use, or further, how and when he came by it—then, the one simple apparent fact, of the Right being exercised, does not suffice—inasmuch as, without Right, every faculty of a proprietor may *de facto* be exercised. Again, one without power to enjoy, to use, to dispose of, or deal with, a particular *res* or a particular Right, may yet be owner of, and, in legal theory, even holder of that very *res*, of that very Right. It follows that, the real Right-owner may have to assert and prove his Right against a *pseudo-*holder. So, one who exercises (acting as the legal holder of) a Right, may have to vindicate his conduct, *i. e.* to furnish proof, that the as-

x

sumed Right belongs to him, and should be legally adjudicated to be his, *de jure* as well as *de facto*.

Full information—other facts—must be sought for, *viz.* such facts, affirmative and negative, as, taken together, warrant and support the inference, that he who exercises the faculty is what he seems and assumes to be, *viz.* jural holder of the Right, or *vice versâ*, that the ousted claimant is entitled to displace the holder and pretender. That information, whether it consist of one or of several facts, if it affirm the Right, is a title. Thus explained, title or manifestation of Right, is a jural edifice, built up, constructed of facts, the absence of any one of which would endanger its stability; each of those facts being weighed and measured and arranged by a legal standard.

A title to property, exhibits, as in a mirror, the continual existence or progress (may-be the occasional suspense, and revival) of an estate or interest, under one or more, various or single, modes and phases of enjoyment, of devolution, either from its first creation as a property or Right, or during such period as the Law (to which it is subject) permits the history of Rights of that class to be inquisitorially sifted and raked up: and a title, if not a complete shield against all opponents or claimants, from whatever quarter, is a contradiction—is at all events not what it should be, and assumes to be—possibly a good imitation, perhaps a shadow, not reality. We hear of, a holding title, a marketable title, a *primâ facie* title, a safe title, a defeasible title, a weak title—qualifications, imperfectly indicating different stages, efforts, or modes of proof—of vindication and manifestation of Right. It therefore follows, that, 1. a title necessarily includes the mode and cause of the immediate, the present holder of the Right enquired about, becoming such holder, as by sale, gift, succession—this fact is, as it were, the roof and completion of that jural edifice which title should be; and, 2. what is a title, what its ingredients and requirements, depends solely (as we have seen the essentials of a contract do,) upon the special rules and provisions of each law-scheme. For what length of time the history of property and ownership must be traced and verified to constitute a title—what modes of devolution, of alienation, of acquisition, are links of Right and therefore of title—what are impediments, burdens, restrictions, in attainment or enjoyment of rights and how removable—such are enquiries which must be variously answered, according as the Right claimed and of which the title is in question, is under English, or Indian, or French, or other specific municipal system.

"*Tituli,*" wrote the jurist Vinnius, "are the "causes from which *res* are severally acquired." And he gives as instances of title; "one has "bought something, or something has been made "a gift or bequeathed to him, who therefore af-"firms that he holds upon such title (*titulus*)."

—elsewhere, "—he who holds against *jus* (*injusté*),
"that is, without *titulus*—" and "—that posses-
"sion which is *injusta*, for want of *titulus*, is to
"be accounted honest because of the intent of the
"*dominus* who transferred it". And, in defining
mere, untechnical, or natural possession, he says,
it is, "that possession which one has without
"*titulus*, or consciousness of being the *dominus*,
"and is therefore put in opposition to civil pos-
"session."—And, "—they who are not owners, al-
"though they possess as well in a civil sense as
"honestly, also under a rightful *titulus*, are yet
"not to be described as possessing in full pro-
"perty (*pleno jure possedere*)."

A later modern expositor of the Roman Civil
Law (Warnkœnig) thus defines *justus titulus*,—
"whenever one has got possession from such *causa*
"as would have conferred ownership of the thing,
"had not some defect crept in (—wherefore *titulus*
"is at this day defined 'a *causa* capable of trans-
"ferring ownership,' or 'a proceeding translative
"of ownership', though defective—), as if you buy,
"and take delivery, from one who is not owner,
"but whom you thought to be owner."

Now it seems, that in the above extracts, *titulus* or 'title' is used in two senses, *viz.* 1. a lawful mode or cause of acquisition, *e. g.* purchase
and sale, gift; 2. the Right, or jural claim to have
and hold, in the complete sense above explained
as what 'title' strictly is. 'Just cause' is the
Roman Civil-Law phrase for the first sense or

idea of 'title:' the second is little else than a paraphrase of Right, or (perhaps more accurately) an
authoritative, because a logical, assertion of Right.
For, a Right is a result. [a]

We have seen that occupation is the origin of
property, *i. e.* of rights in or over or in respect
of any material not before appropriated. Such
a derivation of jural rights is a necessary theory
and postulate whence to deduce and whereon to
erect a proprietary system. Now, although in fact,
under no scheme of laws can *res* be ownerless, yet,
they may be abandoned, they may be unclaimed,
they may be usurped, they may be so carelessly
owned that a stranger can deal with and use them
unmolested and hand them over, as owner, to a
purchaser: moreover, the *indicia* of jural ownership (proofs of title) may be lost, and no longer
reliably traceable. Such instances simulate the
primitive condition of property, that is to say, the
taker and effective holder who desires to hold
on must be allowed to hold, as owner. It is
rational that the nation, the State, should so
construe and allow the condition of such *res* to
be. Again, where there is usurpation or unauthorised enjoyment of another's property; the proprietor looking on the while, tacitly acquiescing
or not adopting any jural mode of remedy or claim
—in such case, the omission of the owner to act, is
certainly not a *titulus* nor a technical *justa causa*
of enjoyment; yet, it is not irrational nor does it

offend the moral sense, that a limit of time should
be fixed, beyond which such careless or dogged
acquiescence should have a jural meaning and
construction put upon it, so as to operate, if not
positively and in a general sense as a forfeiture,
yet as a transfer to the actual and active holder.
And thus it is, the owner of any Right or
proprietary interest always suffers, at his peril, his
advantage of ownership to be dormant. Law does
not favour usurpers, neither does persistence in or
repetition of wrong engender civil right: but civil
benefits and civil remedies, alike, can be available
to those only whose conduct evinces some sense
of their existence and of their value. It may
well be held, that long pertinacious indifference to
the engrossing by strangers of one's possessions
and special interests, is a social offence, and properly visited with forfeiture: it is insensibility to
the worth, to the very existence of civil order;
and a reckless substitution of that primitive state
of things when mere occupancy was Right. Such
penal result of a proprietor's crass neglect, is sha-
dowed in the law-maxim, 'Laws aid the wary, not
the sleeping.' Moreover, such conduct is a premi-
um to disorder, confusion, and spoliation.

Hence it has come about, that "whoso has
"within human memory been in continual posses-
"sion of any thing or continually exercising some
"Right, on that very ground is assumed to have
"legitimately acquired it.—Proof of a prescription
"of this sort is properly had from testimony, viz.

" of those who assert that they have always so·
" seen the matter, nor have they heard from their
" ancestors of its being otherwise."[b] Such is the
antiquity of observance and repute quaintly expressed in English probatory science, 'from time whereof
the memory of man runneth not to the contrary.'

But law-framers have not left so signal a landmark of property and order as that established
(rather, which develops itself) in the above reasoning, to be discovered or ascertained by reasoning
and inference merely. We find arbitrary periods
defined for growth of rights out of mere enjoyment without a *titulus*—for loss of rights by reason
of their being negatively or passively abandoned.

Of this legislation[c] the Roman *usucapio* is the
exemplar and starting point. The term translated
is, use-acquirement; and it is thus vindicated and
described in the 'Digest' or 'Pandects':—

" *Usucapio* was introduced for the public good,
" *viz.* lest ownership of sundry things be left un-
" certain for a long time and often for ever: seeing
" that a fixed period would suffice for the diligence
" of owners." (GAIUS) " *Usucapio* is, the obtaining
" ownership through continued possession for a law-
" defined term." (MODESTINUS)

The generic name for this kind of arbitrary
acquisition and loss of proprietary Right, in
jural science, is, Prescription—it is prescriptive. [d]
The 'law-defined term' has varied considerably
at different epochs and with different peoples;
nor has it been measured merely by the obvious

requirements of reason, or of moral presumption: this is apparent in its earliest and latest instances.

Rome's XII. Tables fixed two years as the period within which legal measures must be taken to assert title to land against an intruder; and but one year for moveables. The Indian limitation law of 1859 stays claims for "any interest in immoveable property" after 12 years—and "for damages for injury to the person and personal property," after one year.

The subject of this last limitation, *viz.* claim to damages or compensation for injury, comes under the same general category, prescriptive title: for, as well put by professor Bell:—

'Prescription is negative or positive. 1. The long abstinence of a creditor from demanding fulfilment of a right or obligation is, on account of the danger of demands upon false evidence, of the probability of payment and loss of documents, of the equity of discouraging forgotten debts, and of the disfavour to one guilty of such negligence, held to be evidence of payment, or of a discharge or abandonment of the obligation; under the name of 'negative prescription.' 2. The 'positive' is the application of this principle to the fortification of a title to land—' [c]

The same writer observes (and his remark has a general import and significance, although made in regard to the Law of Scotland) '—there is no law introducing negative prescription, or any length of abandonment, as an extinction of property. It is

by positive prescription alone that a right of property can be established, however long the true proprietor may have neglected his right. And so the
negative prescription is insufficient to extinguish
any right or claim of property, unless there be an
opposite right in the course of being confirmed at
the same time.' This is true universally. Although civil Law cannot but assign a limit to
doubt and suspense between claimants of property
and rights, it nowhere inflicts forfeiture to the
State of simply neglected interests, as merely
derelict and seized therefore (like to heir-less
property), for common use. There must, in such
case, be a private occupier; some particular de-
scribable holder of the Right, either body-politic,
or body natural; it may be, the holder does not
take by originally effective title, but that he is
one, in whose favor a positive prescriptive title
grows, according to the special provisions of a particular jural scheme and system. Private ownership, as such, must exist somewhere, wherever there
has not been, either voluntary, positive abandonment, or dedication to public use, by the owner—
forfeiture for crime, to the State—or, absolute
defect of representation, upon the owner's death.
It is therefore only on contest of claimants, that
any question of prescription or use-acquirement can
arise. (*p*)

I take from the jurist Thibaut, a few axioms
relative to this head. 'Prescription,' which are of
general application, and which follow in due course.

z

from what has been premised: *viz.* '1. There can be no legal, definite prescription, whether to acquire or extinguish, without some express law. For, conclusions drawn by analogy are inadmissible on account of the singular [*i. e.* special, arbitrary] nature of the provisions relating to this matter— 2. It is requisite that there be a continuous un-interrupted enjoyment of the positive or negative right prescribed for, and the right must be exer-cised by a person claiming it as his own——3. It is requisite that the appointed period of time should have expired——4. The thing must be one to which the doctrines of prescription are ap-plicable [a description of excluded things are given, as goods stolen or forcibly taken, &c.] 5. It is necessary that he who is to lose by prescription should have been legally capable of asserting his right——consequently time does not run if there be no tribunal to which to resort.'

"Prescription", wrote Lord Stair in his 'Institu-tions', "altho' it be by positive law, founded upon "utility more than equity, the introduction whereof "the Romans ascribed to themselves, yet hath it "been since received by most nations; but not "so as to be counted amongst the laws of na-"tions; because it is not the same, but different "in diverse nations, as to the matter, manner, "and time of it——"

In a judgment of an American Court, which as-serts the several Right of each State in the Union to enforce its own bar of limitation, it is observed:

" Prescription is a thing of policy, growing out of
" the experience of its necessity; and the time
" after which suits or actions shall be barred, has
" been, from a remote antiquity, fixed by every na-
" tion, in virtue of that sovereignty by which it
" exercises its legislation for all persons and pro-
" perty within its jurisdiction." (g)

(a) I am disposed to hold, that the word 'title' has never acquired among jurists a scientific or technical meaning: but that, as a colloquial synonyme or name (—for title is etymologically, what any thing is called, nomenclature—)it has the significations noted in the text; and in the English jural art 'conveyancing,' the word has a standard, perhaps a technical meaning. Austin considered the strict and proper sense of 'title' to be, all mediate or interven- ing and investitive facts, through or by aid of which Law indicates the person entitled to property or rights—as distinct from the inference or fiat of Law which gives value to those facts; conclud- ing; "In short, wherever the law confers a right, *not* on a specific "person as being such, the law of necessity confers the right "through the intervention of a title. For, by the supposition, " the person entitled is not determined by the law through any " mark specifically peculiar to himself. And if the right were not "annexed to a title, it follows that the person designed to take " it could not be determined by the law at all."

But it may be said, each of the English statutes which respec- tively conferred (by legalising a crown grant of) 'Blenheim' upon Marlborough, and 'Strathfieldsaye' upon Wellington, was both a law and an 'investitive fact'—a title deed. So, the Right of distant kinsmen or of representative heirs *per stirpes* to a succession, arises from removal, by death, of those nearer heirs who intervened, which removals therefore seem investitive facts. Austin admits, in regard to this term, title, that, in a "large and loose significa- " tion—it is applicable to any fact by which a person is invested " with a right: it is applicable to a law or command which con- " fers a right immediately, as well as to an intervening fact through "which a law or command confers a right mediately."

In some sort, every title is a mere deduction of Law; for, as a contract is a *vinculum* attached by Law (*i. e.* some particular jural system), to certain private acts or conduct; so, a proprietary Right is the result of legal inferences—in each instance a fiat of Law. Although a Right of property (or rather proof of one) is and must be a compound of acts and facts (in the colloquial and ordinary sense) with Law-doctrine; it is this, viz. the rule and dogma, which alone gives the acts or facts legal significance: e. g. the owner of a field puts a stranger in corporal possession of the field by abandoning it to him and his servants, by at the same time delivering to him a written declaration, or by evincing in other modes his intent to transfer the field in full property. Now, those are, undoubtedly, investitive facts; but, whether they are, or not, a title, is pure law-doctrine, varying with the specialties of each system, viz. whether they are, an English feoffment, an ancient Roman *mancipatio*, a mussulman *bye-bil-wufa*, &c.; and the omission of some seemingly insignificant form, as, a signature, a pretended weighment of a pretended price, some formal words oral or written, &c. may render the supposed investitive facts wholly inoperative as a 'title'.

Further, mere proof of the immediate cause, viz. the proceeding (how legally effective soever) of transfer from the late holder, must frequently be but an imperfect manifestation of a title, in the sense of proved ownership; inasmuch as that proceeding cannot intrinsically, *primâ facie*, represent or manifest more than the will of the immediate actors—certainly may not imply exclusive property or power of transfer in the late holder: e. g. if a Hindu childless widow make over, by formal valid acts, land of which she is apparently complete owner, the recipient's 'title', in order to be available, to be valuable, to have any strength or meaning (after the widow donor's death) against the husband's heir, must obviously include proof of the estate being *stree-dhon*, so as to exclude the possibility of its having come to the woman on her husband's death, by descent; nor would that ordinarily suffice, for the bestower of the land in *stree-dhon*, might or might not have had right of disposal.

(b) from Makeldey's *Systema juris Romani hodie usitati* (Hindenburg).

(c) European legislation is here referred to. The Sastras furnish most important and interesting collateral illustration of this necessary phase of positive Law: see Yájnavalkya, Bk. ii, al. 24; and the notes to Röer and Montriou's translation.

(d) These terms are merely arbitrary and artificial, drawn from the old Roman formulary, viz. when the Prætor permitted certain long possessions, not coming within *usucapio* (which therefore did not constitute an affirmative title), to be a good objection in resistance of the owner's suit. The objection was præ-scribed, written over the *intentio* (specification of the legal title to relief), as a preliminary bar to the hearing; the juridical meaning of 'prescription' has outstripped and superseded its early formal significance.

(e) In English Common Law, the term 'prescription' is confined to presumption, from long use, of a *titulus* (as, a lost deed of grant) to such rights connected with land as do not admit of continual positive possession, but are usually curtailments of the dominion of a possessor, *e. g.* a way, non-obstruction of light, pasturage, &c.; which therefore (to speak technically,) lie in grant, and which can be seized by suit only. It is thus put in the books:—'Nothing can be prescribed for, that cannot at this day be raised by grant; for the law allows prescriptions only in supply of the loss of a grant. Ancient grants happen to be lost many times, and it would be hard that no title could be made to things that are in grant, but by shewing of a grant. Therefore upon usage *temps dont*, &c. [*i. e.* 'from time whereof the memory of man runneth not to the contrary'] the law presumes a grant, and a lawful beginning, and allows such usage for a good title; but still it is but in supply of the loss of a grant; and therefore for such things as can have no lawful beginning, nor be created at this day by any manner of grant, or reservation, or deed that can be supposed, no prescription is good.' (Vin. Ab. *Prescription* U.)

In the English system, the term is inapplicable to that which admits of physical custody; this fact being in itself always presumptive of Right, until met in some way and explained. Further, Lord St. Leonards, in his 'Vendors and Purchasers' lays down,— "a title without title-deeds is not one which can be accepted with- "out satisfactory proof that there has been such a long uninter- "rupted possession, enjoyment, and dealing with the property as " to afford a reasonable presumption that there is an absolute "title in fee-simple. But with such proof, a purchaser may be "compelled to take such a title. Of course there are many good "titles of which the origin cannot be shown by any deed or will." So that, naked possession may furnish a critically efficient, as well as a holding claim, Right, and *titulus*.

Kant well explains the intrinsic and logical character of this kind of title and Right, *viz.* a dispensation, by law, of the ordinary necessity for proof and of any specific jural act, as a claim to the recognition and sanctions of Law. He says: '—it is absurd to allege, that an injustice may gradually become a Right by the mere fact of its having lasted long. Use (long continued) supposes Right to the thing [used], far from use being taken as a ground of Right. Consequently, *usucapio*, as acquisition of something by long use, is a contradictory idea. Prescription of claims, as a means of retention [which may be paraphrased 'title to hold'], is not less contradictory, yet furnishing a different idea from the preceding, as respects the argument of appropriation: for it is a negative principle, that is to say, [on the one side] entire non-use of a Right—such non-use as excludes what is needful to assert possession, such as stands for the jural act, relinquishment of Right; and, [on the other side] an exercise of Right in relation to some one else, with a view to shut him out from all claim (by *præscriptio*), and to acquire, by that means, the very subject of his claim: here is contradiction.'

Prescriptive doctrine is concisely summed up by Paulus, in the Digest:—'Age is accounted for a law.'

The Sastras and their glosses, in this as in other instances, evince the aptitude of the Hindu mind (anciently as now) for comprehension and expression of abstract truth: they contain much accurate delineation of juridical principles.

"Where possession *(sambhoga)* is apparent, but not title *(agama)*; "there, title is proof, not possession. This is a settled rule." (MANU, ch. VIII, sl. 200.)

Kulluka Bhutta's comment upon this text is;—'Where there is *sambhoga*, but no *agama*, such as purchase and the like, the proof is the *agama* or getting by the first holder, not *bhoga*.'

Note, he says the 'first' holder, *i. e.*, primitive or first acquirer traceable.

"Title *(agama)* is stronger than possession *(bhoga)*; unless where "this has been continuous, from ancestors. But where there is no "possession at all, title has no strength." (YAJNAVALKYA, BK. II, sl. 27.)

Upon this text the comments of the Mitakshara are logical and significant. It must be premised, that the Sanscrit *sumbhoga* and *bhoga*, alike import 'enjoying', 'being in possession'; *agama* signifies the *causa*, *titulus*, upon which possession is had; *swa-twa* is, the abstract Right.

The Mitakshara——'Acceptance, purchase, and the like, which are the causes of *swatwa*, are, each of them, an *agama*; and the same is stronger than *bhoga*, since, as an index of *swatwa*, *bhoga* is dependent on *agama*. As says Narada—*Bhoga* becomes proof, when it is backed by a perfect *agama*. When the *agama* is defective, *bhoga* cannot be received as proof.—Nor can mere *bhoga* be evidence of *swatwa*, since one may enjoy what belongs to others, by wrongful appropriation; therefore it is declared:—He who asserts *bhoga* alone, without mention of *agama*, should be considered as a thief, because of his urging *bhoga* merely as a pretext.—Wherefore, the text signifies, that *bhoga* together with *agama* is proof; also when it [*bhoga*] is long, uninterrupted, unchallenged or un-opposed, and not concealed from the opposite party. Those five qualifications must there be in *bhoga* in order to make it proof. The latter part of the text, *viz.* " But where there is no *bhoga*, &c." is thus explained. If it be an uninterrupted *bhoga* from time immemorial, it may be admitted as proof without any reference to *agama*—not that there is no regard at all to the existence of *agama;* but that it is of no moment whether *agama* be in fact known or not, since the existence of *agama* is presumed from the *bhoga* itself. Thus, the first part of the half sloka refers to time within memory, and the second part to what is immemorial. Consequently, the substance of the law is this; within time of memory, *bhoga* must have regard to *agama* being ascertained, in order to be proof; for it might easily be ascertained whether there had been any *agama* or not: while, beyond that time, an uninterrupted *bhoga* is of itself proof, without the least reference to *agama*, since it is not possible to ascertain whether there was *agama* or not. By ' time within memory' is meant a century, as the Vedas say, " Man's term of life is one hundred years." Thus, if *bhoga* be continuous for a hundred years, without opposition from, and in the sight of, the other party; and if it be not certain that no *agama* existed, then *bhoga* is taken as an' unfailing index of *agama*, and therefore as indicative of *swatwa*. But even in the case of time immemorial, *bhoga* is no proof, if there be traditionary evidence of there having been no *agama*.' And,—' Not even a hundred *bhogas* can constitute *swatwa*, if there be really no *agama*.'

Elsewhere, the Mitakshara, in explanation of slokas of Yájnavalkya that distinguish the position and holding title of an original intruder upon another's ownership from that of the intruder's descendants (Bk. ii, sl. 27 &c.), says: 'He who effected *agama* of land and the like, if challenged—whence is thy land, &c. ?—is to prove that *agama* (such as gift and the like), by documents, &c. By this it is signified, that the first holder, when unable to prove *agama*, is to be punished. But his son is required to prove, not *agama*, but simply an uninterrupted, unchallenged, and overt *bhoga:* that is, the second is to be punished in case he be unable to prove, not *agama*, but complete *bhoga.* Again, the son of the latter, that is, the third, is to prove, neither *agama* nor complete *bhoga*, but simply continued *bhoga:* by which is signified, that, the third is to be punished in case he be unable to prove, not *agama* nor complete *bhoga*, but only a continued *bhoga.* The reason of all this is, that, as regards the 2nd. and the 3rd., only *bhoga* is material; further, that though material for the 2nd., it is more material for the 3rd.: and the substance and purport is, that, when *agama* is not proved, the suit is lost equally with all three, but there is a difference with regard to punishment. As it is said—He who effected the *agama* is punishable, if he cannot prove it; not his son, nor his son's son: yet, *bhoga* is forfeited [in the absence of such proof] even by the two last.

Thus we have, in venerable and independent Hindu records of jural analysis, the correlative but distinct ideas clearly connected and enunciated, of, 1. actual having or enjoyment; 2. cause, title and ground of having; 3. the Right. To which may be added, 4. the variation between possession, adverse to a dormant claim, as it is original or devolved. According to the Mitakshara, as appears from the above extracts, the difference is not in proof or sufficiency of title, but in the penal responsibility of possessors. The equity of the case has been otherwise dealt with: the following is from a standard authority in English jurisprudence (anterior to existing limitation procedure and modes of claim to realty).

"The different degrees of title which a person dispossessing ano-
"ther of his lands acquires in them in the eye of the law (inde-
"pendently of any anterior right), according to the length of time
"and other circumstances which intervene from the time such dis-
"possession is made, form different degrees of presumption in favor of
"the title of the dispossessor; and in proportion as that presump-
"tion increases, his title is strengthened; the modes by which the
"possession may be recovered vary; and more, or rather different
"proof is required from the person dispossessed, to establish his
"title to recover. Thus, if A. is disseised by B., while the posses-
"sion continues in B. it is a mere naked possession, unsupport-
"ed by any right, and A. may restore his possession, and put
"a total end to the possession of B. by an entry on the lands,

" without any previous action : if B. dies, the possession descends
"on the heir by act of law. In this case the heir comes to the
"land by a lawful title, and acquires in the eye of law an ap-
"parent right of possession ; which is so far good against the per-
"son disseised, that he has lost his right to recover the posses-
"sion by entry, and can only recover it by an action at law. The
"actions used in these cases are called possessory actions, and
"the original writs by which the proceedings upon them are institut-
"ed, are called writs of entry. But if A. permits the possession to
"be withheld from him beyond a certain period of time without
"claiming it, or suffers judgment in a possessory action to be given
"against him by default, or upon the merits ; in all these cases, B.'s
"title in the eye of the law is strengthened, and A. can no longer re-
"cover by a possessory action, and his only remedy then is by an
"action on the right. These last actions are called droiturel actions,
"in contradistinction to possessory actions. They are the ultimate
"resource of the person disseised ; so that if he fails to bring his
"writ of right within the time limited for the bringing of such
"writs, he is remediless and the title of the dispossessor is complete."

(Co. Lit. Butler's notes.)

The importance of 'possession' as a jural fact, irrespective of
valid claim, inevitably leads to unscrupulous, violent and successful effort to change the status, in that respect, of concurrent
claimants. Hence the Roman interdict *unde vi*, to restore, summa-
rily, forcibly-wrested possession; which has analogies and supplements in modern codes. (See Dr. Sullivan's account of the introduction of the English 'assize of novel disseisin,' *Lec.* 31.) Besides,
an actual possessor may of-course exercise the Right of private
coercive resistance (*supra* p. 44) to violence. Enacted law, legislation, can alone create the artificial bar or title of *usucapio* and
its supplement *præscriptio*, in the Roman sense ; generally known
in English Law as 'limitation' *i. e.* a law-defined limit to an
excluded owner's remedy : and which imposition of a limit must
always create, indirectly, a positive title.

(*f*) Thus Coke accounts for wrecked property vesting in the
English crown from "two main maxims of the Common Law ;
"First, that the property of all goods whatsoever must be in some
"person. Secondly, that such goods as *no subject can claim any
"property in* do belong to the king by his prerogative, as trea-
"sure-trove, strays, wreck of the sea, and others—" (2d. Inst. 167*b*)

(*g*) See Story *Conflict of Laws* § 582a no.*.

SECTION IX.

In the last section, possession or 'having' (a homely but effective synonyme) has been dealt with in respect of its relation with title, in its growth and progression, *viz.* from an imperfect, scarcely definable notion of present and vague (because uncertain, fluctuating,) benefit—a jural minimum or point—to an enlarged, substantial jural entity and Right. In this view, every possession, with intent and semblance of owning, has an intrinsic as well as a comparative civil value: the benefit of 'having' rolls on, gathering size and strength, until it reaches and stands (in idea and definition) side by side, as though twin brother, with that other *dominium* formally initiated, which needs not to grow or to improve, because born perfect and full sized. All-important also is possession, irrespective of growth and progress, as an obvious index of *dominium*, which it always represents, presumptively. Possession and *dominium* are alike movable, passing from hand to hand; the absolute type or test of the latter being 'title,' of which, as has been shewn, the lowest significance is, a cause and method of transit, as, sale, gift, exchange. *Dominium*, as a rule, includes or implies disposing power, the faculty of aliening (supra, p. 60); and the term *dominium* or ownership, although specially and properly applicable to full property as above defined (pa. 60), is also applied to every distinct, even fractional jural faculty and Right.

There is scarcely a more difficult problem of jural science than this head of alienation, that is, explanation and analysis of the jural cause and act by which is effected, out of which arises, complete transfer of a Right. A formally pronounced resolve, a mental and express abandonment of the Right, in favor of some other qualified to hold and own that Right, reciprocated by this other one's pronounced acceptance; as—

I, A.B. make over to you C.D. my Right, z, and henceforth z is the Right of you C.D; with a response, I, C.D. accept the transfer and declare myself proprietor of z—

might seem, under all circumstances, to suffice. Yet, this formula can be but an expression of concurrent wills, a convention. Now, alienation—in that it is voluntary and inter-personal, an act of reciprocity, a result or product of distinct volitions—always includes convention, usually jural contract: convention is the basis, the antecedent and inchoate step in all alienation proper; by which is meant, other than the mere operation of death-succession or of judicial sanctions. It follows, that the jural fact 'alienation,' must be a step beyond, something more than, the jural fact 'contract;' seeing that this is but a commencement or part of the former—a first act in the drama of transfer. That first item or part may itself be (as before shewn) either mere words, or

a written record, or a symbolic action: whatever
its character, a sequel is requisite to constitute,
i. e. to complete, the alienation. Were it possible to trace, or rational to expect, in the early
history of jural dealings, any philosophical scheme
or science, rather than a rudely elaborate publication of such few interchanges and simple traffic
of rights as are incident to the beginnings of civil
life, then we might perhaps look for the practical
simplicity of a published intent and acceptance, a
contract, an effective bargain, having been received as
jural completion of even a real transfer, *i. e.* of
some material substance. But, abstract notions of
Right or of ownership have never engaged nor
occurred to the mind of primitive civil communities. Things, *i. e.* all enjoyable and tangible objects
that rude men comprehend to be passable from
owner to owner—such as, wild or easily raised
fruits of the earth, spoil of the chase, cattle,
pasturage, rough implements of toil or chase, dwell-
ings and places of shelter, natural or rudely artificial—were and are doubtless continually, in the
very earliest days, among any people, of the
progressive idea of *meum* and *tuum*, made over from
one holder to another, as well with partial as with
entire and exclusive interest, by corporal act, by
material signs and clumsy symbols; and this, prior
to any literate or graphic representation of ideas
and wishes being known or thought of. In the
earliest times, even, as we know, in a more advanced epoch,[a]   and among primitive peoples at
this day, not the mental resolve or agreement, not

the conventional idea, but the ceremonial, the
acted formality, the published and witnessed de-
monstration is alone regarded.   Binding by mere
words of good faith, abstract realization of Right
or of transfer of Right, can there have no place
(at any rate, in a civil sense or as a jural rule—(b)):
such are tokens of Reason's growth and cultivation,
of an advanced civil experience.   So that, long
before the possible elaboration of contract, we
trace alienation as a jural formality and fact.
Slowly and gradually has supervened understanding
and analysis of the component parts of this vul-
garly simple and single, but scientifically 'complex
work and process.

It is thus apparent, that transfer of the position
of proprietor, and of jural possession, are severally
facts, but such facts as, according to each jural
system, raise the jural conclusion of—property, or
possessory right having shifted, under a contract or
convention; further that, in the logic of jurisprudence, no mere mental act, no evidence of will, of
agreement, not carried out by actual, potential, or
constructive delivery of the subject *res*, works a
positive change in ownership.   A contract creates an
obligation and a Right : from a sale-bargain arises,
not any real or positive relation with the subject
agreed to be transferred, but a personal claim to
have the transfer made, a *jus ad rem*—Right to
acquisition of the thing.   That Right is distinct
from any act or indication of transfer.

I proceed to a closer analysis of the act of

transfer, in its separate and distinctive character. An act of transfer, in conception and in fact, is necessarily two-sided : it is compounded of two distinct jural facts and acts, *viz.* on the one side, parting with, abandoning, for a purpose (*i. e.* the yielding to another), of some Right-external (—material, or lying in obligation merely—); on the other, accomplishment of the purpose, *viz.* the taking, occupation by that other, of the Right parted with. But, there can be no interval (—or an ideal one, a mathematical point, without parts or magnitude—), no suspense of ownership, no sensible extinction and revival, no solution of tie, if it be a real Right, between person and *res*, only a change of the person : it is the very incidence of the new taking and title, which unrivets the vinculum of the old. And the discovery of this necessity calls attention to the third idea and fact, *viz.* the precedent or concurrent convention, already noted ; of which the influence and efficacy is felt and apparent in construing, in weighing, in appreciating the (logically, and usually in deed) sequent act of transfer. "Something external" wrote Kant, "is ac-"quired, either, by an act of individual will (*facto*); "or, by an act of the united wills of two (*pacto*); "or, by an act of the common will of all (*lege*)."

The second instance of the category is what we are now dealing with : invariably, concurrence of wills, merely united, or general, precedes the bipartite act of change in ownership : when united wills have matured into contract, this has become, as

above explained, an independent element and item
—a stage, as well as a step—in the process of
jural alienation.

From much that has been said, it is apparent, that the delivery, or making over, which
is the main ingredient, the completion, the essential result and meaning of alienation, is by no
means identical with material handing over of
any substance or thing: this may, as observed by
Austin, be 'pre-appointed evidence of a *titulus*',
and, therefore, essential in the proof of ownership,
'and sometimes (for that reason) feigned to have
taken place'. But, unless physical contact be made
part of the technical title, it is a non-essential fact,
not importing or necessarily indicative of jural
tradition. (See Kant's distinction of physical from
jural possession, *supra* pa. 66.)

On the other hand, unreserved alienation of
any sort of Right, imports, *ex vi termini*, by its
very name, that all jural claim, facilities and
modes of enjoyment, as held by the transferring
owner, have passed to the new owner: whether
or not therefore, the physical power to use or
handle the subject of transfer has or not passed,
there cannot but be an actual or a virtual giving
over of the subject, whatever it be, *viz.* either
de facto, or symbolized, or, at the least, assumed, as a fact accomplished.

It follows, that, in order to describe or to
understand, what is that delivery and giving over
which is a component of civil or jural alienation,

further scrutiny must be made, of, what 'possession' is—what, the taking or acquiring, the
maintaining, the parting with or losing, jural
possession.

It was a Roman maxim, and one correctly
enunciating an important general juridical principle,
that, 'no one can himself vary the cause of his
possession.' Here is meant, the 'just cause' above
described as one of the uses and meanings of
Title. A power over, or custody of, a subject of
property having been acquired through some specific *causa, titulus,* and means, which *causa* turns
out to be, either in itself defective, as a transfer
of and title to the particular *dominium* or Right
it had been assumed to confer, or else inadequate
to the (perhaps dishonest) wishes and intentions
of the holder and acquirer—in either case, neither
of them, the victim of error nor the dissatisfied
holder, can, singly, of his own mere motion
and will, remedy and patch up the defect—supply
what is wanting—much less alter the very character of the proceeding and basis upon which his
claim and his possession, such as they are, are
erected—from which they spring. So much is self-
evident: thus—if the holder could not, originally,
have created his own *titulus* or derivative Right—
which, in its very definition and essence, must
have included several concurrent wills, as well as
acts of distinct actors—neither can the *titulus*
which he has, be added to or changed by any
inferior or less intricate machinery. Time (creating

judicial presumption (—though not in every case, *e. g.*
of plain trust or of unbroken agency—) or positive
law, may put age in place of a *titulus*, and so
give fruition to his wishes and his patience: but,
the holder himself can by no device or eagerness
invest his holding with any new garment of Right,
or actively give to himself another *titulus:* the attempt to do so, is, assuming to personate an absent, possibly a non-existent, seller or donor,⁔ to
exercise another's *arbitrium;* it is, representation
by one individual of antagonist actors in a bipartite
transaction.

Yet was it also a rule of the old *jus civile,*
that, conscious loss of physical power to eject a
de facto holder, even mere apprehension and
belief of inability, by the ousted owner, and
consequent inaction, in so far furnished a mode
of, or substitute for, jural as well as material
transfer of land, as to work a change in the
character (therefore in the ground and cause)
of possession—and this, even where the holder had obtained his holding as agent or as
depositary. Of the less considered and more easily
handled sort of *res,* now known as 'personalty,'
viz. what can be shifted from place to place with
the person, jural possession was, for the time,
lost, whenever the subject was actually appropriated by another, in any way, whether stealthily
(*subreptum*) or violently.

This entire doctrine is a result and inference
from another and more obvious one, *viz.* that, every

jural taker and possessor must have the *animus possidendi*, *i. e.* intent, consciousness, sentiment, of having: if he, actually or virtually, abandon or resign the *animus*, or, if the idea of its retention become impracticable and illusory—if, for instance, a jewel be lost or dropt into the ocean, or, a house be openly appropriated by a brigand force— the injured or loser may or not, in respect of the loss from which he suffers, become, and on just grounds, a *petitor* or complainant, seeking what is his—he may, perchance, pursue the of- fender as for a public outrage; but in no sense does he himself possess or hold that by loss of which he is aggrieved, either directly or vicari- ously. In such case—*i. e.* wherever all power to use or to have is at an end—the usurper, even though he be a fraudulent agent or bailee, can scarcely be said to have varied his title: rather, he has renounced his title, and pro- claimed himself a wrong-doer; choosing the risks of this new character and status, one clothed with the chances of mere possession growing, through the owner's inaction, into proprietary title and Right.

Holding as jural possessor, and its consequences, in contrast with a mere holding title, are curiously exemplified in the English Common law of real property.

" By the doctrine of the feudal law, no person who " had an estate of less duration and extent than for " his own life or for the life of another man, was

"considered to be a freeholder; and none but a free-
"holder was considered to have the possession of
"the land. It is true, that estates were sometimes
"held for terms of years. In that case, the pos-
"session of the termor was considered to be the
"possession of the freeholder; but still the ter-
"mor held the possession, though he held it for
"the freeholder; and the freeholder, by trusting
"the termor with it, exposed himself to lose it, by
"the termor's negligence or treachery. If the
"termor left the possession vacant; if he permit-
"ted himself to be disseised of it; if he under-
"took to alien it either by act in *pais*, or by
"matter of record; if he claimed the fee; or if
"he affirmed it to be in a stranger;—in all these
"cases, the freeholder exposed himself to the loss
"of the possession, as much as if they were his
"own acts. Thus the termor held the possession,
"but he was said to hold it *nomine alieno*, in
"contradistinction to the freeholder himself, who
"was said to hold it *nomine proprio*. Hence
"Britton expressly defines an estate of freehold
"to be, the possession of the soil by the freeholder;
"and the author of the 'Doctor and Student' says,
"that the possession of the land is called, in the
"law of England, the franktenement or freehold:
"so nearly synonymous in those days was the
"possession to the freehold. In this manner, the
"possession of the termor differed from that of a
"mere bailiff, who had no possession. The same
"principles obtained with respect to the transfer of

"the freehold. Nothing further was necessary
"than a delivery of the possession, or, as it is
"called by our law-writers, livery of seisin. The
"freehold could be transferred by no other means.
"But, here a difference is to be observed with
"respect to the effect of the livery of a termor for
"years and the livery of a mere bailiff. On ac-
"count of the solemnity upon which the entry of
"the termor into the lands was grounded, the
"connection between him and the reversioner, and
"his actually holding the possession of the land
"(though he held it for the freeholder), the livery
"of the former was a transfer of the possession;
"but the livery of the latter was absolutely with-
"out effect.—Long leases for years also came into
"use, and more settled and accurate notions were
"had, of tenancies by sufferance and at will. All
"these were considered to be in the same situation
"as the termor for years. Their possession was
"held to be the possession of the immediate free-
"holder; but as they had, or rather held, the pos-
"session, and were in by the act of the freeholder
"in some cases, and by his privity or forbearance in
"all, they were considered to be in, as of the seisin
"of the fee. It sometimes happened, that persons
"had the possession who had not the right; such
"were tenants by disseisin, deforcement, abate-
"ment, or intrusion. Still, as they had the posses-
"sion, they might, by livery of it, transfer it to
"another. Thus, by the old feudal law, on the one
"hand, the freehold could not be transferred but

"by livery of seisin; on the other, livery of seisin
"could not be made by any person who had
"the possession, without transferring the freehold.
"This transfer of the fee was called a feoffment.
"No writing was necessary for this purpose;
"and when charters came into use, the trans-
"fer of the fee was supposed to be produced,
"not by the charter, but by the livery which
"it authenticated. But the material variation, with
"respect to the form of transferring property
"by livery, was, that originally it was usual
"to make the feoffment on the land, before
"the peers of the court, who subscribed the
"charter of feoffment with their names; and
"the entry of the feoffee upon the land was
"afterwards recorded in the lord's court; but in
"progress of time, the feoffment was allowed to
"be good, though it were attested by strangers
"only, and the recording of the feoffee's entry
"was dispensed with. This, undoubtedly, lessened,
"very considerably, the solemnity and notoriety of
"feoffments—" (c)

Admitting then, the incontrovertible tenet, well
defined (nor less ably proved and illustrated) by
Savigny, that, 'Physical power is the *factum* which
must exist in every acquisition of possession—,'
we have to abstract from the essential idea of
that power, and therefore from the idea of possession, all notion of corporeal contact: yet, with that
power must be combined the intent and the
consciousness which together are *animus possi-*

dendi, in order to generate the condition of things signified by 'possession.'

The result may be dogmatically stated—possession, as a jural fact, is; 'the power, with (*plus*) the sentiment, of having'—and this, whether the application be to a thing tangible and visible, or to enjoyment of a jural faculty or Right. I say, enjoyment, to avoid probable confusion, in this class of *res*, of possession or having, with claim and title to have. Jural *i. e.* rightful claim, is one thing; jural, rightful, or actual having, is another—the two united are plenary, rightful possession.

The particular term 'possession' seems scarcely applicable, in its usual and conventional sense (whether scientific or colloquial), to what is occasional merely, or, in its entirety, intangible, to what can be taken—sensibly or consciously had—only by fruition, by active exercise and use; *e. g.* a Right of way, to pluck fruit. To this class may be specially applied the dogma of Kant;—"every object whatever, exterior to my will, in "just so far as it is in my power, may be ac-"counted mine, juridically, without being in my "possession."

The name 'possessor' is incorrectly given, as a jural description, to one whose claim and Right is but to detain; as, if one have a bare pledge or a deposit. The apparent possession is vicarious, and in a special manner; the origin, cause, and meaning of the interest or relation created (which is not purely substitutive, like that of the feudal termor) alike negative all idea of any self-asserting, proprietary effort or condition in him who *de facto* holds; another, the owner, is still possessor, in spite of his mode of dealing with—of the use he has made of and put to—his delegation of, that power and physical faculty which is an incident or part of his possession. [d]

What is the handing over, the alienation of possession, of title, and of the two united, I assume to be apparent from the preceding deductions and illustrations.

It also follows, that, symbolical (which is, typical and ideal) delivery, is not to be confounded with potential, custodial, subjecting, or even virtual delivery: the one is a supposition, an acted resolve; the other a fact, a resolve carried out. The former is illustrated by the handing over of a clod of earth, in token of transfer of a tract of land; the latter, by handing over the key of a locked up ware-house, containing merchandize purchased, to the purchaser: taking the key, is actual assumption of custody.

"That which I possess in my name, I can "possess as another's nominee; not that I thereby "change the *causa* of possession, but I cease to "be possessor, and, by the service I give, I "establish another's possession: nor is it the same "thing, to possess, and, as another's nominee to "possess. For he is the possessor in whose name

"possession stands. The delegate ministers to
"another's possession." CELSUS

These dogmatical yet logical sentences of the
Digest, explain and justify the apparently exceptional transfer of possession, which occurs when
the owner parts with and makes over his dominical
Right and his *animus possidendi*, while retaining
his physical relation with and actual power over
the subject possessed, even as before the transfer :
the change is ideal and metaphysical, but strictly
juridical and true ; the fact of representation or of
agency being, ofcourse, admitted.

'I, A. holding as jural possessor, now make over
to you B. (by record, or token, or words, as may
be,) my entire Right and interest in that which
I hold ; henceforth holding, not of or for myself,
but for and of you, on account &c. (whatever the
commission or delegation may be).' [a]

This doctrine or position, is perhaps rather a crucial application of propositions already advanced,
as to possession and alienation, than any thing new
or even supplemental.

The same reasoning and conclusions apply, when
an owner desires to clothe his agent, by and
through whom he holds, with the ownership: here,
a new character has to be given to the position already occupied by the transferee, him to whom
the transfer is to be made. It is the converse, or
correlative of the former instance, *viz.* retention,
by the party transferring, of a vicarious and limited
possessory power; so, in this, of the agent, the

abstract Right only has to pass, and no physical change or movement need occur: the transaction is in will, not in action—the object and scope of the change is, not to clothe with power, but to withdraw restrictions that modify and hamper the exercise of existing physical power.

Savigny sums up the problem of vicarious acquisition, or acquisition through foreign agency, and such as excludes personal or direct act of the acquirer, in the question—

"How is it possible to acquire through the acts "of another party the consciousness of physical "dominion over a subject?"

An obvious and, although indirect, no imperfect solution of the problem may be thus stated; the notion and reality of such physical dominion is typified or instanced (and is therefore explained and illustrated) in the pursuit of, or in ability to pursue a possessory remedy against a stranger who has dispossessed the agent: such remedy, representing as it does a substantive Right (*supra,* p. 42), is more than an ideal equivalent of that physical relation or power which is required in order to complete the new jural possession.

"A man seems to have to himself *(apud se)* "whatever he has a legal remedy for; since, that "is had *(habetur)* which can be sued for." ULPIAN. *(f)*

There is yet another kind or phase of alienation to be treated of in this Section, *viz.* 'involuntary alienation.' To all but lawyers, this term may

c 2

seem to include a contradiction, in its negative
element—a transfer against will. It is a transfer
lege simply, the third category of Kant's analysis,
supra, p. 190 : it is the voice of the Law, the
general will, in place of the *arbitrium* and desire
implied in private traffic of rights : it is, a sanction, to enforce or to punish, when the Law's
command is disobeyed, when a Right is violated : it is a process in execution of a judgment
of Law.

In some sense, prescriptive title may be considered a result—a *fiat*—of involuntary alienation ; being
the Law's substitute for a proprietor's will, therefore a transfer *lege.* But, prescription differs from
judicial alienation in this, that, although *invito
domino,* it is a presumption from the owner's
conduct, a conclusion generated by that conduct,
a jural interpretation of that conduct—not an adjudication of contested rights, nor a penal sentence of deprivation. As before explained (pa. 177),
prescription is a title, not a penalty : and, although
what constitutes prescriptive title, in each jural system, is a postulate, a dogma of the science of proofs
and of procedure, that postulate is but to assist
and define the rational presumption—a dogmatical
assuming of Reason's office, perhaps—and is something less than a judicial mandate, or a sanction.

Alienation of private rights, when made *lege, i. e.*
by (as a result of) the general and public will,
in contradistinction to individual or private will, is,
—either (1), an adjudication, simply, carried out

by, or under terror of, the Law's sanctions, *e. g.*
in a suit to enforce a contract of sale, the judge
decrees, in his office of arbiter and guardian of
civil liberty and of good faith, that the thing,
or the Right, be given over, as contracted for
——or (2), an indirect, accidental consequence of
adjudication, *e. g.* the judge finds a debt to be
due, or, that loss and injury has occurred, as complained, and estimates the value (money-worth)
which the claimant is to get, from the debtor or
the wrong-doer; in order to realise or to make
over that value to the claimant, conversion (*viz.*
sale), alienation, or else coercive custody, of property,
by officers of the Law, may be an inevitable mode
of action——or (3), the judge, administering criminal Law, sentences one convicted of crime to
forfeit property to the State (either in the form of
value or of debt, or generally all rights of a
certain class, or all that the criminal has, or a
specific subject of property), which, by the sentence, becomes public property. This third instance is rather extinction than alienation of property: it is simply infliction, as imprisonment of
the person, or forced labour would be—it is immediately within the definition of civil sanctions
(*supra*, p. 15).

Conveyance, active transfer, of a private Right,
under the first general category, of alienations
without will (*i. e.* will of the owner), although effected without any apparent specific *animus*, as it
is without any physical aid, of the owner, and by

a public officer, is entirely in accordance with, indeed in direct support of, that owner's civil liberty (*supra*, p. 33); he, 'of his own act, causes, though he does not effect, the alienation. Logically and jurally therefore, this alienation is not involuntary; but its incidents (because of their analogy) are properly classed and analysed here.

The second instance, *viz.* compulsory conversion, compensatory transfer—is the remedial action of Law, and a true involuntary alienation; no private or particular will can be implied here; proprietary rights of the helpless or the dishonest debtor, and of him to whom injurious loss is imputed, are given over *lege*, in order to adjust, to rectify, the dues and the damage adjudicated. The Right of remedy is thus recognised and applied. With respect to the title or the extent of Right so compulsorily alienated, it can be but a change of position, *viz.* from the proprietor or seeming proprietor-debtor, to the successful suitor: the Law's action cannot in such case (any more than the owner himself could) vary or improve the *causa* or title of a possessor. Finally, this judicial interference with and paramount adjustment (acting as a forfeiture) of private rights, seems to range under the *dominium eminens* (*supra*, p. 71). (a)

(a) Take the gradual progress of the *Jus Civile.*—" There seems " to have been one solemn ceremonial at first for all solemn trans- " actions, and its name at Rome appears to have been *nexum.* " Precisely the same forms which were in use when a conveyance " of property was effected seem to have been employed in the " making of a contract. But we have not very far to move onwards

"before we come to a period at which the notion of a Contract
"has disengaged itself from the notion of a Conveyance. A double
"change has thus taken place. The transaction with the copper
"and the balance when intended to have for its office the transfer
"of property, is known by the new and special name of Mancipa-
"tion. The ancient Nexum still designates the same ceremony,
"but only when it is employed for the special purpose of solemnis-
"ing a contract.—Nexum, therefore, which originally signified
"a Conveyance of property, came insensibly to denote a contract
"also, and ultimately so constant became the association between
"this word and the notion of a Contract, that a special term,
"Mancipium or Mancipatio, had to be used for the purpose of
"designating the true nexum or transaction in which the property
"was really transferred.—The old Nexum has now bequeathed to
"maturer jurisprudence first of all the conception of a chain unit-
"ing the contracting parties, and this has become the Obligation.
"It has further transmitted the notion of a ceremonial accompany-
"ing and consecrating the engagement, and this ceremonial has
"been transmuted into the Stipulation." *(Ancient Law.)*

The Mosaic account of Abraham's purchase *(Gen.* c. 23) of a
family burial-place, neither alludes to symbol nor to record, but
merely to wide publication of the contract of sale, and to payment
of the price; in virtue of which the field "stood" to the purchaser.

"And Ephron was dwelling in the midst of the sons of Heth.—And Ephron
"answered Abraham, saying, Pray, my Lord hear me! the land is 400 shekels of
"silver—and Abraham weighed to Ephron the silver which he spake in the ears of
"the sons of Heth, 400 shekels of silver, current with the trader. And the field
"of Ephron, which was in Machpelah, which was before Mamre, the field, and
"the cave which was in it, and all the trees which were in the field, which
"were in all its border round-about, stood to Abraham for a purchase ['passed
"over to Abraham for a property' (Kalesch)], *before the eyes of the sons of*
"*Heth, among all entering at the gate of his city.* And afterwards Abraham
"buried Sarah his wife in the cave of the field of Machpelah—And the field,
"and the cave which was in it stood ['passed over' (Kalisch)] to Abraham for a
"possession of a burying place from the sons of Heth." (Colenso)

But the part of the description which I have italicised, clearly
shows, that the peculiar Jewish publicity, 'among all entering at
the gate'—*i. e.* as the commentator Kalisch notes, 'in the presence
of all the citizens,' not the mere contract, nor even the payment,
was relied on, as the fact and the proof of transfer. See however
Jeremiah, ch. 32, v. 7 &c.

(*b*) I interpose this caution, because I consider the phase or stage of civilization which closely assimilates distinctions of Right, jural faculties and remedies, to minute or strict analysis of the ethical claims of man upon man, to be, but a development and matured application of that moral intelligence which is essentially and necessarily human—in other words, of Reason: it is the new application, new working out of Reason, which potentially exists (though latent) even in the most primitive, in the savage, as in the advanced and polished, of mankind. Need the earnest student of history or the traveller among undeveloped races be informed, that rude, unlettered, crude-minded men have shown a nice sense of honor, a nice feeling and appreciation of justice, goodness, righteous dealing? This consideration will have to be pursued and enlarged on, in a subsequent section; as it bears upon the growth and varieties of civil Law.

(*c*) Butler's note, *Co. Lit.* 330*b*.

(*d*) The treatment, in the text, of jural possession, does not accord, in terms, with distinctions and modes often applied to it; but the difference is unsubstantial, and this explanation (agreeing even in terms with the views of able jurists) appears to me intelligible, definite, and logically consistent. Sir Erskine Perry's translation of Savigny's treatise, uses the phrase 'derivative possession' to denote what I have called 'vicarious;' this includes a part and excludes other part of the component idea in derivation; that is to say, it excludes all notion of jural transfer, as of jural substitution. A pledgee creditor's custody represents, besides the owner's jural possession, also a specific interest and jural power in the creditor, and which interest justifies his compulsory representation of the debtor and of all rights of the latter, including the possessory right; hence, in the *Jus Civile*, the creditor's possession or custody served to continue the prescription (use-acquirement) of the non-holding debtor.

The Roman remedy of 'interdict' was to protect lawful (*i. e.* plausible and peaceable) custody, irrespective of the jural interest or relation which that custody represented.

It is not correct to say (as Dr. Sullivan does, Lec. 31, *in fin.*), that the English borrowed the distinction between the Right of possession and the Right of property from the *Jus Civile*. The substantial distinction must be familiar to every system of proprietary rights, and was so especially in the early feudal relation of lord and vassal; the latter having a possession and usufruct (precarious or assured) dependent upon the lord's *dominium*. A bailiff, a farmer, a tenant, always, each, had a possession, although, in each case, one differently defined, perhaps merely representative, even merely natural or casual, perhaps *quasi* dominical.

(*s*) Savigny argues,—"Whoever is in a condition, generally, to "acquire possession for another, by his own acts, is not the less "competent to do so, because, up to that moment, he, the agent, "may have had juridical possession of the subject." And he instances, 1. "Whoever gives a thing as a gift, and at the same "time hires it, may not say any thing in terms as to the pos-"session, but his intention is, that a contract of hiring should "immediately ensue between himself and the donee ; it is, there-"fore, a necessary consequence, that the donee should be pos-"sessor, and he himself the occupant of another's possession—2. "The same thing happens with *usufructus* ; whoever, therefore, "gives away or sells an article, and retains the *usufructus* for "himself, does, in fact, transfer the possession and the property, "and only proceeds to enjoy, like any other fructuary, the pos-"session of another. 3. If a thing is pledged, but at the same "time the use of it is permitted to the pledger, the possession "[*i. e.* such possession as may belong to a pledgee,] of the thing "is thereupon acquired by the creditor.—4. In a general partner-"ship, delivery of all the individual goods is looked upon as made, "directly that the contract is completed——"

Still, the transfer (or its equivalent), and the contract, are distinct. Together, they form the 'alienation.' The transfer may be other than actual, or ostensible, or physical, *i. e.* where express contract, or usage, or the necessity of the case (as in commercial co-partnership—and here, joint interest or proprietorship may be treated as an incident of status—) justifies a substitution of the *animus* for the act ; in other words, substitutes the declaration, that possession has passed, for overt change—the will for the deed. The case is exceptional, and requires, in each instance, to be accounted for. It is familiar to jurists under a somewhat barbarous name, *constitutum possessorium*. Lindley, in a note to his translation of Thibaut's *Pandekten Rechts* (*i. e.* to the text defining what this mode or Right is), says, the doctrine is wholly denied by several jurists, and is termed by one 'a monstrous offspring of practice.' Savigny merely insists, that a *constitutum* is not to be presumed.

English commerce, the Law-Merchant, has introduced a laxity, which varies, not the juridical rule, but its application. "In "Scotland [as was in Rome], property is not transferred, either "nominally or effectually, without delivery of the commodity—" (Bell's Commentaries). In English Law, however, the sale of a specific subject, where nothing remains to be done by the seller before it is to be delivered, passes the property in the subject to the purchaser, without delivery. In the words of Lord Wensleydale, (in *Wait* v. *Baker*, 2 Exch.) "—property does not pass until "there is a bargain with respect to a specific article, and every "thing is done which, according to the intention of the parties to "the bargain, was necessary to transfer the property in it." Thus, the English Law treats the fact, or legal inference, of appropriation, to which purely possessory remedies are, or not, attached, according to circumstances, (and see the nicety of the inference exemplified in the cases *Tempest* v. *Fitzgerald*, reported 3 Barnewall & Alderson, and *Atkinson* v. *Bell*, 8 Barnewall & Cresswell), as virtual and jural transfer—in other words, as equivalent to, or as constructive, delivery, or, as a conveyance of Right, as may be; while the Scottish Law requires, that the purchaser be put in the position of the seller, and that the sort of dominion and control, whatever it be, that the latter had, be made over in fact, nothing less. So that, the difficulty in doubtful English cases usually resolves itself (the contract being assumed) into one of two questions,—was there appropriation? or, was there delivery? In Scotch cases, the last question alone is material.

The French code, in terms, overleaps all logical or scientific distinction. The framers of that code, able as they were, were not jurists, but practical statesmen. Seeing the devices that had been used to avoid the extraneous ceremony of tradition, they boldly cut the knot by declaring ;—"A gift duly ac- "cepted shall be complete by the mere consent of the "parties ; and the property of the subject of gift shall be "transferred to the donee, without need of other delivery." (*Art.* 938.) And, "Property in goods is acquired and trans- "ferred, by succession, by gift, by testament, and by "the effect of obligations." (*Art.* 711.) And, speaking of Sale, "It is complete between the parties, and property is "acquired of right to the buyer, as respects the seller, as "soon as agreement is come to as to the thing and the price, "although the thing have not yet been given over or the price "paid." (*Art.* 1583.)

Thus, the *constitutum* or agency of the seller—his change of *status*, as it were—is declared to be the normal effect of every immediate obligation to alienate. As a French commentator (Marcadé) explains it, "—by the consent alone, the obligation to "deliver becomes fictitiously accomplished, and the delivery is "accounted made."

The English cases do not go so far. A valid contract of sale of a specified subject, and a compliance by the seller with all conditions on his part, entitle him to recover the price ; because the purchaser has become invested with jural faculties to complete the transfer—it is for him to exercise them. But the French dogma of assumed positive delivery is not adopted. And the very form and necessity of those artificial enactments *(Co. Civ.)*, as indeed of all devices to supply the element of transfer or to bridge over the admitted interval between a contract and its performance, prove the doctrine and analysis of alienation, as explained in the text. Property is no doubt an ideal relation, but, by reason of the substance and material entity related, it is not simply an abstraction.

Nor can it be denied, that a laxity has been introduced by the English cases which invest the vendee of goods with an indefinite but absolute proprietary right *(jus in re)*, at least, in terms, by force and virtue of the mere bargain or contract—a real or *quasi-real* Right, which is, nevertheless, irrespective of and may not include possessory Right, *i. e.* any claim to use or to handle, to have ; and this, although the single and distinct purpose of the contract on the vendee's part be, to get that proprietary possession—moreover, the holding Right of the seller (when it exists, *e. g.* when the price is due and unpaid,) not being a possessory Right and yet not a mere lien or pledge : see the cases, *Milgate* v. *Kebble*, 3 Manning & Grainger ; *Martindale* v. *Smith*, 1 Qu. B. ; *Fitt* v. *Cassanet*, 4 M. & G. ; *Dodsley* v. *Varley*, 12 Adolphus & Ellis.

Surely, here is a backward progress, a reverting to the confusion between obligation and transfer, contract and conveyance, of very primitive jurisprudence. The confusion would seem to have insensibly grown out of an inexact use of the term 'property,' *viz.* to represent the claim of a purchaser who has not received the thing as bargained for : his Right is perfect, *i. e.* to have the thing made his ; but the inference of actual appropriation from concurrence of intentions merely, is premature and unscientific. It is presuming a *constitutum*. (Yet, see per Campbell, C. J. *arguendo* in *Schuster* v. *McKellar*, 7 Ellis & Blackburn 719).

The *primâ facie* inconsistency in the incidents of the Roman *emptio-venditio* (as of the Scottish contract of sale), *viz.* that, although until delivery, the seller remains propietor, yet, after the bargain and before delivery, the commodity is at the purchaser's risk, is thus explained by Ortolan :—

"The seller remaining proprietor, as a consequence, if "there be an increase, by bearing fruit, by alluvion, from "any cause whatever, he it is who becomes proprietor of "the fruits, of the accretions; if the commodity deteriorate, if "it perish, his right as proprietor is lessened by so much, "or is extinguished. The Law speaks not, in such case, of "the Property. But what is the effect of the contract of "sale? It is, to produce obligations : the seller is under "obligation to deliver and make over the commodity to the "purchaser : and, if, after the sale there be fruits or accretions, "certainly he is under obligation to deliver those up : if the "commodity have lessened, or deteriorated without fault of "the owner, he shall not be then bound to make it over to "the purchaser otherwise than in its diminished or deteriorated "condition : should it have perished without fault of his, then "his obligations are put an end to." And this seems a rational "conclusion.

The above considerations of ideal, in lieu of actual and corporeal transfer, are ofcourse irrespective of those exceptional rights or privileges sometimes granted to creditors, to demand annulment or disregard of such transfer when made, as it may be, without publication or notoriety *(clam)*, because of its being a breach of commercial faith, and lessening, in an unfair and deceptive mode, the available assets of a debtor. Such special provisions have no bearing upon the principles governing the idea or the fact of jural possession.

(f) This view or dogma certainly does not include the doctrine of the English Chancery, that a vendee by contract, but who is compelled by the vendor's breach of faith to sue for performance of that contract, is to be regarded as, not merely having a right *in personam*, but as the equitable (therefore, jural) owner and possessor. This is one of many maxims and ethical syllogisms which guide the remedial action and jurisdiction of that paramount, prescriptive *imperium* vested in the Chancellor; but which do not modify nor affect the jurisprudence of property.

(g) The *pignoris capio* of early Roman judicature, the prætorian

emptio bonorum and *missio in possessionem*, the later *distractio bonorum* and *pignus prætorium*, each and all exemplify this coercive civil transfer of an owner's proprietary rights, wholly or partially, conditionally or absolutely. The *cessio bonorum* (parent of modern bankruptcy and insolvency laws) was introduced in mercy to the debtor. In Dalrymple's *Essay towards a general history of feudal property in Great Britain* is an interesting and instructive episode (written 1757) on the progress, there, of judicial alienation, which I extract.

"With regard to the involuntary, or legal alienation, which arises from "attachment for debt, the progress of it, natural and feudal, seems to be this. "The notion of borrowing under a promise of paying, is in general not very "natural among a rude people; their conception of obligation is but weak in "any case, and that of their obligation to fidelity is still weaker. All uncivilized "nations are observed to be cruel and treacherous; instead then of a promise to repay, "or of a written document in evidence of that promise, the borrower gives a pledge, as "a more solid security. Thus the old word in the English and Scotch law books, "*namium*, which at present we translate by the word Distress, signified anciently from "the Saxon, *pignoris prehensio*, the seizing or distraining of the pledge. From "the *Regiam Majestatem* and Glanville, it appears, that in consequence of prior "agreements betwixt the parties, this pledge, upon failure of payment, either "remained with the creditor, or, on application to the judge, was sold by his "order; and it is not improbable, that at that time, no moveables unless so "pledged, could be sold for debt; nor even when pledged could they be sold, till "after a competent time, and delay of payment; for so it is laid down by "Glanville and in the *Regiam Majestatem*: and a statute of Robert I. made "at a time when even moveables not pledged could be sold for debt, declares, "that even then they could not be sold for forty days after the attachment. "Before these days were elapsed, they were kept rather as a security for the "debt, till the debtor still delaying to pay, they were employed to extinguish it.

"The progress of the attachment of immoveables is the same. In the law "of the books of the fiefs they could not be attached for debt; nor could "they be attached by the Saxon law; nor for several reigns after that of "William the Conqueror; nor in the time of Glanville: on the contrary, the "only writs of execution at Common Law in England, were the *fieri facias* on "the goods and chattels, and the *levari facias* to levy the debt or damages "on the lands and chattels; neither is there the least hint of such attachment "in the Scotch *Regiam Majestatem*, or the Scotch *Quoniam attachiamenta;* "although in this last the method of attaching moveables for debt is most "exactly described, even the words of the brief, the duty of the sheriff, the "proof of the debt, the sale, or if no body will buy, the appraisement; yet "the attachment of immoveables is not mentioned at all. Nor at these periods "could the law, unless with an exception to be afterwards mentioned, be "possibly otherwise: the limited notions of power over property, added "to the interest of the lord against bringing in any vassal who was

"stranger to him, were insuperable bars to any further attachment. It
"is true, by the *Regiam Majestatem*, (lib. 3. cap, 5.) and Glanville,
"(lib. 10. cap. 8.) it appears, that land might be pledged for debt; and
"from the same passages, compared with cap. 3 of the first authority, and
"cap. 6. of the other, it appears, that in consequence of bargains concerning
"such pledging of land, a practice had crept in, that the principal sum not
"being paid, the land either remained with the creditor, or on application to the
"judge was sold by him. But some of those cases being in consequence of agree-
"ments, were branches rather of voluntary than involuntary alienation, and they
"belonged more to the rules of private transactions, than of public Law: and
"further, as no right of pledge was supported by the king's courts without
"possession; the possessor of the land pledged, seemed in this circumstantiate
"state to have acquired a connection with, and power over it, which facilitated
"the notion of his retaining it, although the attachment of land by other cre-
"ditors in general, who were not already in possession, was, it is certain, utterly
"unknown. I say by other creditors in general; for though in the reign of
"Henry III. we soon after find, that the king, and the surety for the king's
"debtor purging his debt to the king, could enter upon the land for
"the debt, and keep it till the debt was paid, yet this was a preference
"special to the king; and as the surety had paid off the debt to the king, he
"seemed to come in his place, and to have a right to enjoy his privileges.
"But as the voluntary alienation of land was first freely introduced among
"trading people in boroughs, so the involuntary alienation of it was first
"freely introduced among the same people in the same places. Thus in
"Scotland, in the laws of the boroughs, which were composed in the reign of
"David I. the method of attaching and selling land for debt, is completely laid
"down. By those laws, the creditor might enter upon the lands of his
"debtor, and after certain delays sell them: the only restraint this attach-
"ment admitted, was a right of redemption given to the relations of the
"debtor; a right derived from the most ancient Law, and at that time
"not totally eradicated even in boroughs. This attachment thus taking
"its rise on the laws of the boroughs, and among trading men, was
"afterwards extended to all the subjects indiscriminately; so that by a
"statute in the reign of Alexander II. upon application of the creditor,
"it became the duty of the sheriff to advertise the debtor to sell
"his land in fifteen days, which if the debtor did not do, the sheriff was
"impowered to sell it himself.—In the same manner it was, that the statute
"*de mercatoribus*, introduced the benefit of statute-merchant first in England
"in the thirteenth year of Edward I. By that statute, which was transplanted
"afterwards likewise into Scotland, the merchant creditor was allowed, upon
"failure of payment, to take possession of the whole of his debtor's land,
"till he was paid off his debt: in that land too he was infeofed by the
"Law; and upon the same plan of attachment with this statute-merchant,
"the statute-staple was, two reigns after, invented. It is true, that the same
"year in which the statute-merchant was introduced, execution upon judge-
"ments, and common recognizances, by the writ of *elegit*, which was common

"to all the subjects, was likewise introduced. But the difference of execution
"given upon this writ, and that given upon the statute-merchant, proves a
"very wide difference in the attachment allowed among merchants, and that
"allowed among the other subjects. The security by statute-merchant, gave
"possession of the whole of the land to the creditor; but the writ of *elegit*
"gave him possession of no more than a half: originally men could
"not alienate at all, afterwards they were allowed to alienate, but not
"beyond half of the feud: now, this principle, or rather rule, was
"strong at the time the writ of *elegit* was invented, and the statute
"*Quia Emptores* had not yet been introduced; therefore whatever stretches
"might be found necessary from the circumstances of merchandise, yet with
"regard to the kingdom in general, a small deviation only was made from
"the Common Law, and the *elegit* was permitted to affect no more by the
"operation of Law, than a man was supposed capable of alienating by his
"own deed. As the feudal law relaxed of its severity, and the commerce
"of land grew more into use, the attachment of land by statute-merchant,
"and statute-staple, was allowed to all the subjects in general. The statute-
"merchant became first by practice, and afterwards by a statute of Henry
"VIII. one of the common assurances of the kingdom: and though the
"same statute of Henry VIII confined the benefit of the statute-staple
"within its ancient bounds, so as to operate only for behoof of the mer-
"chants of the staple, and only for debts on the sale of merchandize
"brought to the staple; yet it framed a new sort of security, which all
"the subjects might use. This security is known by the name of a recog-
"nizance on 23 Henry VIII. cap. 6. and in it the same process, execution,
"and advantage, in every respect, takes place, as in the statute-staple. But
"in later times, when land came to be absolutely in commerce, this attach-
"ment was thought insufficient; and therefore the act of the 13th of queen
"Elizabeth, and the subsequent acts concerning bankrupts, established a
"complete attachment of such lands as belonged to the persons specified in
"those acts: instead of a half, those statutes laid the whole of the land
"open to the creditor, and instead of a possession, which was all he had
"by the *elegit*, or statute-merchant, or statute-staple, they gave him the
"means of procuring a sale of the whole for the payment of his debt."

SUPPLEMENT.

In anticipation of the second part of this work, these general notes and suggestions are added, as a help to students.

Civil rights, as described in Section V. range under three heads or classes;

1. Inherent personal attributes: in regard to which civil Law rather recognises than establishes rights; *e. g.* Right to life, to self-respect, to good faith.

2. Civil relations, or adherent personal attributes, *i. e.* of status; these are various in kind and in origin; as, claims of paternity, of office or of rank.

3. External acquisitions, being claims to have or to enjoy things, services, benefits; *e. g.* land or fruits of land, men's labour.

The third class is divisible into; 1. such acquisitions or claims as consist in some definite relation to things; as, property in or out of land or other substance whatsoever, and are therefore rights of universal exclusion; or, 2. such as are claims against some determinate person; *e. g.* rights under a contract, or other Right (*i. e.* remedy) against some person, as, for infringement of any Right ranging under either of the classes 1. 2.

The subdivision No. 1 of 'external acquisitions' is equivalent to Austin's *jus in rem*, usually rendered, Right over or in a thing (—a more correct translation would seem to be, Right towards or with reference to a thing—), denoting, says Austin, "the compass and not the subject of the "Right." His original English definitions cover and distinguish phases of Right, *viz.*

"Real rights may be defined in the following manner: "Rights residing in persons, and availing against other per-"sons generally." and,

" The following definitions will apply to personal rights:
" Rights residing in persons and availing exclusively against
" persons specifically determinate: or, Rights residing in
" persons and answering to duties which are incumbent
" exclusively on persons specifically determinate."

Austin adds,

" As every imaginable right belongs to one of these
" classes [*jus in rem* and *jus in personam*], or else is
" compounded of rights belonging to each of these classes,
" it is manifest that a full exposition of this all-pervading
" distinction were nearly equivalent to a full exposition of
" the entire science of Law."

A specialty attends one mode of status-rights, in the
several kinds of power, of control over the will, the liberty, the *arbitrium* of the subject-person, whether child,
ward or servant, which distinguishes it from other claims
in personam. Such status-relations entitle to the exercise
of a class or series or repetition of claims upon determinate persons, as distinguished from particular claims
having separate authorizations. In viewing, classing or
accounting for the former, we regard the personal specialty
or position of the claim-holder: in the latter, we regard
the claim or the act conferring authority.

The former Right, although met by a correlative obligation in a person or persons determinate *e. g.* the ward,
clearly does not belong to the same category or class
as rights represented by persons merely, *i. e. vincula*
(bonds), dues, whether contractual or the result of injury.
These reflect nothing adherent to the Right-holder's person;
they issue, entire, from acts, from the person, of the Right-
bound. Austin, however, treated status-rights as having
a double aspect, 1. *in personam* as regards the person
who is the object of the Right (*e. g.* the ward), 2. as
general or negative, and binding all persons, not any
determinate person, and therefore, in this aspect, as
strictly personal rights. Kant classes as mixed or per-

sonal-real rights, the parental and the dominical; a view substantially adopted by Austin, in his explanation of 'rights *in rem* over persons.'

It may be said; childhood, wardship and service are, severally, terms indicative of a subjection and rule, more analogous to political domination than to proprietary; but distinct from both the one and the other. The first, *viz.* 'filial subjection,' is, in origin, a purely natural ordinance: the last, *viz.* 'obligation to serve,' is simply, either contractual or punitive; meaning by 'punitive' all gradations of involuntary and unrequited or compelled servitude. The ordinary relation of 'master and servant' has its beginning, its continuance and its force in contract; but, while the relation lasts, any interference (as explained) with the servant that can in any way trespass upon what he is under obligation to render to his master, whether it be an interference with the servant's ability or with the servant's will to give his contracted services, is, or may be a wrong in a double sense, *viz.* an injury to the servant personally and directly, also an injury to the master's position, to the master's property and existing Right in the presumed benefit of services which are thus placed out of his reach, or diminished in value, by the wrong-doer. So, on the other hand, any illegal interference (*e. g.* defamation of the servant) which deprives the servant of his correlative advantages in the mutuality of contractual status, is a wrong to the servant. And a case may be supposed where a reciprocal injury to the status-Right of each is the result of one wrongful act, *e. g.* the master is induced by some maliciously false report to dispense with the service, or (a case more strictly in point) to change its character prejudicially to the interests of both.

Austin objects to Kant's distinctive name, personal-real (calling it, an innovation upon the established language of the science,) as unnecessary, since this is, Austin

E 2

affirms, but the same kind of Right as 'to or in a thing.' But, the objection seems hypercritical. A capital obstacle in study of jural science (so Austin himself has emphatically acknowledged) is, the absence of any established language. And we are warned in the Digest, 'there is a risk in every civil-law definition—' (JAVOLENUS). For risk, may be read, doubt, uncertainty. Rights and distinctions of rights are variously defined. So indeed must it be with all abstract moral reasoning: no original thinker implicitly adopts or falls in with the terminology of any predecessor—a rule, of which Austin is a distinguished example.

There is, undoubtedly, ground for Austin's conclusion—"To fix the notion of 'status' with perfect exact-"ness, seems to be impossible."

The compensatory or remedial Right (pa. 42) is always *in personam*, virtually if not in terms; for, it necessarily affects and aims at a particular invader of a Right, which Right must operate restrictively, either upon some determinate person, or upon all without exception. Of the latter sort, immunity from bodily hurt; of the former, a Right of usufruct, are instances. Judgments or adjudications affirming or establishing rights, of-course vary in description, as the rights themselves do, *viz. in re, in personam, &c.:* but the judicial act commonly includes some order entitling to a new specific acquisition or claim. Every thing given by a judgment to the complainant, is a new, remedial, established Right, in substitution—perhaps, but solemn, authoritative renewal—of the Right which was the cause and subject of the litigation: *e. g.* an order, that a contract be specifically performed—that an instrument to convey or assure property be executed—that a like instrument, or a written obligation, be cancelled or delivered up —that a nuisance be abated—that a sum of money be paid—that possession of any *res*, as land, be given or restored (either as an order to or upon the person merely, or directly by forcible interference *i. e.* by legal process)— that a certain Right be not exercised during a definite time or under a certain contingency—&c.

The word 'obligation' has several jural meanings. It has been already used as the general correlative of Right: it has however distinctively a three-fold sense; *viz.* 1. the tie of contract; 2. the result of infraction of a Right, *e. g.* injurious damage to property; or, 3. a mode of action or of abstinence specially commanded by a law; as, to pay a tax; not to grow tobacco.

The obligation 'by law,' as a class, includes all jural duties, obligations, requirements, other than those advisedly self-imposed, *i. e.* framed by the will of the obliged in concert with some particular fellow-will.

It therefore includes, among others, all duties that result from acts entailing involuntary obligation, *viz.* wrongs. Some of this wide class (by law) are not specifically defined, indeed are scarcely capable of exhaustive description.

The facts that originate, or lead to remedy upon contract, *i. e.* resulting from contract-obligations, are, the incidents of each species of contract as well as the incidents of (*viz.* what constitutes) every possible breach: they are, necessarily, numerous (perhaps innumerable), elastic, and varying with the ever-changing, multiform necessities and desires of men.

Contract is a voluntary variation of the civil boundary of each man's liberty (pa. 33). Obligation from delict or wrong is a penal and compensatory variation of the same boundary, *viz.* sanctioned extension of the line limiting A's range of civil action, into and across the correlative line or boundary-limit of B. Pursuing the metaphor, civil obligations are identical with the entire boundary that limits each one's range. The contract-obligation and the delict-obligation vary in their formation or immediate origin, not in operation; for each is the voice of Law: in each case the obligatory tie and fact is, specifically, that the State has said, *ita jus esto*, which may be explained and paraphrased—so the Law commands.

Roman and other jurists have treated of *quasi*-contract and of *quasi*-delict; and, in English Law is a head of 'implied' contract and 'implied' covenants. I venture to think each of these sub-divisions superfluous, even if scientifically admissible. For instance: Law declares, that one who, of his own accord and without authority, assumes to represent another in his social status and responsibilities, *e. g.* as a trader or artificer, or, to act as though he held (when not holding) a commission or delegation —is vested with proportionate liability, that he incurs, by so volunteering, a risk of damage to himself, however well-meant or disinterested or morally justifiable his officiousness. Here is a *quasi*-contract. Now, as regards the person on account of whom the acts of interference are performed, we find no definite station within the broad jural domain of 'contract and wrong' specially appropriate to this class of proceeding; unless, indeed, on the one hand, the beneficial effect of the assumed status be held juridically tantamount to assent of the person represented —and, on the other, failure or prejudice in result, be held to determine, *ex post facto*, the wrongful character of that assumption. But this, obviously, can not be admitted. Subsequent assent may well be logically retracted, so as to legalise (or waive complaint for) a prior equivocal act. When no such assent is given, the interference, if not a punishable offence, is either an immaterial injury, *i. e.* an act infringing Law, but innocuous (*sine damno*)—or, it generates a delict-obligation, an actionable wrong, within the definition lately promulgated by the highest authority, *viz.*—'something which prejudicially affects plaintiff in some legal right.' (*Rogers* v. *Dutt*, 6 Moore's Pr. Council Indian cases)

The implied undertaking (*assumpsit*) or contract, in English Law, is simply evidence of a conventual obligation, or, at the most, a jural postulate, a conclusive presumption proving the *vinculum* or legal tie: *e. g.* I send to a baker for a loaf of bread—surely, the public character of the baker's calling, and my requiring the loaf, are facts significant of a purchase—in other words, those facts are evidence, and, unexplained, lead inevitably to the conclusion of an ostensible offer, on my part, to pay for the loaf—in English-law technical phrase they 'raise an *assumpsit.*'

Neither is mental intention, nor is the holding out a resolve (as an inducement for reciprocity or trust) to be shewn by words (whether written or spoken) alone: there are, to the eye of common-sense, many other tokens of either fact.

Again, if an instrument of transfer simply testify, that a seller, for a certain price, 'grants' to the purchaser the thing sold, but does not contain any words of contract or any express provision beyond the mere fact of purchase and sale; nevertheless, if it turn out, that the seller has no Right (although he believed himself entitled) to the subject of sale, and the purchaser be, in consequence, ousted or turned out of the enjoyment upon which he had entered and which he supposed he had bought, then, under English Common Law, the disappointed purchaser might complain of breach of the 'implied covenant' contained, wrapt up in the word of transfer, 'grant,' *viz.* the implied covenant or undertaking that he, the seller, had the power and title to do what he then assumed to do: if he had not, although may-be self-deceived, he cannot escape from his contract; for, *ex vi termini* (by the very import of the term) alienation supposes and includes contract, as shewn in Section IX.

Quasi-contract, Austin describes as denoting—"any inci-"dent by which one party obtains an advantage he ought "not to retain, because the retention would damage "another; or by reason of which, he ought to indemnify "the other. The prominent idea in *quasi*-contract seems "to be, an undue advantage which would be acquired by "the obligor, if he were not compelled to relinquish it or "to indemnify." And see 'Ancient Law' pa. 343.

Every fault or offence is a breach of obligation. It is either, a violation of a civil Right, or, an act which violates or endangers public order, public decency, the well-being and peace of the State: it may be both at once, as, killing or personal injury to a magistrate or State-officer: it may affect the whole community in another sense, as, breach of a contract to supply the army with clothes.

With regard to the division of offences into *culpa* and *dolus:* as inexcusable negligence is *culpa;* so, a great *culpa* has been deemed jurally equivalent to *dolus.* This was Roman doctrine, and indicates intermediate degrees or stages of wrong; *viz.* 1. between what is civilly imputable as an adjustment of loss, not being any breach of moral Law— and *culpa*, a fault; 2. between an injurious, culpable act, immoral perhaps as evincing general rashness or carelessness, but not a result of vicious will in the particular instance—and *dolus*, designed wrong.

Self-preservation, self-protection, mutual protection, are natural Rights; as, revenge, retaliation for wrong, are natural and universal propensities. The State, in absorbing all rightful power to punish and to protect, overrules, disallows and supersedes those rights and those propensities (at all events, in ordinary exercise and occurrence), analysing their origin, their motive, their necessity—thus substituting Order and Reason for Disorder and Passion. In this view, and as a civil legal substitute for wild instinctive vengeance, penal laws are closely allied to the philosophy of moral action, and depend upon moral definitions and distinctions.

Mr. Senior, in his biography of the French advocate, Berryer, notes the terrible elasticity of national morals that may consist even with advanced civilization (as far as this is evinced by refined manners, and learning,) *viz.* as instanced in the dislocation of social bonds wrought by the political revolution of France at the close of the 18th century. He says—" Mons. Berryer's narratives of his con-" tests on questions depending on marriage, divorce, and " legitimacy, are interesting. They describe a community " unsupported by religion, delicacy, or morality—in which " virtues had so often been declared to be criminal, and " crimes to be virtuous, that public opinion had been des-" troyed, and with it, conscience and even the self-respect of " individuals."

That portion of the manners of a nation which, although they go, with the rest, to fashion its individuality, do not pass into Law, form a conventional code, having conventional sanctions depending upon the 'reflex sentiments.' With a vain or sensitive people, such by-laws of the social system have paramount sway. Sterne's apostrophe, "Hail, ye " small sweet courtesies of life!" alluded to no part of the universal code, recognized by all, but to those lighter yet important virtues characteristically designated by the Parisian *les petites morales*. Honour, gallantry, modes of dress, of address, of taking food, a polite demeanour—here is the area of the minor moralities or modes, which vary even beyond the variations of civil Law, and the infraction of which are *mala prohibita*, frequently entailing severe, if not cruel, resentment and retribution. Such rules are sometimes found (illogically and unreasonably) translated into civil Law, *e. g.* where mere cast-distinctions, ritual formalities, fanciful or speculative notions in things indifferent, are civilly enforced, as with the Hindus and other ancient peoples. See Mr. Grote's exposition of *nomos;* 'Plato,' vol. 1, p. 249 &c.

On a mere impressional view, formal enactment seems scarcely indispensable for criminal any more than for civil rules of municipal Law. Common (or judicially-promulgated) Law frequently includes both classes; official legislation, as to both, substantially, recognises or amends rather than creates rules. A Jeffreys can enlarge a penal code by construction; as the resources of a Mansfield find new aids to commerce in the yet unfathomed depths of contract-law.

Nevertheless, it may be adopted as a principle of modern jurisprudence, that the application of punishment, in other words, the criminal Law, does not admit of enlargements or novelty by construction or analogy. Direct and literal command, the voice of Power, is here needed: there is no necessity, no excuse for elasticity, for equitable extension of the laws of crime. Social arrangements, from their indefinite variety and complication, do furnish a reason and a demand for elasticity in rules and modes of intercourse: punishment, penal sanction, is something else—it is not inflicted to satisfy any individual or any section of the community, but to vindicate the principle and the existence of order, every infraction of which (at least in theory, constitutionally) concerns all, in equal degree. Hence, the origin or formal approval, the precise demarcation, the promulgating of this all important class of civil laws, consistently and wisely rests with the proper legislative function. Popular opinion or customary observance cannot, with an advanced community, originate or gradually introduce an unpromulgated crime.

"Crimes" writes Mr. Stephen "are actions punished by "the Law:" and he instances the English statute 34. Hen. viii, which prohibited reading of the New Testament to all save a privileged class, as showing the arbitrary character of the definition of crimes in any system—that it is the mere creature of sovereign will, of legislative power.

The editor of the 5th edition of Hawkins' 'Pleas of the Crown' (published 1777) thus notices the encrease of Eng-

lish penal enactments during the preceding sixty years :—
" The encrease of commerce, opulence, and luxury, since that
" period, has introduced a variety of temptations to fraud
" and rapine, which the legislature has been forced to repel,
" by a multiplicity of occasional statutes creating new of-
" fences and inflicting additional punishments."

In one sense, every sanction, although the sequel of a civil
remedy merely, is penal and criminal; inasmuch as it threat-
ens and indicates suffering for disobedience. But, in such
case, an appeal is made to the sense of compensating justice
in the mind of the wrong-doer; terms are offered to him;
Law but demands his co-operation to repair a fellow citizen's
loss, adjudged to have resulted from his error, his ignorance, his carelessness or his wrong-headedness; if he slight
the Law's demand, he necessitates a resort to coercive and
retributive action, ultimately—a very different affair from
the direct retribution following an act in contravention of
a mandate of criminal law.

Dr. Whewell, with his wonted philosophical accuracy,
distinguishes between the *fact* and the *idea* of rules of
conduct; applying the former to existing systems of human
Law, the latter to the universal principle, to be dis-
cerned by Reason, which is, therefore, the real standard of
'right and wrong'—the veritable *nomos* of Plato's Socrates.
The 'positive laws' of Austin's school are the 'fact' of each
defined, contrived system, whatever that be, and whatever its
relation to the real standard. If, with Paley and Bentham
and Austin, we make 'utility' a key-note, a criterion whereby to adjust the harmony of any regulated system—to test
what is, by what ought to be; still, that utility and its
standard are, an idea, an opinion—at the least, a reasoned
result—and easily distinguishable from the positive facts of
a national code or law-scheme, evolved, generated, and nur-
tured, as such must be, by the accidents of each nation's
history.

Equity, as a juridical term, I consider to denote, the difference (overplus or balance) between each people's promulgated national Law or civil scheme of conduct—and the collective moral sense or conscience of the same people. English Equity was originally an appeal to the royal conscience from the rules administered by the Courts, to supplement their shortcomings, to modify their rigour and severity. This delicate and difficult function of the Executive happening to be delegated to members of the Roman hierarchy, accounts for much of its character, both in substance and form. Equity is, the national morality, as understood and interpreted by the administrator for the time being, formalized and adapted to the exigency presented.

The simplest and most direct mode of arriving at a conception of inter-national Law is; to realise and complete in one's mind the idea of mankind without civil Law, *i. e.* in a (supposed) primary stage or condition, not having any special or artificially organised rules of government or of conduct. Yet, in such a state of things, mankind can not be counted lawless: no man with reference to any other man is free from obligation, if and when the two are any way brought into contact, in action, in interest, in affairs of life; whenever their interests or wishes clash. For every such case, there undoubtedly is a law, self-existent, and discoverable. We cannot imagine any mode of collecting or grouping families of men, however unfettered by civil rules, however various, however strange to each other, which, reflection upon and observation of the condition of material as of moral nature, do not at once convince us, involves some mutual link, of sympathy, of needs, of possible society and its consequent obligations. If so, is not this a Law of nations? For, the original, the self-existent Law, binding the entirety, is obviously not repealed or abrogated by the circumstance (whether accidental or necessary), that, some of the groups or families have coalesced under new or artificial bonds. The original link remains; having, in addition, some reference to and bearing upon the subordinate civil formation. The civil structure does not supersede or vary the fundamental necessity, *viz.* that Man is linked to Man, more than potentially, as a universal and natural truth.

Austin seems indignantly to repudiate the notion of growth of Law from popular habit or from opinion; condemning the several Roman definitions of (what may be called) inevitable Law: *viz.* a *jus* which Nature has ordained among all men; a *jus* established by habits; a *jus* raised and contrived by the learned.

To reject all historical and philosophical bases or building up of human coercive rules, and to substitute the naked authoritative command as an arbitrary, self-existent cause of Law, is one thing—to insist that the many accidental, moral, and political elements or motive-powers which go to produce Law, are not separately or collectively, cognizable as Law, until promulgated or recognised by those political organs (legislative or judicial) whose fiat of recognition announces and inaugurates birth of Law, is another. The former sentiment or dogma annihilates, it is submitted, all science of jurisprudence or of Law,— at any rate, reduces what should be a science, substantively, to a mere dialectic formulary and terminology: the latter proposition, however, is a fundamental truth, and rightly distinguishes the result, the consequence, from the process of formation. This view it is, which underlies, which accounts for, the seeming (the really superficial) antagonism between Austin and Savigny.

Austin himself thus describes certain modes of unwritten Law; *viz.*

"Owing their existence, as positive Law, to sovereign or "inferior judges, although they are shaped by the judi- "cial legislators on customs current in the community or "on opinions of private jurisconsults."

He also admits,—"Much of the positive Law obtaining
"in any community, is custom turned into Law by the
"adjection of the legal sanction"—and elsewhere, "Certain
"laws are so obviously suggested by utility, that a per-
"son of small experience (if not affected with insanity)
"would naturally surmise their existence." And, when defining 'privileges'—"They are mere anomalies: exorbi-
"tant or irregular commands proceeding from the legis-
"lature; or, what in effect is exactly the same thing,
"eccentric customs tacitly sanctioned by the legislature."

Dr. Maine treats customary formation of Law as the
secondary epoch in juridical history, *viz.* that succeeding
the purely despotic or patriarchal, in which every occasional solution of differences among the governed was the
birth of a legislative decree or *themis*, an *ex post facto*
but heaven-inspired rule of right: to which simple archaic
plan, succeeded the customary.

The same jurist crystallizes the conditions of mankind
under the *quasi*-instinctive operation of primitive social
habit, into varying *formulæ* of status—a negation of 'agreement,' in any sort, direct and immediate, or remote; and
thus concludes his able historical analysis—"We may say,
"that the movement of the progressive societies has hith-
"erto been a movement from status to contract."

Holding, as I do, that any narrative of the operation of
human wants and wills and dispositions, can but illustrate
and apply (thus pointing the inferences of) ethical and jural
truth; I would say—Voluntary union of wills and of human
purposes was always, in fact, convention and agreement;
when a civil sanction was added, it became contract, *i. e.*
the civil *vinculum*. It is perhaps difficult to over-rate the
silent and, as it were, instinctive influence of the original family-grouping upon what we, may call (borrowing
a term of geology) the world's juridical formations.

The archaic or primitive social fabric is portrayed in strong
relief by Dr Maine, who describes its ever-living influence—

"older probably than the State, the Tribe, and the House,
"it left traces of itself on private Law long after the
"House and the Tribe had been forgotten, and long after
"consanguinity had ceased to be associated with the com-
"position of States. It will be found to have stamped it-
"self on all the great departments of jurisprudence, and
"may be detected, I think, as the true source of many
"of their most important and most durable characteristics."

Connexion in blood, real or simulated; a despotic
father's commands; a perpetual corporate entity; undivided
responsibility; slavery; elastic absorption of strangers into
the union—such were, severally, characteristics of the
varied *nuclei* or kernels, from and around which primitive States grew or were fashioned. To those characteristic landmarks and stages of the earliest social progress,
succeeded more mature indications, belonging to the youth
or to the early manhood of civilization, *e. g.* the *themistes*
(despotic judicial awards), customs, codified texts, and,
above and before all, contract or compact, *i. e.* deliberate,
systematic joining of individual wills; for—"The necessity
"of depending upon assurances made by other men, gives
"birth to a Right in the person to whom the assurances
"are made—" (whewell): and the necessity must always
have existed, that is, as soon as two independent wills
existed. The earliest compacts may be compared to
mastication of food by a child, followed, as it must be,
by the elaborate sequences effecting conversion of that
food into blood; and (completing the analogy) the contracts of an advanced civilization may be compared to
the same physical operation by the mature jaws of the
conscious man of science. Are not the two operations,
with their consequences, essentially identical?

That mankind are one, in race and origin, is (although not
universally received,) an ably worked result of learned inves-
tigation—a synthetical deduction from established results.
From the physical and moral wants, from the congenital

(or, at least, natural) differences of the first human progeny, and from the changes wrought by migrations, we may obtain a sufficient approximation to what the early jural steps of mankind really were, to serve as a starting point for research into what is reliable in history. Yet we must proceed warily. Hermann, speaking of the Trojan war, the theme and scene of the Iliad, says :—

"Although not a few of its earlier traditions may be "founded on fact, and contain traces of real transactions, "these are so interwoven with myths and enveloped in "allegory, that the most penetrating genius is incompetent "to restore them to a complete and connected historical "whole. This remark is still more applicable to the do-"mestic history of a people. There can be none, till a "nation has by its own spontaneous energy attained that "individuality, in which by displaying peculiarities of "character, it becomes distinct from all others. In the "case of the Greeks, this national character was develop-"ed through a course of violent commotion, revolution, "and migration, closing with the invasion of the Hera-"clidæ and its consequences."

Perhaps no safer authority or instance could be given than this extract, in order to exhibit, generally, the extent to which archaic research, in the field or mine of history, can furnish the facts, the actual proceedings of the earliest struggles in politico-social order. We are thus compelled to reason, for the most part, from results. We garner the facts of juridical science, by which to illustrate, to test, to trace that internal frame-work of axioms, that circulating original principle, which must be the life and support of the structure,—i. e. of jurisprudence.

Austin, in his 'Notes on codification' lays down :—"The "historical school of jurisprudence, so far as they are "right, concur with every body. Their peculiar views of "the value of history, exclusive of philosophy, are wrong.— "Law (as it ought to be) is not deducible from principles "knowable *a priori*, but from principles which must be "obtained (through induction) from experience. No ex- "perience of actual institutions, independently of the "principles which are obtained by experience of Human "Nature can be of any value."

Such views seem scarcely reconcileable with the same acute reasoner's denunciation of "the fustian which is styled "the Law of Nature!"

Kant, with logical correctness, distinguishes the giver of the 'command' *i. e.* the legislator who imposes the civil obligation, from the author or source of the 'law' (which the legislator may or may not be,) to which that obligation is attached, and which the command enforces.

Austin divided the *jus gentium* of the Pandects into three parts: 1. a 'conceit' and 'absurdity' of Ulpian alone—the mere fancy of that jurisconsult's brain: 2. a *jus naturale* answering to modern ideas of a Natural Law, "imported into the Roman Law from hypotheses of "Greek philosophers concerning the rationale of Law and "morals, by the jurists who are styled 'classical,'—of "excerpts from whose writings, the Pandects are principally "composed:" 3. a body of subsidiary Law which the *prætor peregrinus* thus produced, *viz.*—"Perpetually en- "gaged in judging between foreigners and citizens of "Rome, and between foreigners of different dependent "States, these magistrates were led to compare the several "systems of Law which obtained in the several commu- "nities composing the Roman empire. And, comparing "the several systems obtaining in those several commu- "nities, they naturally extracted from those several "systems, a system of a liberal character; free from the "narrow peculiarities of each particular system, and meeting "the common necessities of the entire Roman world."

It is certainly questionable, whether the accidental con- vergence or co-administration of several particular systems, *i. e.* of several peculiarities, must produce any better or more liberal system. It may be here noted, that Romulus and his companions had certainly a choice of civilisations to copy from: and, as they brought their religion, so they could not but import or reflect much from the jural schemes of an advanced people, *viz.* Etruria; impressed however, and directed by the prædatory independence which characterised the Quirital migration.

CPSIA information can be obtained at www.ICGtesting.com
Printed in the USA
BVOW06s0122100614

355911BV00005B/347/P